Money, Markets, and Mobility

CELEBRATING THE IDEAS OF
ROBERT A. MUNDELL
NOBEL LAUREATE IN
ECONOMIC SCIENCES

EDITED BY
THOMAS J. COURCHENE

 JOHN DEUTSCH INSTITUTE FOR THE STUDY OF
ECONOMIC POLICY, QUEEN'S UNIVERSITY

 INSTITUTE FOR RESEARCH ON PUBLIC POLICY
INSTITUT DE RECHERCHE EN POLITIQUES PUBLIQUES

Published in cooperation with
McGill-Queen's University Press
Montreal & Kingston • London • Ithaca

ISBN: 0-88911-818-3 (bound)   ISBN: 0-88911-820-5 (pbk.)
© John Deutsch Institute for the Study of Economic Policy
Queen's University, Kingston, Ontario K7L 3N6
Telephone: (613) 533-2294   FAX: (613) 533-6025
and Institute for Research on Public Policy
1470 Peel St., Suite 200, Montréal, Québec H3A 1T1
Telephone: (514) 985-2461   FAX: (514) 985-2559
Printed and bound in Canada

National Library of Canada Cataloguing in Publication

Main entry under title:

   Money, markets and mobility : celebrating the ideas of Robert
A. Mundell, Nobel Laureate in economic sciences / Thomas J.
Courchene, editor.

Proceedings of conference, Money, markets and mobility : celebrating
   the ideas and influence of the 1999 Nobel Laureate Robert A.
   Mundell held May 24-25, 2000 at Queen's University.
Co-published by: Institute for Research on Public Policy.
ISBN 0-88911-818-3 (bound).--ISBN 0-88911-820-5 (pbk.)

   1. International finance. 2. International economic relations.
3. Mundell, Robert A., 1932-. I. Courchene, Thomas J., 1940-
II. Mundell, Robert A., 1932-   III. John Deutsch Institute for the
Study of Economic Policy IV. Institute for Research on Public Policy

HG205.M65 2002   332'.042   C2002-901012-8

With Thanks

Co-sponsors:

Royal Bank of Canada

Donner Canadian Foundation

School of Policy Studies (Queen's University)

Principal's Development Fund (Queen's University)

Credits:

Cover Design — Mark Howes
SPS Publications Unit (Queen's University)

Nobel Prize Photo — Hans Mehlin, Nobel e-Museum

Cover Photo — Jack Chiang, The Kingston Whig-Standard

Contents

Acknowledgement ... ix

Homage to Robert Alexander Mundell:
Nobel Prize Press Release ... xi

Introduction ... 1

I: The 1999 Nobel Lecture in Economic Sciences

Robert A. Mundell
A Reconsideration of the Twentieth Century ... 17

II: Optimum Currency Areas: Analytical Perspectives

Ronald McKinnon
Mundell, the Euro and Optimum Currency Areas ... 41

Richard G. Harris
The New Economy and the Exchange Rate Regime ... 59

III: Optimum Currency Areas: Empirical Perspectives

Michael B. Devereux and Philip R. Lane
Exchange Rate Flexibility and Monetary Policy Choice
for Emerging Market Economies ... 87

v

IV: The Macro Mix

Russell S. Boyer
Reflections on the Mundell-Fleming Model on its
Fortieth Anniversary ... 119

Pierre Fortin
Problems of Monetary and Exchange-Rate Management
in Canada ... 139

V: Real Trade Theory

James R. Melvin and Robert Waschik
Factor Flows: Immigration in a Specific Factor Framework ... 165

VI: International Economy

Sylvia Ostry
Perspectives on the Evolution of the Global Trading System ... 197

VII: North American Currency Integration: Policy Panel

John McCallum
Engaging the Debate: Costs and Benefits of a North
American Common Currency ... 227

Herbert Grubel
Toward North American Monetary Union ... 245

George M. von Furstenberg
Unilateral and Multilateral Currency Integration:
Reflections on Western Hemispheric Monetary Union ... 253

VIII: The Future of National Currencies

Robert A. Mundell
Exchange Rate Systems and Currency Integration:
Prospects for the Twenty-First Century ... 269

vi

Appendix

Robert A. Mundell
A Plan for a European Currency ... 295

Contributors

vii

Acknowledgements

In May of 2000, Queen's University conferred an Honorary Doctor of Law on Kingston-born Robert A. Mundell, the recipient of the 1999 Nobel Prize in Economic Sciences. As part of the Queen's festivities, the John Deutsch Institute for the Study of Economic Policy hosted a conference to celebrate Mundell's ideas and his contributions to Canadian and international economics. The result is this Festschrift in honour of Robert Mundell.

Hence, our first debt of gratitude is to Robert Mundell and to the other contributors to this volume.

As always for JDI publications, all centres around Sharon Sullivan. She manages the conference, coordinates the process of compiling the final versions of papers and then orchestrates the production of the volume.

It is also a pleasure to thank Marilyn Banting for her editing skills and the School of Policy Studies Publications Unit for valuable back-up in preparing aspects of this volume.

We are also pleased to recognize cooperation of Jack Chiang of the Kingston Whig Standard and Bob Mundell's wife, Valeria Natsios, for providing photographs for the volume.

Finally, we are delighted to recognize again our co-sponsors: Royal Bank of Canada, Donner Canadian Foundation, School of Policy Studies (Queen's University) and Principal's Development Fund (Queen's University).

Charles M. Beach   Thomas J. Courchene   Hugh Segal
Director   Editor   President
John Deutsch Institute   IRPP

King Gustav of Sweden
presents
Robert A. Mundell
with the
1999 Nobel Prize in Economic Sciences

Homage to Robert Alexander Mundell: Nobel Prize Press Release

The Royal Swedish Academy of Sciences awarded **the Bank of Sweden Prize in Economic Sciences in Memory of Alfred Nobel, 1999**, to

Professor **Robert A. Mundell**, Columbia University, New York, USA

for his analysis of monetary and fiscal policy under different exchange rate regimes and his analysis of optimum currency areas.

Economic policy exchange rates and capital mobility

Robert Mundell has established the foundation for theory which dominates practical policy considerations of monetary and fiscal policy in open economies. His work on monetary dynamics and optimum currency areas has inspired generations of researchers. Although dating back several decades, Mundell's contributions remain outstanding and constitute the core of teaching in international macroeconomics.

Mundell's research has had such a far-reaching and lasting impact because it combines formal — but still accessible — analysis, intuitive interpretation and results with immediate policy applications. Above all,

---

Reprinted with permission from the Royal Swedish Academy of Sciences 1999 (www.nobel.se/economics/laureates/1999/press.html).

Mundell chose his problems with uncommon — almost prophetic — accuracy in terms of predicting the future development of international monetary arrangements and capital markets. Mundell's contributions serve as a superb reminder of the significance of basic research. At a given point in time academic achievements might appear rather esoteric; not long afterwards, however, they may take on great practical importance.

* * * * *

How are the effects of monetary and fiscal policy related to the integration of international capital markets? How do these effects depend on whether a country fixes the value of its currency or allows it to float freely? Should a country even have a currency of its own? By posing and answering questions such as these, Robert Mundell has reshaped macroeconomic theory for open economies. His most important contributions were made in the 1960s. During the latter half of that decade, Mundell was among the intellectual leaders in the creative research environment at the University of Chicago. Many of his students from this period have become successful researchers in the same field, building on Mundell's foundational work.

Mundell's scientific contributions are original. Yet they quickly transformed the research in international macroeconomics and attracted increasing attention in the practically oriented discussion of stabilization policy and exchange rate systems. A sojourn at the research department of the International Monetary Fund, 1961–1963, apparently stimulated Mundell's choice of research problems; it also gave his research additional leverage among economic policymakers.

The Effects of Stabilization Policy

In several papers published in the early 1960s — reprinted in his book *International Economics* (1968) — Robert Mundell developed his analysis of monetary and fiscal policy, so-called stabilization policy, in open economies.

The Mundell-Fleming Model

A pioneering article (1963) addresses the short-run effects of monetary and fiscal policy in an open economy. The analysis is simple, but the conclusions are numerous, robust and clear. Mundell introduced foreign trade and capital movements into the so-called IS-LM model of a closed economy, initially developed by the 1972 economics laureate Sir John Hicks. This allowed him to show that the effects of stabilization policy hinge on the degree of international capital mobility. In particular, he demonstrated the far-reaching importance of the exchange rate regime: under a floating exchange rate, monetary policy becomes powerful and fiscal policy powerless, whereas the opposite is true under a fixed exchange rate.

In the interesting special case with high capital mobility, foreign and domestic interest rates coincide (given that the exchange rate is expected to be constant). Under a *fixed exchange rate*, the central bank must intervene on the currency market in order to satisfy the public's demand for foreign currency at this exchange rate. As a result, the central bank loses control of the money supply, which then passively adjusts to the demand for money (domestic liquidity). Attempts to implement independent national monetary policy by means of so-called open market operations are futile because neither the interest rate nor the exchange rate can be affected. However, increased government expenditures, or other fiscal policy measures, can raise national income and the level of domestic activity, thereby escaping the impediments of rising interest rates or a stronger exchange rate.

A *floating exchange rate* is determined by the market since the central bank refrains from currency intervention. Fiscal policy now becomes powerless. Under unchanged monetary policy, increased government expenditures give rise to a greater demand for money and tendencies towards higher interest rates. Capital inflows strengthen the exchange rate to the point where lower net exports eliminate the entire expansive effect of higher government expenditures. Under floating exchange rates, however, monetary policy becomes a powerful tool for influencing economic activity. Expansion of the money supply tends to promote lower interest rates, resulting in capital outflows and a weaker exchange rate, which in turn expand the economy through increased net exports.

Floating exchange rates and high capital mobility accurately describe the present monetary regime in many countries. But in the early 1960s, an analysis of their consequences must have seemed like an academic curiosity. Almost all countries were linked together by fixed exchange rates within the so-called Bretton Woods System. International capital movements were

xiii

highly curtailed, in particular by extensive capital and exchange rate controls. During the 1950s, however, Mundell's own country — Canada — had allowed its currency to float against the US dollar and had begun to ease restrictions. His far-sighted analysis became increasingly relevant over the next ten years, as international capital markets opened up and the Bretton Woods System broke down.

Marcus Fleming (who died in 1976) was Deputy Director of the research department of the International Monetary Fund for many years; he was already a member of this department during the period of Mundell's affiliation. At approximately the same time as Mundell, Fleming presented similar research on stabilization policy in open economies. As a result, today's textbooks refer to the *Mundell-Fleming Model*. In terms of depth, range and analytical power, however, Mundell's contribution predominates.

The original Mundell-Fleming Model undoubtedly had its limitations. For instance, as in all macroeconomic analysis at the time, it makes highly simplified assumptions about expectations in financial markets and assumes price rigidity in the short run. These shortcomings have been remedied by later researchers, who have shown that gradual price adjustment and rational expectations can be incorporated into the analysis without significantly changing the results.

Monetary Dynamics

In contrast to his colleagues during this period, Mundell's research did not stop at short-run analysis. Monetary dynamics is a key theme in several significant articles. He emphasized differences in the speed of adjustment on goods and asset markets (called *the principle of effective market classification*). Later on, these differences were highlighted by his own students and others to show how the exchange rate can temporarily "overshoot" in the wake of certain disturbances.

An important problem concerned deficits and surpluses in the balance of payments. In the postwar period, research on these imbalances had been based on *static* models and emphasized *real* economic factors and *flows* in foreign trade. Inspired by David Humes's classic mechanism for international price adjustment which focused on *monetary* factors and *stock* variables, Mundell formulated *dynamic* models to describe how prolonged imbalances could arise and be eliminated. He demonstrated that an economy will adjust gradually over time as the money holdings of the private sector (and thereby its wealth) change in response to surpluses or deficits. Under fixed exchange rates, for example, when capital movements are sluggish, an

xiv

expansive monetary policy will reduce interest rates and raise domestic demand. The subsequent balance of payments deficit will generate monetary outflows, which in turn lower demand until the balance of payments returns to equilibrium. This approach, which was adopted by a number of researchers, became known as the *monetary approach to the balance of payments*. For a long time it was regarded as a kind of long-run benchmark for analyzing stabilization policy in open economies. Insights from this analysis have frequently been applied in practical economic policymaking — particularly by IMF economists.

Prior to another of Mundell's contributions, the theory of stabilization policy had not only been static, it had also assumed that all economic policy in a country is coordinated and assembled in a single hand. By contrast, Mundell used a simple dynamic model to examine how each of the two instruments, monetary and fiscal policy, should be directed towards either of two objectives, external and internal balance, in order to bring the economy closer to these objectives over time. This implies that each of two different authorities — the government and the central bank — is given responsibility for its own stabilization policy instrument. Mundell's conclusion was straightforward: to prevent the economy from becoming unstable, the linkage has to accord with the relative efficiency of the instruments. In his model, monetary policy is linked to external balance and fiscal policy to internal balance. Mundell's primary concern was not decentralization itself. But by explaining the conditions for decentralization, he anticipated the idea which, long afterwards, has become generally accepted, i.e., that the central bank should be given independent responsibility for price stability.

Mundell's contributions on dynamics proved to be a watershed for research in international macroeconomics. They introduced a meaningful dynamic approach, based on a clear-cut distinction between stock and flow variables, as well as an analysis of their interaction during the adjustment of an economy to a stable long-run situation. Mundell's work also initiated the necessary rapprochement between Keynesian short-run analysis and classical long-run analysis. Subsequent researchers have extended Mundell's findings. The models have been extended to incorporate forward-looking decisions of household and firms, additional types of financial assets and richer dynamic adjustments of prices and the current account. Despite these modifications, most of Mundell's results stand up.

The short-run and long-run analyses carried out by Mundell arrive at the same fundamental conclusion regarding the conditions for monetary policy. With (i) *free capital mobility*, monetary policy can be oriented towards either

xv

(ii) an *external objective* — such as the exchange rate — or (iii) an *internal (domestic) objective* — such as the price level — but not both at the same time. This *incompatible trinity* has become self-evident for academic economists; today, this insight is also shared by the majority of participants in the practical debate.

Optimum Currency Areas

As already indicated, fixed exchange rates predominated in the early 1960s. A few researchers did in fact discuss the advantages and disadvantages of a floating exchange rate. But a national currency was considered a must. The question Mundell posed in his article on "optimum currency areas" (1961) therefore seemed radical: when is it advantageous for a number of regions to relinquish their monetary sovereignty in favor of a common currency?

Mundell's article briefly mentions the advantages of a common currency, such as lower transaction costs in trade and less uncertainty about relative prices. The disadvantages are described in greater detail. The major drawback is the difficulty of maintaining employment when changes in demand or other "asymmetric shocks" require a reduction in real wages in a particular region. Mundell emphasized the importance of high labor mobility in order to offset such disturbances. He characterized an optimum currency area as a set of regions among which the propensity to migrate is high enough to ensure full employment when one of the regions faces an asymmetric shock. Other researchers extended the theory and identified additional criteria, such as capital mobility, regional specialization and a common tax and transfer system. The way Mundell originally formulated the problem has nevertheless continued to influence generations of economists.

Mundell's considerations, several decades ago, seem highly relevant today. Due to increasingly higher capital mobility in the world economy, regimes with a temporarily fixed, but adjustable, exchange rate have become more fragile; such regimes are also being called into question. Many observers view a currency union or a floating exchange rate — the two cases Mundell's article dealt with — as the most relevant alternatives. Needless to say, Mundell's analysis has also attracted attention in connection with the common European currency. Researchers who have examined the economic advantages and disadvantages of EMU have adopted the idea of an optimum currency area as an obvious starting point. Indeed, one of the key issues in this context is labor mobility in response to asymmetric shocks.

xvi

Other Contributions

Mundell has made other contributions to macroeconomic theory. He has shown, for example, that higher inflation can induce investors to lower their cash balances in favor of increased real capital formation. As a result, even expected inflation might have a real economic effect — which has come to be known as *the Mundell-Tobin effect*. Mundell has also made lasting contributions to international trade theory. He has clarified how the international mobility of labor and capital tends to equalize commodity prices among countries, even if foreign trade is limited by trade barriers. This may be regarded as the mirror image of the well-known Heckscher-Ohlin-Samuelson result that free trade of goods tends to bring about equalization of the rewards to labor and capital among countries, even if international capital movements and migration are limited. These results provide a clear prediction: trade barriers stimulate international mobility of labor and capital, whereas barriers to migration and capital movements stimulate commodity trade.

References

Mundell, R.A. (1961), "A Theory of Optimum Currency Areas", *American Economic Review* 51, 657–665.
_____ (1963), "Capital Mobility and Stabilization Policy under Fixed and Flexible Exchange Rates", *Canadian Journal of Economics* 29, 475–485.
_____ (1968), *International Economics* (New York: MacMillan).

Introduction

Thomas J. Courchene

Robert A. Mundell — Canada's Nobel Laureate

In this volume we honour the magnificent contributions of Robert A. Mundell, arguably the foremost postwar thinker in international macro-economics and the global monetary order. Mundell was not the first Canadian to win a Nobel Prize in Economics and he will not be the last. But his Nobel Prize is surely a quintessentially "Canadian" Nobel Prize in the sense that his intellectual achievements are closely allied with the challenges that Canada, as a small open economy, faces in the global economic order — domestic and external balance, perfect capital mobility, fixed versus flexible exchange rates, optimal currency areas and the like. What Mundell perceived, and what few others did, was that all economies in our progressively global and mobile world would eventually take on the then-distinguishing features of the Canadian economy. Hence, we as Canadians can take special pride in his Nobel Prize since his accomplishments are to an important degree routed in his Canadianness — and this is apart from the fact that he has maintained his close Canadian ties and citizenship.

Queen's University is especially proud of Mundell's achievement as he is a Kingston native. Indeed, this conference celebrates not only Robert Mundell's Nobel Prize but, Queen's conferring on him an Honorary Doctor of Laws.

Introduction

The role of this introduction is to focus briefly on selected aspects of Bob Mundell's career and, then, to present a brief outline of the volume.

Robert Mundell: A Profile

Robert A. Mundell was born in 1932 in Latimer, Ontario, essentially a crossroads near Loughborough Lake on the outskirts of Kingston. On the occasion of his delivering Queen's School of Policy Studies' inaugural Gibson Lecture in 1990, Bob and his wife Valerie and I finally managed to locate Latimer's abandoned one-room schoolhouse that Mundell asserts was so central to his intellectual formation. In his typically mischievous way, he claims he never really went to grade one: rather, he was able to pick and choose simultaneously from the offering of grades one through eight.

In 1945, the Mundell family moved to Kingston — actually to the Gate House of the Royal Military College since Bob's father was in the army — and Bob took his first year of high school at Kingston Collegiate Vocational Institute. Bob's father retired from the army during this year and the Mundell family moved west to British Columbia, where Bob completed high school and, later, graduated from the University of British Columbia.

He began his graduate work at the University of Washington, then continued at the Massachusetts Institute of Technology (MIT) and the London School of Economics, receiving his PhD in 1956 from MIT. Then began a series of short-term professorships across North America and Europe — to Chicago in 1956–57 as a post-doctoral fellow, then back to UBC for a year and on to Stanford in 1958–59 and the Bologna Institute for Advanced International Studies for 1959–61 before joining the staff of the International Monetary Fund (IMF) in 1961. His time at the LSE introduced him to James Meade and his writings which, combined with his Bologna experience, enabled Mundell to observe first hand both the introduction of the Common Market in 1956 and the Treaty of Rome in 1958, events whose trajectory he would eventually influence as the "intellectual godfather" of the euro. And, of course, his IMF years introduced him to Marcus Fleming, the Deputy Director of the Research Department of the IMF.

By 1963 Bob was back in Canada (McGill) for a year, then off to the Brookings Institution in Washington, DC for 1964–65 and finally to the University of Chicago, where he stayed long enough (1966–71) to develop the what might be termed the Mundell School of "open-economy macro-economics", many of the disciples of which have gone on to achieve renown on their own.

While I am not a Chicago PhD, I did have the incredible good fortune to have been a Chicago post-doctoral student in 1968–69 and to get to know Bob and his work during these creative Chicago years. Chicago's senior faculty were simply grand — among them Friedman, Harberger, Becker, Zellner, Fogel and Coase. International economics was held down by two Canadians: Mundell and Harry Johnson. Harry's lectures were, at one level, a student's delight. The anlytical core of each topic was carefully developed and then all of the relevant recent literature was integrated into this core — a *tour de force*, to be sure, but one that typically left a student believing that there were precious few loose ends that would provide topics for theses. Bob was exactly the opposite, at least from my limited experience. Mundell would walk into class and present the students with an interesting issue or challenge (sometimes the issue came from the class) and then would proceed to develop a model to tackle it, or at least get the model up and running more or less in the right direction. In the process of this modelling, the air was ripe with thesis topics. Our late Queen's colleague, Doug Purvis, himself a leading Chicago School disciple until his tragic death in 1993, pursued what was likely the optimal strategy — get your ideas from Bob, but write your thesis under Harry!

In 1972, Mundell was again back in Canada, this time as Chair of Waterloo's Economics Department. Finally, in 1974, Bob went to Columbia which, apart from short-term visitorships, has remained his intellectual home to this day. As the Nobel Website notes, these visitorships since moving to Columbia included: the Annenberg Professor of Communications at USC in 1980; the Repap Professor of Economics at McGill in 1989–90; Richard Fox Professor of Economics at the University of Pennsylvania in 1990–91; and a return visit to Bologna in 1997–98. Along the way Bob has received the Guggenheim Prize in 1971, the Jacques Rueff Medal in 1983, the AEA Distinguished Fellow Award in 1997, and he became a Fellow of the America Academy of Arts and Sciences in 1998. Post Nobel Prize, Robert Mundell has received honorary degrees from numerous universities world-wide, including, of course, Queen's University.

While the above Nobel Prize Press Release from The Royal Swedish Academy of Sciences focuses largely on Mundell's contributions from his pre-Columbia period, he has continued to have a remarkably influential career. One of his recent achievements has already been alluded to: his

Introduction

campaign for a single European currency and, more generally, for currency reform in Canada and elsewhere. I need not stress his key and early analytical role in the introduction of the euro. Suffice it to say that although his Nobel Prize was long overdue, it is entirely fitting that Bob won the prize in the year that the euro was inaugurated.

Closer to home, Bob's 1990 paper "The Overvalued Canadian Dollar" represents one of the early contributions in the direction of raising the issue of exchange-rate fixity and monetary union between the United States and Canada. He has followed this with dozens of interviews, articles and public appearances in support of currency consolidation in the Americas.

Among his other recent contributions, the most impressive and most far-reaching would surely have to be his role as the intellectual force behind the "supply-side revolution". This was a natural for Bob in the sense that this was a macro-mix issue. Mundell's recipe, adopted by President Ronald Reagan (with the help of Jack Kemp and others) was that the appropriate macro mix was tight money to control inflation and tax cuts to stimulate growth. It is important to note in this context that the top marginal personal income tax rate in the United States in 1979 was 70%. During the Reagan years, this was reduced to 28% (there is a brief 33% tax rate while the personal exceptions are taxed back). It is also important not to minimize the "demonstration effect" abroad of this U.S. tax cut. Indeed, the sweep of this global revolution is such that I am sure that there is not a single developed country where top marginal tax rates have not been lowered substantially. And Canada is no exception.

While the combination of the Nobel press release and the above review of some of the other major milestones hopefully serves as an appropriate *tour d'horizon* of Robert Mundell's intellectual career, it nonetheless misses much of what Mundell the person is all about. His interests have always transcended economics. He has always been a keen student of philosophy (how else would we know that Plato was a hard currency advocate, while Aristotle a soft-currency man?). Likewise for history (how else would we know that the looting of Constantinople in 1203 led to the proliferation of fluctuating exchange rates in the middle ages?). Bob is also an accomplished painter. No doubt it was this combination of history and art and philosophy that played a role in his devoting considerable effort over the last 25 years or so to rebuilding and restoring a twelfth-century Medici castle in Tuscany, Santa Columba, more recently called Palazzo Mundell. His Website is liberally sprinkled with pictures of his wife Valerie Natsios and their young son Nicholas, usually with Palazzo Mundell as backdrop.

4   *Introduction*

Mundell remains devilishly young at heart, always good humoured and, as his student Rudi Dornbusch notes, he often comes across as a good natured *enfant terrible*. Indeed, at the Nobel Prize award ceremony, and again at his Queen's Honorary Degree ceremony, Bob concluded his respective addresses with a rendition of "I Did It My Way".

Outline of *Money, Markets and Mobility* ...

Beyond the formal recognition of an Honorary Doctor of Laws from Queen's, *our way* to celebrate Mundell's achievements was to hold a conference in his honour and to publish the *Festschrift*. An annotated outline of this celebratory volume follows.

Mundell's Nobel Lecture

Thanks to the Nobel Foundation and to Mundell, the volume appropriately begins with Bob's Nobel Prize Lecture. Recognizing that his was the last Nobel Prize in Economics in the twentieth century and with his typical flair for the dramatic, Mundell entitled his lecture *A Reconsideration of the Twentieth Century*. He divides the century into three distinct and almost equal parts. The first part, 1900–33, is the story of the international gold standard, its breakdown during World War I, its managed restoration in the 1920s and its demise in the early 1930s. The second part, 1934–71, begins with the devaluation of the dollar and the establishment of the $35 gold price and ends when the United States took the dollar off gold. The third part of the century, 1972–99, starts with the move to flexible exchange rates and continues with the subsequent outbreak of massive inflation and stagnation in the 1970s, the blossoming of supply-side economics in the 1980s, and the return to monetary stability and the birth of the euro in the 1990s.

In Mundell's view, the twentieth century ended with an international monetary system inferior to that with which it began. In the penultimate paragraph he elaborates as follows:

> Today, the dollar, the euro and yen have established three islands of monetary stability, which is a great improvement over the 1970s and

1980s. There are, however, two pieces of unfinished business. The most important is the dysfunctional volatility of exchange rates that could sour international relations in time of crisis. The other is the absence of an international currency.

Fortunately, in the final paper in the volume, Mundell addresses this "unfinished business".

McKinnon on Optimum Currency Areas

The Nobel Prize Lecture aside, our Mundell *Festschrift* begins with an analytical focus on optimum currency areas (OCA). The author, Stanford's Ronald McKinnon, is ideally suited to delve into this issue since his own *American Economic Review* article "Optimum Currency Areas" (September 1963, pp. 717–725) remains a key contribution to the development of the OCA literature. McKinnon's role here is to try to marry the two Mundells, as it were — the Mundell of the seminal 1961 AER paper and the Mundell who later was hailed, as already noted, as the godfather of the euro. As McKinnon emphasizes, the key to bridging these two Mundells lies in two rather obscure articles presented at a 1970 conference in Madrid and published in the conference volume edited by H.G. Johnson and A.K. Swoboda, *The Economics of Common Currencies* (1973). As McKinnon elaborates, the more analytical of these two articles notes that a country suffering an adverse shock can better share the loss with a trading partner if both countries hold claims on each other's output in a common currency. If, however, a country holds its claims in its own currency and devalues in response to an adverse shock, it then absorbs the loss itself. The more policy oriented of the two is entitled *A Plan for a European Currency* and it is one of Mundell's first papers arguing for a common European currency. Because Mundell's role in the evolution of the euro is not well known or understood, I have (following Ron McKinnon's suggestion) included *A Plan for a European Currency* as an Appendix to this volume.

Harris on Open Economy Endogenous Growth

Richard Harris' "The New Economy and the Exchange Rate Regime" is, in an important sense, the most Mundellian of the contributions in this volume.

Essentially, Harris takes the endogenous growth model and proceeds to internationalize it in the context of both fixed and flexible exchange-rate regimes. In an economy with two sectors — an old (resource-based) economy and a new (human-capital/information-based) economy — Harris focuses on the implications for productivity under both fixed and flexible rate regimes when the economy is hit by two shocks: a fall in prices in the old economy (e.g., a fall in resource prices) and the advent of a new general purpose technology (GPT) which presents new opportunities for productivity increases. The results of the analysis are striking. If flexible rates are used to buffer (i.e., offset) the fall in commodity/resources prices, productivity falls for two reasons: (i) more labour and capital remains employed in the old, lower productivity economy and (ii) the home country price of the GPT rises in tandem with the depreciating home currency and, therefore, its adoption becomes less pervasive. In contrast, a non-buffered economy (i.e., a fixed-exchange-rate regime) experiences higher productivity in response to the two external shocks because more labour and capital shifts from the old to the new economy and because the GPT is less expensive, both relative to a buffering scenario. In addition to making an important contribution to the optimal currency area debate, Harris' model is likely to trigger a lively literature in the general area of open-economy, endogenous-growth models.

Devereux/Lane on International Macro Simulation

The paper by Michael Devereux and Philip Lane, "Exchange Rate Flexibility and Monetary Policy Choice for Emerging Market Economies", is a convenient bridge between the previous two papers on optimal currency areas and the later session on open-economy macro models. Drawing on one of the results of the Mundell-Fleming model, namely that if the economy is subject to foreign disturbances such as real interest rates or demand shocks, then it is better to let the exchange rate adjust so as to cushion the effect of the shock, Devereux-Lane paramaterize an open-economy model to address the issue of whether developing economies would be better off with fixed or flexible exchange rates in the face of those foreign shocks. The authors compare fixed exchange rates with four variants of flexible rates — a money growth rule, a price stability rate, a Taylor rule (targeting inflation and output) and an optimal policy rule (defined as adjusting either money or interest rates to ensure that the domestic price of non-traded goods equals marginal cost). The conclusions of the simulation suggest that more exchange-rate variability is necessary than is typically allowed within the usual operating rules for monetary policy. The authors recognize that their model ignores shocks emanating from the domestic financial system which, in turn, may place limitations on the ability to conduct monetary targeting as an operating rule. Moreover, the model ignores the reality that developing countries typically cannot issue marketable debt in their own currencies, which also may constrain exchange-rate operations. Nevertheless, as these simulation models embrace more and more characteristics of the real world they will be increasingly able to provide important benchmarking in terms of what to expect from alternative exchange-rate regimes for small, open economies in an integrating global economic order.

Boyer on the Mundell-Fleming Model

Noting that the May 2000 Conference in honour of Mundell was the fortieth anniversary of the origins of the Mundell-Fleming model, Russell Boyer elects to focus his paper on the manner in which the Mundell-Fleming model developed over the 1960–63 period, drawing from Mundell (1960), (1961a), (1961b), Fleming (1962) and, finally, Mundell's classic perfect capital mobility article in 1963. Boyer begins by developing the general framework that underlies both the Mundell and Fleming contributions and presents the implications for the macro mix under both exchange-rate regimes. He then takes us through Mundell's modifications to this basic model — first, shifting the definition of monetary policy from (a) a given level of the money supply to (b) maintaining a constant rate of interest and finally to (c) an open market operation or the change in central bank domestic assets in the context of a definition of money consisting of both foreign and domestic assets and, second and simultaneously, effectively increasing the degree of capital mobility until the familiar FF (external balance) curve becomes horizontal in r-Y space. While the punch line is well known — monetary policy is potent under flexible exchange rates but ineffective under fixed rates (and vice versa for fiscal policy) — the evolution of the model is both instructive and fascinating. As Boyer notes, the elegance and power of the Mundell analysis not only led to its immediate adoption but as well its longevity, ample evidence for which is that "as a device for expounding the effects of macroeconomic policies, the Mundell model diagram is still unsurpassed at the undergraduate textbook level". Boyer adds that this is proof positive of Mundell's dictum — hard writing makes easy reading.

Fortin on the Macro Mix

In 1964, Bob Mundell published "Problems of Monetary and Exchange Rate Management in Canada" in the *National Bank Review*. This article constituted an assessment of Canadian macro policy in light of Bob's classic papers on monetary and fiscal policies under fixed and fluctuating exchange rates, highlighted in the Boyer paper. Fortin opts to use this same title to direct attention to some key Canadian macro-policy issues in the current time frame. He starts from an intriguing premise. Given that he, along with Mundell and others, believes that a North American Monetary Union is the preferable long-term future for the Canadian currency but is an unacceptable option over the nearer term, the critical policy issue then becomes one of improving the theory and practice of monetary and exchange-rate management. Toward this end, he addresses three broad questions: Has the inflation target been too low? Has actual output tended on average to be too much below potential output? Have monetary conditions become harder to manage? While Fortin answers all three questions in the affirmative, this is vintage Fortin in that much of the richness and insight of the analysis lies in the process of getting to "yes".

Melvin/Waschik on Real Trade and Factor Mobility

In all the excitement about Mundell's contributions to international money and macro policy — optimal currency areas, perfect capital mobility, fixed versus flexible exchange rates, the macro mix, and more recently, the euro and supply-side economics — it is easy to forget that Bob began his career as a trade theorist. James Melvin and Robert Waschik not only remind us of Bob's trade theory work, but they motivate their own contribution "Factor Flows: Immigration in a Specific Factor Framework" by drawing on Mundell's 1957 influential *American Economic Review* article, "International Trade and Factor Mobility". The starting point of the Melvin-Waschik analysis is Mundell's result that, under certain assumptions, commodity trade and factor mobility are substitutes in the sense that both lead to the same trade equilibrium, namely that all factors will receive the same real incomes. It is also well-known that the so-called specific-factor models represent one case where factor-price equalization will not hold. (The specific-factor model employed by Melvin and Waschik is one where the production of both goods requires labour, but one also requires land while the other also requires capital.) Accordingly, Melvin and Waschik utilize a specific-factor model and explore the extent to which factor prices can differ. The results are quite dramatic. In one of their examples, wages in autarky in the home country are nine times that of the foreign country. However, commodity trade increases the disparity to 11 times! With labour mobility, wages will be equalized — they fall to 23% of autarky levels in the home country and they double in the foreign country. For both countries, a full equilibrium with trade and factor mobility is preferred to migration only. Given that the returns to the specific factors are also affected differentially by trade and by factor mobility, this has the obvious potential for political conflict between labour and the specific factors in terms of how far to pursue trade in goods and/or in factors.

Ostry on the Evolution of the Global Trading Order

No volume focusing on money, markets and mobility would be anywhere near comprehensive without some analysis of the evolution of those supra-national institutions primarily responsible for freeing up trade in goods and services. Sylvia Ostry's "Perspectives on the Evolution of the Global Trading System", precisely and ideally fills the bill. Ostry begins by noting that the Uruguay Round and its creation, the World Trade Organization (WTO), embraced a series of "new issues" that have one common factor: they involve not only the border barriers or "shallow integration" of the original General Agreement on Tariffs and Trade (GATT) but, also and primarily, the domestic policy reconciliation or "deeper integration" of the WTO. Phrased differently, the *negative integration* (the "thou shalt nots") of GATT has given way to the *positive integration* of the WTO, in effect requiring reconfiguring of domestic infrastructure in terms of governance, legal systems, regulatory systems and the like. Intriguingly, corresponding to the "new issues" are a series of "new players" such as Internet-driven non-governmental organizations (NGOs). Accordingly, and appropriately, a major part of Ostry's analysis is devoted to elaborating on the three broad roles for, or types of, NGOs: "mobilization networks" whose chief objective is to rally support for a specific set of activities; "technical networks" designed to provide specific information related to WTO issues; and a "virtual-secretariat" role to inform and to assist developing countries in their WTO relationships. Thus, further progress in freeing international trade in goods and services requires directing attention to both institutional/structural issues and to policy issues. Sylvia Ostry opts more for the latter when she concludes that where there is a political will there is a policy way, which she hopes will soon lead to a serious rethinking of global policy.

McCallum, Grubel and von Furstenberg on Common Currencies

Setting aside the Nobel Prize Lecture, the volume began with some analytical perspectives relating to optimal currency areas and currency consolidation. The two concluding sections return to this theme, the first of which is in the form of a policy roundtable focusing on the pros and cons of a North American common currency.

John McCallum (then with the Royal Bank, now the Secretary of State for International Financial Institutions) opens the roundtable with "Engaging the Debate: Costs and Benefits of a North American Common Currency". For McCallum, a North American common currency means either dollarization or a currency board: he rejects any option based on a North American version of the euro. After he further rejects dollarization as politically unacceptable and a currency board as a slippery slope toward dollarization, McCallum is left with flexible rates, and the core of his contribution is basically a defence of the floating-rate *status quo* on grounds of sovereignty and policy flexibility, on the one hand, and a dismissal of the common currency arguments that flexible rates have undermined living standards and reduced Canadian productivity relative to the United States, on the other.

Herbert Grubel is one of the most ardent proponents of Canada-U.S. currency integration. In his paper, "Toward North American Monetary Union", Grubel focuses on some of the new and/or lower profile rationales for monetary union (implicitly directing the reader to his 1999 Fraser Institute publication for more mainstream rationales). One of his principal arguments is that the degree of labour-market flexibility and the nature of adjustment mechanisms are *not independent* of the exchange-rate regime. Specifically, Grubel argues that the removal of the exchange rate as a shock absorber would lead to much enhanced labour-market and institutional flexibility: indeed the famous European Commission report, *One Market, One Money* argued that monetary union would enhance labour market flexibility. The upshot of all of this, according to Grubel, is that those empirical studies that suggest that shocks are difficult to accommodate under fixed exchange rates must be seriously discounted if the data they rely on

Introduction

were generated under flexible rates. As a concluding comment, Grubel notes that the wholesale acceptance of the Keynesian assumption of downward rigid wages led to inflation and deficits as solutions to unemployment. Now that price stability and balanced budgets have triumphed over inflation and deficit financing, attention has turned to the importance of flexible rates to deal with unemployment and imperfect labour market flexibility. Grubel's parting shot is that the time has come for exchange-rate flexibility to join inflation and deficits on the scrap heap of policies inspired by Keynesian economics.

In "Unilateral and Multilateral Currency Integration: Reflections on Western Hemispheric Monetary Union", George von Furstenberg broadens the discussion beyond a Canada-U.S. currency union. His view is that while dollarization may be a useful immediate option for some countries in our hemisphere, it is a second-best option in the short run and unsustainable in the long run. This long-run unsustainability will arise because if the option of monetary union is not available, then rather than losing seigniorage indefinitely countries will, in tandem, reclaim co-ownership and co-management of their monetary assets in a multilateral monetary union with like-minded countries. The Americans could attempt to counter this somewhat by making dollarization more attractive, for example, by returning some of the seigniorage to the dollarizing country. But even this will unlikely be enough. Von Furstenberg concludes that eventually dollarization (or unilateral monetary union as he calls it) will be doomed and destabilizing unless it evolves toward a multilateral form from within. Hence, his policy recommendation is that it is time for the United States to take a careful look at Europe's multilateral model of monetary union and to develop a variant that could become beneficial for the western hemisphere as a whole.

Mundell on Currency Evolution

It is entirely fitting that Bob Mundell has the last word, specifically "Exchange Rate Systems and Currency Integration: Prospects for the Twenty-First Century". This paper fulfills two roles. Firstly, it is a natural extension and elaboration of the series of issues dealt with by McCallum, Grubel and von Furstenberg. Secondly, it is a perfect "bookend" to Mundell's Nobel Lecture. The latter paper (and century) essentially ends with the introduction of the euro in 1999 whereas this paper begins with the advent of the euro and what this might augur for the twenty-first century.

12   *Introduction*

The analysis is far reaching, focusing as it does on alternative approaches to currency integration, on alternative approaches to monetary rules, on the pros and cons of dollarization and its alternatives from a Canadian perspective, on the need for both external and internal stability and, finally, on the advantages of a world currency. His concluding paragraph is instructive:

> The link between language and currency has often been noted. Language is a medium of communication and currency is a medium of exchange. National, ethnic and liturgical languages are here to stay, but a common world language, understood as a second language everywhere, would obviously facilitate international understanding. By the same token, national or regional currencies will be with us for a long time in the next centuries, but a common world currency, understood as the second most important currency in every country, in which values could be communicated and payments made everywhere, would be a magnificent step toward increased prosperity and improved international organization.

* * *

All that remains is for me to express my sincerest thanks, as well as those of the John Deutsch Institute for the Study of Economic Policy and our co-sponsors in this venture, to the authors and to Robert Mundell for their contributions to this volume.

It is a privilege and an enormous pleasure for me to invite you to sample our celebratory tribute to Robert Alexander Mundell, the 1999 Nobel Laureate in Economic Sciences.

Introduction

Money, Markets and Mobility

Part I:

The 1999 Nobel Lecture in Economic Sciences

A Reconsideration of the Twentieth Century

Robert A. Mundell

By comparison with past centuries, the twentieth has produced extremes. Its earliest part was a benign continuation of the pax of the nineteenth century. But this calm before the storm was followed by World War I, communism, hyperinflation, fascism, depression, genocide, World War II, the atom bomb and the Soviet occupation of Eastern Europe. There followed a period of comparative stability, punctuated by the balance of terror of the Cold War, the Nato Alliance and decolonialism. Toward the end of the century the Cold War ended, the Soviet Empire was dismantled, democracy emerged in Eastern Europe, the *Pax Americana* flourished and the euro came into being. The clue to the twentieth century lies in the links between its first and last decades, the "bookends" of the century.

In 1906, Whitelaw Reid, the U.S. Ambassador to Britain, gave a lecture at Cambridge University with the title, *The Greatest Fact in Modern History*, in which the author, a diplomat, journalist and politician, was given as his subject, the rise and development of the United States! It cannot have

---

This article is a revised version of the lecture Robert A. Mundell delivered in Stockholm, Sweden, December 10, 1999, when he received the Bank of Sweden Prize in Economic Sciences in Memory of Alfred Nobel. The article is copyright The Nobel Foundation 1999 and is reprinted with permission from the Royal Swedish Academy of Sciences 1999 <http://www.columbia.edu/~ram15/nobelLecture.html>.

been obvious then that the rise of the United States was the "greatest fact in modern history" but it was true that in a matter of only two centuries a small colony had become the biggest economy in the world. The first decade of the century hinted at what the last decade confirmed, *viz.*, American preponderance. Forget the seventy-five years between 1914 and 1989!

An underlying theme of my lecture today is the role of the United States in what has been aptly called the "American century". I want to bring out the role of the monetary factor as a determinant of political events. Specifically, I will argue that many of the political changes in the century have been caused by little-understood perturbations in the international monetary system, while these in turn have been a consequence of the rise of the United States and mistakes of its financial arm, the Federal Reserve System.

The twentieth century began with a highly efficient international monetary system that was destroyed in World War I, and its bungled recreation in the inter-war period brought on the great depression, Hitler and World War II. The new arrangements that succeeded it depended more on the dollar policies of the Federal Reserve System than on the discipline of gold itself. When the link to gold was finally severed, the Federal Reserve System was implicated in the greatest inflation the United States has yet known, at least since the days of the Revolutionary War. Even so, as the century ends, a relearning process has created an entirely new framework for capturing some of the advantages of the system with which the century began.

The century can be divided into three distinct, almost equal parts. The first part, 1900–33, is the story of the international gold standard, its breakdown during the war, mismanaged restoration in the 1920s and its demise in the early 1930s. The second part, 1934–71, starts with the devaluation of the dollar and the establishment of the $35 gold price and ends when the United States took the dollar off gold. The third part of the century, 1972–1999, starts with the collapse into flexible exchange rates and continues with the subsequent outbreak of massive inflation and stagnation in the 1970s, the blossoming of supply-side economics in the 1980s, and the return to monetary stability and the birth of the euro in the 1990s. The century ends, however, with our monetary system in deficit compared to the first decade of the century and that suggests unfinished business for the decades ahead.

Mismanagement of the Gold Standard

The international gold standard at the beginning of the twentieth century operated smoothly to facilitate trade, payments and capital movements. Balance of payments were kept in equilibrium at fixed exchange rates by an adjustment mechanism that had a high degree of automaticity. The world price level may have been subject to long-term trends but annual inflation or deflation rates were low, tended to cancel out, and preserve the value of money in the long run. The system gave the world a high degree of monetary integration and stability.

International monetary systems, however, are not static. They have to be consistent and evolve with the power configuration of the world economy. Gold, silver and bimetallic monetary standards had prospered best in a decentralized world where adjustment policies were automatic. But in the decades leading up to World War I, the central banks of the great powers had emerged as oligopolists in the system. The efficiency and stability of the gold standard came to be increasingly dependent on the discretionary policies of a few significant central banks. This tendency was magnified by an order of magnitude with the creation of the Federal Reserve System in the United States in 1913. The Federal Reserve Board, which ran the system, centralized the money power of an economy that had become three times larger than either of its nearest rivals, Britain and Germany. The story of the gold standard therefore became increasingly the story of the Federal Reserve System.

World War I made gold unstable. The instability began when deficit spending pushed the European belligerents off the gold standard, and gold came to the United States, where the newly-created Federal Reserve System monetized it, doubling the dollar price level and halving the real value of gold. The instability continued when, after the war, the Federal Reserve engineered a dramatic deflation in the recession of 1920–21, bringing the dollar (and gold) price level 60 percent of the way back toward the prewar equilibrium, a level at which the Federal Reserve kept it until 1929.

It was in this milieu that the rest of the world, led by Germany, Britain and France, returned to the gold standard. The problem was that, with world (dollar) prices still 40 percent above their prewar equilibrium, the real value of gold reserves and supplies was proportionately smaller. At the same time monetary gold was badly distributed, with half of it in the United States. In addition, uncertainty over exchange rates and reparations (which were fixed

A Reconsideration of the Twentieth Century

in gold) increased the demand for reserves. In the face of this situation would not the increased demand for gold brought about by a return to the gold standard bring on a deflation? A few economists, like Charles Rist of France, Ludwig von Mises of Austria and Gustav Cassel of Sweden, thought it would.

Cassel (1925) had been very explicit even before Britain returned to gold:

> The gold standard, of course, cannot secure a greater stability in the general level of prices of a country than the value of gold itself possesses. Inasmuch as the stability of the general level of prices is desirable, our work for a restoration of the gold standard must be supplemented by endeavours to keep the value of gold as constant as possible ... With the actual state of gold production it can be taken for certain that after a comparatively short time, perhaps within a decade, the present superabundance of gold will be followed, as a consequence of increasing demand, by a marked scarcity of this precious metal tending to cause a fall of prices.

After gold had been restored, Cassel pursued his line of reasoning further, warning of the need to economize on the monetary use of gold in order to ward off a depression. In 1928 he wrote:

> The great problem before us is how to meet the growing scarcity of gold which threatens the world both from increased demand and from diminished supply. We must solve this problem by a systematic restriction of the monetary demand for gold. Only if we succeed in doing this can we hope to prevent a permanent fall of the general price level and a prolonged and world-wide depression which would inevitably be connected with such a fall in prices.

Rist, Mises and Cassel proved to be right. Deflation was already in the air in the late 1920s with the fall in prices of agricultural products and raw materials. The Wall Street crash in 1929 was another symptom, and generalized deflation began in 1930. That the deflation was generalized if uneven can be seen from the percentage loss of wholesale prices in various countries from the high in 1929 to September 1931 (the month that Britain left the gold standard): Japan, 40.5; Netherlands, 38.1; Belgium, 31.3; Italy 31.0; United States, 29.5; United Kingdom, 29.2; Canada, 28.9; France, 28.3; Germany, 22.0.

The dollar price level hit bottom in 1932 and 1933. The highlights of the price level from 1914 to 1934 are given in Table 1.

Table 1: Wholesale Prices, 1914-33

Year	1930 = 100	Year	1930 = 100
1914	78.4	1924	113.5
1915	80.5	1925	119.7
1916	98.9	1926	115.7
1917	135.9	1927	110.5
1918	152.0	1928	112.1
1919	160.3	1929	110.1
1920	178.7	1930	100.0
1921	113.0	1931	84.3
1922	111.9	1932	75.3
1923	116.4	1933	76.2

Source: Wholesale Price Index, Bureau of Labor Statistics. Adapted from Table 21 in Jastram (1982: 206).

For decades economists have wrestled with the problem of what caused the deflation and depression of the 1930s. The massive literature on the subject has brought on more heat than light. One source of controversy has been whether the depression was caused by a shift of aggregate demand or a fall in the money supply. Surely the answer is both! But none of the theories — monetarist or Keynesian — would have been able to predict the fall in the money supply or aggregate demand in advance. They were rooted in short-run closed-economy models which could not pick up the gold standard effects during and after World War I. By contrast, the theory that the deflation was caused by the return to the gold standard was not only predictable, but was actually, as we have noted above, predicted.

The gold exchange standard was already on the ropes with the onset of deflation. It moved into its crisis phase with the failure, in the spring of 1931,

A Reconsideration of the Twentieth Century

of the Viennese Creditanstalt, the biggest bank in Central Europe, bringing into play a chain reaction that spread to Germany, where it was met by deflationary monetary policies and a reimposition of controls, and to Britain, where, on September 21, 1931, the pound was taken off gold. Several countries, however, had preceded Britain in going off gold: Australia, Brazil, Chile, New Zealand, Paraguay, Peru, Uruguay and Venezuela, while Austria, Canada, Germany and Hungary had imposed controls. A large number of other countries followed Britain off gold.

Meanwhile, the United States hung onto the gold standard for dear life. After making much of its sensible shift to a monetary policy that sets as its goal price stability rather than maintenance of the gold standard, it reverted back to the latter at the very time it mattered most, in the early 1930s.

Instead of pumping liquidity into the system, it chose to defend the gold standard. Hard on the heels of the British departure from gold, in October 1931, the Federal Reserve raised the rediscount rate in two steps from 1 to 3 percent dragging the economy deeper into the mire of deflation and depression and aggravating the banking crisis. As we have seen, wholesale prices fell 35 percent between 1929 and 1933.

Monetary deflation was transformed into depression by fiscal shocks. The Smoot-Hawley tariff, which led to retaliation abroad, was the first: between 1929 and 1933 imports fell by 30 percent and, significantly, exports fell even more, by almost 40 percent. On June 6, 1932, the Democratic Congress passed, and President Herbert Hoover signed, in a fit of balanced-budget mania, one of its most ill-advised acts, the Revenue Act of 1932, a bill which provided the largest percentage tax increase ever enacted in American peacetime history. Unemployment rose to a high of 24.9 percent of the labor force in 1933, and GDP fell by 57 percent at current prices and 22 percent in real terms.

The banking crisis was now in full swing. Failures had soared from an average of about 500 per year in the 1920s, to 1,350 in 1930, 2,293 in 1931, and 1,453 in 1932. Franklin D. Roosevelt, in one of his first actions on assuming the presidency in March 1933, put an embargo on gold exports. After April 20, the dollar was allowed to float downward.

The deflation of the 1930s was the mirror image of the wartime rise in the price level that had not been reversed in the 1920–21 recession. When countries go off the gold standard, gold falls in real value and the price level in gold countries rise. When countries go onto the gold standard, gold rises in real value and the price level falls. The appreciation of gold in the 1930s was the mirror image of the depreciation of gold in World War I. The dollar

Robert A. Mundell

price level in 1934 was the same as the dollar price level in 1914. The deflation of the 1930s has to be seen, not as a unique "crisis of capitalism", as the Marxists were prone to say, but as a continuation of a pattern that had appeared with considerable predictability before — whenever countries shift onto or return to a monetary standard. The deflation in the 1930s has its precedents in the 1780s, the 1820s and the 1870s.

What verdict can be passed on this third of the century? One is that the Federal Reserve System was fatally guilty of inconsistency at critical times. It held onto the gold standard between 1914 and 1921 when gold had become unstable. It shifted over to a policy of price stability in the 1920s that was successful. But it shifted back to the gold standard at the worst time imaginable, when gold had again become unstable. The unfortunate fact was that the least experienced of the important central banks — the new boy on the block — had the awesome power to make or break the system by itself.

The European economies were by no means blameless in this episode. They were the countries that changed the status quo and moved onto the gold standard without weighing the consequences. They failed to heed the lessons of history — that a concerted movement off, or onto, any metallic standard brings in its wake, respectively, inflation or deflation. After a great war, in which inflation has occurred in the monetary leader and gold has become correspondingly undervalued, a return to the gold standard is only consistent with price stability if the price of gold is increased. Failing that possibility, countries would have fared better had they heeded Keynes' advice to sacrifice the benefits of fixed exchange rates under the gold standard and instead stabilize commodity prices rather than the price of gold.

Had the price of gold been raised in the late 1920s, or, alternatively, had the major central banks pursued policies of price stability instead of adhering to the gold standard, there would have been no Great Depression, no Nazi revolution and no World War II.

Policy Mix Under the Dollar Standard

In April 1934, after a year of flexible exchange rates, the United States went back to gold after a devaluation of the dollar. This decreased the gold value of the dollar by 40.94 percent, raising the official price of gold 69.33 percent

A Reconsideration of the Twentieth Century

to $35 an ounce. How history would have been changed had President Herbert Hoover devalued the dollar, three years earlier!

France held onto its gold parity until 1936, when it devalued the franc. Two other far-reaching events occurred in that year. One was the publication of Keynes' *General Theory*; the other signing of the Tripartite Accord among the United States, Britain and France. One ushered in a new theory of policy management for a closed economy; the other, a precursor of the Bretton Woods agreement, established some rules for exchange rate management in the new international monetary system.

The contradiction between the two could hardly be more ironic. At a time when Keynesian policies of national economic management were becoming increasingly accepted by economists, the world economy had adopted a new fixed exchange rate system that was incompatible with those policies.

In the new arrangements, which were ratified at Bretton Woods in 1944, countries were required to establish parities fixed in gold and maintain fixed exchange rates to one another. The new system, however, differed greatly from the old gold standard. For one thing, the role of the United States in the system was asymmetric. A special clause allowed any country the option of fixing the price of gold instead of keeping the exchange rates of other members fixed. Because the dollar was the only currency tied to gold it was the only country in a position to exercise the gold option. There thus came into being the asymmetrical arrangements in which the United States fixed the price of gold whereas other countries fixed their currencies to the dollar. Another difference of the new system from the old was that not even the United States was on anything that could be called a full gold standard. The dollar was no longer in the old sense "anchored" to gold; it was rather that the world price level, and therefore the real price of gold, was heavily influenced by the United States. Gold had become a passenger in the system.

Was a new system created at Bretton Woods? From the early planning it seemed that this would be the case. The British and American plans both contained provisions for a world currency: John Maynard Keynes had his "bancor", and Harry Dexter White had his "unitas". But these forward-looking ideas were soon buried. No doubt the Americans came to believe that a world currency would clip the wings of the dollar. There was not therefore a Bretton Woods "system" but rather a Bretton Woods "order" outlining the charter of a system that already existed.

World War II brought a repetition of the monetary imbalances of World War I. The devaluation of the dollar and gathering war clouds in Europe made the dollar a safe haven and the recipient of gold to pay for war goods.

The United States sterilized the gold imports and imposed price controls. It was therefore able to run deficits without going off gold. Because gold was still "overvalued" in this era of "dollar shortage", interest rates remained incredibly low. By 1945, the public debt had soared to 125 percent of GDP.

At the end of the war, the U.S. price level doubled as a result of the end of price control, the unleashing of pent-up demand and the expansionary monetary policies of the Federal Reserve System that continued to support the bond market. The postwar inflation halved the real value of the public debt, increased tax revenues as a result of "bracket creep" in the steeply-progressive income tax system (which rose to 92.5 percent), halved the real value of gold and eliminated its overvaluation. After further inflation during the Korean War and the onset of steady "secular" inflation, gold became undervalued.

Meanwhile, Germany and Japan, in the aftermath of their paper-money inflations, under the auspices of the U.S. occupation authorities, had currency reforms in which 10 units of old money were exchanged for 1 unit of new currency; both reforms took place in 1948, with the exchange rate for Germany set at DM 4.2 = $1, and for Japan at Y360 = $1. The exchange rates later proved to undervalue German and Japanese labor and the two economies performed spectacularly in the post-war period, fulfilling their destiny of overtaking Britain and France as the second and third largest economies in the world.

Until the 1960s, U.S. macroeconomic policy was based more on closed-economy principles than on the requirements of an international monetary system. Monetary and fiscal policy were directed at the needs of internal balance and the balance of payments was all but ignored. In 1949 the United States had peaked at over 700 million ounces of gold, more than 75 percent of the world's monetary gold. Gold losses began soon after, but the effect of these sales on the money supply was sterilized by equivalent purchases of government bonds by the Federal Reserve System. The gold losses were at first looked upon as a healthy redistribution of the world's gold reserves but toward the late 1950s they were recognized as dangerous.

The Federal Reserve System was required to keep a 25 percent (reduced from 40 percent in 1945) gold cover behind its currency and deposit liabilities. If gold reserves fell below this level, interest rates would have to be raised. If the fall in gold reserves reached the level of required reserves, the United States would be forced to take account of its balance-of-payments constraint like any other country. The problem of the appropriate mix for

A Reconsideration of the Twentieth Century

monetary and fiscal policy came to the foreground during the administration of President John F. Kennedy, who took office in 1961.

At this time I played a part in the story. Newly arrived in the Research Department at the International Monetary Fund (IMF) in the fall of 1961, I was asked to look into the theoretical aspects of the monetary-fiscal policy mix. The main problem in this post-Sputnik era was sluggish growth and subpar employment in the United States in contrast to Europe and Japan (precisely the reverse of the situation today), and a now worrisome balance of payments deficit. Three schools of thought had emerged. Keynesians, led by Leon Keyserling, the first Chairman of the Council of Economic Advisers, pushed for easy money and an increase in government spending. The Chamber of Commerce argued for fiscal constraint and tighter money. The Council of Economic Advisers, following the Samuelson-Tobin "neo-classical synthesis", advocated low interest rates to spur growth and a budget surplus to siphon off excess liquidity and prevent inflation.

In my analysis, I showed that none of the above policies would work, and would lead the economy away from equilibrium. The correct policy mix was to lower taxes to spur employment, and tighten monetary policy to protect the balance of payments. My paper was circulated by the IMF to its members in November 1961 and published in *IMF Staff Papers* in March 1962.

It gradually came to be realized that the policies of the Kennedy administration were not working: the wrong policy mix had produced increasingly disequilibrating effects: a steel strike, a stock market crash, and stagnation. At the end of 1962, Kennedy announced a reversal of the policy mix, with tax cuts to spur the economy and interest rates to protect the balance of payments. Legislative delays meant that the tax cut had to wait until the summer of 1964 but its anticipation positioned the economy for the great expansion of the 1960s.

The adoption of my policy mix helped the United States to achieve rapid growth with stability. It was not intended to and could not solve the basic problem of the international monetary system, which stemmed from the undervaluation of gold. Nevertheless the problem of the U.S. balance-of-payments was intricately tied up with the problem of the system. With very little excess gold coming into the stocks of central banks from the private market, and the U.S. dollar the only alternative component of reserves, the U.S. deficit was the principal means by which the rest of the world was supplied with additional reserves. If the United States failed to correct its balance of payments deficit, it would no longer be able to maintain gold convertibility; on the other hand, if it corrected its deficit, the rest of the world would run short of reserves and bring on slower growth or, worse, deflation. The last scenario hinted at a repetition of the problem of the interwar period.

Two basic solutions were consistent with preserving the system. One solution was to raise the price of gold. The founding fathers of the IMF had put a provision in the IMF Articles of Agreement for dealing with a gold scarcity or surplus: a change in the par values of all currencies, which would have changed the price of gold in terms of all currencies and left exchange rates unchanged. In the 1968 election campaign, candidate Richard M. Nixon chose Arthur Burns as his emissary on a secret mission to sound out European opinion on an increase in the price of gold. It turned out to be favorable and Burns recommended prompt action immediately after the election. Nothing, however, came of it.

The other option was to create a substitute for gold. This course was in fact adopted. In the late summer of 1967, international agreement was reached on an amendment to the IMF articles to allow the creation of Special Drawing Rights (SDRs), gold-guaranteed bookkeeping reserves made available through the IMF, with a unit value equal to one gold dollar, or 1/35 of an ounce. Somewhat less than SDR 10 billion were allocated to member countries in 1970, 1971 and 1972, but they proved to be inadequate — too little and too late — to meet the main problems of the system.

On August 15, 1971, confronted by requests for conversion of dollars into gold by the United Kingdom and other countries, President Nixon took the dollar off gold, closing the "gold window" at which dollars were exchanged for gold with foreign central banks. The other countries now took their currencies off the dollar and a period of floating began.

But floating made the embryonic plans just forming for European monetary integration more difficult, and in December 1971, at a meeting at the Smithsonian Institution in Washington, D.C., finance ministers agreed on a restoration of the fixed exchange rate system without gold convertibility. A few exchange rates were changed and the official dollar price of gold was raised but the act was almost purely nominal since the United States was no longer committed to buying or selling gold.

The world thus moved onto a pure dollar standard, in which the major countries fixed their currencies to the dollar without a reciprocal obligation with respect to gold convertibility on the part of the United States. But U.S. monetary policy was too expansionary in the following years and, after another ineffective devaluation of the dollar, the system was allowed to break

A Reconsideration of the Twentieth Century

up into generalized floating in the spring of 1973. Thus ended the dollar standard.

What lessons can be learned from the second third of the century? One is that the policy mix has to suit the system. Another is that a gold-based international system cannot survive if war-related inflation makes gold undervalued and the authorities are unwilling to adjust the gold price and create a sufficient quantity of gold substitutes. A third lesson is that the superpower cannot be disciplined by the requirements of convertibility or any other international commitment if it is at the expense of vital political objectives at home; the tail cannot wag the dog. A fourth lesson is that a fixed exchange rate system can work only if there is mutual agreement on the common rate of inflation. Europe was willing to swallow the fact that the dollar was not freely convertible into gold in the 1960s, but when U.S. monetary policy became incompatible with price stability in the rest of the world (and in particular Europe), the costs of the fixed-exchange-rate system were perceived to exceed its benefits.

A final lesson is that political events, and in particular the Vietnam War soured relations between the Atlantic partners and created a tension in the 1960s that can only be compared with the pall cast over the international system by disputes over reparations in the 1920s. Fixed-exchange-rate systems work better among friends than rivals or enemies.

Inflation and Supply-Side Economics

With the breakdown of the system, money supplies became more elastic, accommodating not only inflationary wage developments but also the monopolistic pricing of internationally traded commodities. Each time the price of oil was raised in the 1970s, the Eurodollar market expanded to finance the deficits of oil-importing countries; from deposits of $223 billion 1971 they would explode to $2,351 billion in 1982 (International Monetary Fund, *IMF International Statistics Yearbook*, 1988 p. 68).

Inflation in the United States had now become a major problem. It had taken twenty years, from 1952 to 1971, for U.S. wholesale prices to rise by less than 30 percent. But after 1971, it took only eleven years for U.S. prices to rise by 157 percent! This mainly peacetime inflation was greater than the war-related inflations from World War II (108 percent over 1939–48),

World War I (121 percent over 1913–1920), the Civil War (118 percent over 1861–1864) or the War of 1812 (44 percent over 1811–1814). The greatest inflation in U.S. history since the War of Independence took place after the United States left gold in the decade after 1971.

That inflation in the 1970s was worldwide can be seen from the price indexes of the G-7 countries in Table 2, noting the index values for 1971 in comparison with the standard base of 100 in 1980. Only in Germany did consumer prices in the decade of the seventies fall short of doubling. In Italy and the United Kingdom, prices more than tripled. The breakdown in monetary discipline was worldwide, engulfing all the G-7 countries and to an even greater extent most of the rest of the world.

Table 2: Consumer Prices in G-7 Countries, Selected Years 1950–98

Country	1950	1971	1980	1985	1990	1998
United States	29.2	49.1	100	130.5	158.5	197.8
Japan	16.3	44.9	100	114.4	122.5	134.4
United Kingdom	13.4	30.3	100	141.5	188.7	243.6
Germany	39.2	64.1	100	121.0	129.4	144.8
France	15.6	42.1	100	157.9	184.2	213.7
Italy	13.9	28.7	100	190.3	250.6	346.3
Canada	28.4	47.5	100	143.0	177.9	203.7

Source: *IMF International Financial Statistics* (International Monetary Fund, various years).

In the United States, three back-to-back years of two-digit inflation (1979–81) created a crisis situation. The price of gold hit $850 an ounce in early 1980, and silver went to $50 an ounce. On March 14, 1980, President Jimmy Carter announced his new program: an oil import fee, and credit controls. The plan was a disaster and real output plummeted in the second

A Reconsideration of the Twentieth Century

quarter. In December 1980, a month after the presidential elections, the prime interest rate hit a record of 21.5 percent! The United States seemed to be on the brink of financial disaster.

Gone were the days when, with David Ricardo, economists could think of money as a "veil". The existence of big government and progressive income taxes guarantees non-neutrality. One route was through the fiscal system. With steeply progressive tax rates, rising from zero to 70 percent at the federal level, and up to 85 percent counting state and local taxes, inflation was pushing taxpayers into higher and higher tax brackets even at unchanged real incomes. Taxes had to be paid on interest receipts even though the bulk of the high interest rates represented inflation premiums. Soaring tax revenues coupled with government's high marginal propensity to spend led to an increasing share of government in the economy. No wonder the stock market hated inflation!

Supply-side economics began as a policy system alternative to short-run Keynesian and monetarist demand-side models. It was based on a policy mix that delivered price stability through monetary discipline, and economic stimulation of employment and growth through the tax and regulatory systems. It was partly a continuation of my work on the policy mix in the early 1960s. In the spring of 1974 I presented a paper at a conference on global inflation in Washington, an excerpt of which was reported (Rowland Evans and Robert Novak, 1981, p. 63) as follows:

> While the Ford administration was insisting that only a tax increase could fight inflation, Mundell argued that an immediate $10 billion *reduction* was essential to avoid even bigger budget deficits fueled by "stagflation," the lethal combination of inflation and stagnation inherited from Nixon by Ford.

With my arrival at Columbia University in the fall of 1974, a "club" of what later would become dubbed as "supply-siders" met from time to time at a Wall Street restaurant to discuss economic policy and particularly what to do about the rising inflation and unemployment. The conclusion was that cuts in marginal tax rates were needed to create output incentives to spur the economy, and tight money would produce price stability. The need for tax cuts and tight money became more urgent as inflation increased in the late 1970s and inflation, via "bracket creep", was pushing taxpayers into ever-higher income tax brackets. Within a short time, a political convert, Jack F. Kemp, Congressman from Buffalo, parlayed the ideas into a bill calling for a 30 percent tax cut, most of which would be enacted in a sweeping 23 percent tax cut spread over three years, followed by an indexing of the tax brackets for inflation. In the election campaign of 1980, Kemp was a candidate for the presidency but bowed out after Ronald W. Reagan agreed to incorporate the Kemp-Roth bill in his agenda for the economy. After Reagan's election, the first phase of the new policy mix was introduced with the Economic Recovery Act of 1981.

Meanwhile, the Federal Reserve, under the chairmanship of Paul Volcker, at long last woke up and tightened monetary policy. After a steep, but short, recession, the economy embarked on one of its longest-ever expansions at the same time that inflation was increasingly brought under control. The new policies shifted the Phillips curve downward and to the left, allowing unemployment and inflation to decrease at the same time.

There was a sequel to the tax cut, the arms buildup, the policy of disinflation and Reagan's landslide re-election. The Tax Reform Act of 1986, the second phase of the supply-side revolution, lowered the marginal tax rate in the highest tax bracket to 28 percent, the lowest top marginal rate since 1932. The 1982–90 expansion was the second longest up to that time and, along with the arms buildup, helped to convince the leaders of the Soviet Union to leave Eastern Europe free to choose its own system.

Growth continued until the nine-month downsizing recession of 1990-91, which probably cost President George H. W. Bush re-election. Expansion resumed in the spring of 1991 and continued at least until the end of the decade, making the combined period 1982–2000 the greatest expansions in the history of any country. Over the period no less than 37 million new jobs were created! The Dow-Jones Average soared from below 750 in the summer of 1982 to over 11,000 by the turn of the century.

Meanwhile, the withdrawal of the Soviet Union from Eastern Europe — itself, as already noted, partly due to the success of supply-side economics — made unification of Germany possible and brought with it renewed impetus for European monetary and political integration. The fiscal spending associated with German spending on its new states gave a jolt to the exchange-rate mechanism (ERM) of the European Monetary System (EMS). A few countries left the exchange-rate mechanism, and others opted for devaluation within it. Nevertheless, by January 1, 1994, the European Monetary Institute came into being, and, by the middle of 1998, so did its successor, the European Central Bank. On January 1, 1999, the euro was launched with eleven members. A new era in the international monetary system was unfolding.

A Reconsideration of the Twentieth Century

The introduction of the euro redraws the international monetary landscape. With the euro — upon its birth the second most important currency in the world, — a tri-polar currency world involving the dollar, euro, and yen came into being. The exchange rates among these three islands of stability will become the most important prices in the world economy.

The creation of the euro will doubtless lead to its widespread adoption in Central and Eastern Europe as well as the former CFA franc zone in Africa and along the rim of the Mediterranean. Expansion of the wider euro area — counting not only currencies entering with an enlargement of the European Union, but also currencies fixed to the euro — will eventually give it a transactions area larger than that of the United States and will, inevitably, provoke countervailing expansion of the dollar area in Latin America and parts of Asia. Other currency areas are likely to form, adapting to local needs the example of Europe. But stability for the near future will be best assured by stabilization with one of the "G-3" areas.

The 1970s was a decade of inflation, but the 1980s was a decade of correction and the 1990s a decade of comparative stability. The experiment with flexible exchange rates in the 1970s started off as a disaster, from the standpoint of economic stability, but nevertheless, it set in motion a learning mechanism that would not have taken place in its absence. The lesson was that inflation, budget deficits, big debts and big government are all detrimental to public well-being and that the cost of correcting them is so high that no democratic government wants to repeat the experience. Consequently virtually all of the developed OECD countries had drastically reduced budget deficits and whittled inflation rates down to those of the pre-1914 international gold standard.

In many respects economic performance in the 1990s compares well with that of the first decade of the century. Prudent finance then as now produce similar effects. But in two respects our modern arrangements — I am trying to avoid the word "system" — compares unfavorably with the earlier system: the current volatility of exchange rates and the absence of a global currency.

The volatility of exchange rates is especially disturbing among countries each of which have achieved, according to local definitions and indexes, price stability. The volatility therefore measures real-exchange-rate changes and involves dysfunctional shifting between domestic and international-goods industries and aggravates instability in the financial markets.

How much flexibility is good? If we think of the euro as the "ghost of the mark" could we look at past variations in the mark-dollar rate as an augur of the dollar-euro rate in the future? Between 1971 and 1980 the mark doubled against the dollar, to $1 = DM 1.7; between 1980 and 1985, it halved, to $1 = DM 3.4; between 1985 and the crisis of 1992, it more than doubled, to $1 = DM 1.39; and it has since fallen to $1 = DM 1.9. The mark-dollar rate has fluctuated up and down by more than 100 percent, a mountain of volatility that would make the ERM crisis of 1992 seem like a little hillock. Comparable movements of the dollar-euro rate would crack Euroland apart.

Nor does looking at the yen-dollar rate give us more comfort. The dollar has gone down from 250 yen in 1985 to 79 yen in 1995, and then it went up to 148 yen in 1998 (with forecasters expecting it to hit 200!), and down to 105 yen in early 2000.

The twentieth century will not see fixed exchange rates again among the G-3. But it is entirely possible that a new international monetary system will emerge in the twenty-first century. Convergence of inflation rates has become remarkable, better than that associated with parts of the Bretton Woods era, comparable to the gold standard itself, as Table 3 shows:

Table 3: Inflation Rates Among the Big Three

	1995	1996	1997	1998	1999		
					I	II	III
United States	2.8	2.9	2.3	1.6	1.7	2.1	2.3
Japan	-0.1	0.1	1.7	0.6	-0.1	-0.3	0.0
Euro Area*	1.8	1.5	1.8	1.0	0.8	1.0	1.1

Note: *Germany cost-of-living index for 1995–98, the European Monetary Union Index of Consumer Prices for 1999.

Source: IMF *International Financial Statistics*, January 2000, 57.

It may seem a long way off, but I believe that given such the degree of inflation convergence some sort of monetary union of the three areas would not be impossible. The same conditions would result from a three-currency fixed-exchange-rate system with agreement over a common inflation rate and a fair distribution of seigniorage. If such a fixed-exchange-rate arrangement among countries that had converged is conceivable, it would not be such a far step toward a reformed international monetary system with a world money of the kind initially proposed back in the days of Bretton Woods.

To conclude this section, what lessons can we take from the last third of the twentieth century? One is that flexible exchange rates, at least initially, did not provide the same discipline as fixed rates.

A second is that the costs of inflation are much higher in a world with progressive income tax rates.

A third is that the need for, and means of, attaining monetary stability can be learned. A fourth is that the policy mix can shift the Phillips curve.

Experience breeds its own reaction: Plato the inflationist gave birth to Aristotle, the hard-money man. The reaction in the 1980s gave a boost to central bank independence. Governments forced into the Maastricht mold had to cut back on spending growth as well as deficits. Supply-side economics pointed to one of the mechanisms for strapping down ministers of finance.

One lesson, however, has yet to be learned. Flexible exchange rates are an unnecessary evil in a world where each country has achieved price stability.

Conclusions

It is time to wrap up the century in some conclusions. A first conclusion is that the international monetary system depends on the power configuration of the countries that make it up. Bismarck once said that the most important fact of the nineteenth century was that England and America spoke the same language. Along the same lines, the most important fact of the twentieth century has been the rise of the United States as a superpower. Despite the incredible rise in gold production, Gresham's Law came into play and the dollar elbowed out gold as the principal international money.

The first third of twentieth century economics was dominated by the confrontation of the Federal Reserve System with the gold standard. The gold standard broke down in World War I and its restoration in the 1920s created the deflation of the 1930s. Economists blamed the gold standard instead of their mishandling of it and turned away from international automaticity to national management. The Great Depression itself led to totalitarianism and World War II.

The second third of the twentieth century was dominated by the contradiction between national macroeconomic management and the new international monetary system. In the new system, the United States fixed the price of gold and the other major countries fixed their currencies to the convertible dollar. But national macroeconomic management precluded the operation of the international adjustment mechanism and the system broke down in the early 1970s when the United States stopped fixing the price of gold and the other countries stopped fixing the dollar.

The last third of the twentieth century started off with the destruction of the international monetary system and the vacuum sent officials and academics into a search for "structure". In the 1970s the clarion call was for a "new international monetary order" and in the 1990s a "new international monetary architecture". The old system was one way of handling the inflation problem multilaterally. Flexibility left each country on its own. Inflation was the initial result but a learning mechanism educated a generation of monetary officials on the advantages of stability and by the end of the century fiscal prudence and inflation control had again become the watchword in all the rich and many of the poor countries.

Today, the dollar, the euro and yen have established three islands of monetary stability,which is a great improvement over the 1970s and 1980s. There are, however, two pieces of unfinished business. The most important is the dysfunctional volatility of exchange rates that could sour international relations in time of crisis. The other is the absence of an international currency.

The century closes with an international monetary system inferior to that with which it began, but much improved from the situation that existed only two-and-a-half decades ago. It remains to be seen where leadership will come from and whether a restoration of the international monetary system will be compatible with the power configuration of the world economy. It would certainly make a contribution to world harmony.

A Reconsideration of the Twentieth Century   *35*

Bibliography

Anderson, Martin. *Revolution.* New York: Harcourt Brace Jovanovich, 1988.

Bartley, Robert. *The Seven Fat Years.* New York: Free Press, 1992.

Cassel, Gustav. *The Restoration of Gold as a Universal Monetary Standard* (1925).

_____. *Postwar Monetary Stabilization.* New York: Columbia University Press, 1928.

Evans, Rowland, and Robert Novak. *The Reagan Revolution.* New York: E. P. Dutton, 1981.

Fleming, J. Marcus. "Domestic Financial Policies Under Fixed and Floating Exchange Rates." IMF Staff Papers, November 1962, 9(3), pp. 369–79.

International Monetary Fund. *IMF International Statistical Yearbook.* Washington, DC: International Monetary Fund, 1988.

IMF International Financial Statistics. Washington, DC: International Monetary Fund, various years.

Jastram, Roy. *Silver: The Restless Metal.* New York: Wiley, 1981.

Johnson, H. Clark. *Gold, France, and the Great Depression, 1919–1932.* New Haven, CT: Yale University Press, 1997.

Johnson, Harry G. and Swoboda, Alexander K., eds. *The Economics of Common Currencies.* London: George Allen & Unwin Ltd., 1973, pp. 114–32.

Keynes, John Maynard. *A Tract on Monetary Reform.* London: Macmillan, 1923.

Mundell, Robert A. "The Monetary Dynamics of International Adjustment Under Fixed and Flexible Exchange Rates," *Quarterly Journal of Economics,* May 1960, 84(2), pp. 227–57.

_____. "A Theory of Optimum Currency Areas." *American Economic Review,* September 1961a, 51(4), pp. 657–65; reprinted in Mundell (1968).

_____. "Flexible Exchange Rates and Employment Policy." *Canadian Journal of Economics and Political Science,* November 1961b, 27(4), pp. 509–17; reprinted in Mundell (1968).

_____. "The International Disequilibrium System." *Kyklos,* 1961c, 14(2), pp. 154–72; reprinted in Mundell (1968).

_____. "The Appropriate Use of Monetary and Fiscal Policy for Internal and External Stability." *IMF Staff Papers,* March 1962, 9(1), pp. 70–79.

_____. "Capital Mobility and Stabilization Policy Under Fixed and Flexible Exchange Rates." *Canadian Journal of Economics and Political Science*, November 1963, 39(4), pp. 475–85; reprinted in R. Caves and H. Johnson, eds., *Readings in International Economics*. Burr Ridge, IL: Richard D. Irwin, Inc. (for the American Economics Association), 1967, pp. 487-99.

_____. "A Reply: Capital Mobility and Size." *Canadian Journal of Economics and Political Science*, August 1964, 30(3), pp. 421–431; reprinted in Mundell (1968).

_____. "The Dollar and the Policy Mix: 1971." *Essays in International Finance*, Princeton University, May 1971, (85), pp. 1–28.

_____. "The Future of the International Financial System," in A. Acheson, J. Chant, and M. Prachowny, eds., *Bretton Woods Revisited*. Toronto: University of Toronto Press, 1972, pp. 91–104.

_____. "The International Monetary System: The Missing Factor." *Journal of Policy Modeling*, October 1995, 17(5), pp. 479–92.

_____. "Jacques Rueff and the International Monetary System," in *Actualité de la pensée de Jacques Rueff*. Proceedings of a colloquium held on the centenary of the birth of Jacques Rueff, Paris, November 7, 1996.

_____. "Updating the Agenda for Monetary Reform," in Mario I. Blejer, Jacob A. Frankel, Leonardo Leiderman, Assaf Razin (and in cooperation with David M. Cheney), eds., *Optimum Currency Areas*. Washington, DC: International Monetary Fund, 1997a.

_____. *The International Monetary System in the 21ˢᵗ Century: Could Gold make a Comeback?* Latrobe, PA: Center for Economic Policy Studies, St. Vincent College, 1997b.

_____. "Uses and Abuses of Gresham's Law in the History of Money." *Zagreb Journal of Economics*, 1998, 2(2), pp. 3–38.

Neikirk, William R. *Volcker: Portrait of the Money Man*. New York: Congdon & Weed, 1987.

Reid, Whitelaw. *The Greatest Fact in Modern History*. New York: Crowell, 1907.

Wanniski, Jude. "It's Time to Cut Taxes." *Wall Street Journal*, December 11, 1974.

_____. *The Way the World Works*. New York: Basic Books, 1978.

Young, John Parke. *European Currency and Finance*. Washington, DC: U.S. Government Printing Office, 1925.

Money, Markets and Mobility

Part II:

Optimum Currency Areas:
Analytical Perspectives

Mundell, the Euro and Optimum Currency Areas

Ronald McKinnon

Robert Mundell was awarded the 1999 Nobel Prize in Economics for path-breaking theoretical contributions published in the 1960s on the ways monetary and fiscal policies work in open economies. His ideas are deeply embedded in textbooks on how the foreign exchanges constrain national macroeconomic policies.

But does Mundell deserve the additional sobriquet of "intellectual father of the euro"? Since 1970, he has enthusiastically advocated European monetary unification (EMU), and seems vindicated by the formal advent of the euro on January 1, 1999.

Therein lies a paradox. For more than a decade before the appearance of the EMU, the fierce debate on whether a one-size-fits-all European monetary policy was appropriate for a diverse set of European countries pitted politicians, who on the continent were mainly in favour, against economists, who generally were much more doubtful. The doubters who opposed EMU used arguments drawn from Mundell's own work! Specifically, Mundell's earlier classic article, "The Theory of Optimum Currency Areas" published in 1961 in the *American Economic Review* comes down against a common

---

I would like to thank Antonin Murphy for his thoughtful comments.

monetary policy — and seems to argue in favour of making currency areas smaller rather than larger.

This paradox, where Mundell seems to be on both sides of the debate over European monetary unification and on the adoption of common monetary standards in other parts of the world, can be resolved by noting that there are *two* Mundell models: earlier and later. In two important papers* written in 1970, but not published until 1973 and then only in an obscure conference volume, Mundell presents a different, and surprisingly modern, analytical perspective. If a common money can be managed so that its general purchasing power remains stable, then the larger the currency area — even one encompassing diverse regions or nations subject to "asymmetric shocks" — the better.

Let us consider each Mundell model in turn.

The Earlier Mundell with Stationary Expectations

Like most macro economists in 1961, Mundell still had a postwar Keynesian mindset in believing that national monetary and fiscal policies could successfully fine-tune aggregate demand to offset private sector shocks on the supply or demand side. Underpinning this belief was the assumption of stationary expectations. As a modelling strategy, he assumed that people took the current domestic price level, interest rate, and exchange rate (even when the exchange rate was floating) as holding indefinitely. Stationary expectations underlies not only in his theory of optimum currency areas (1961), but as well the standard textbook Mundell-Fleming model (Mundell, 1963) of how monetary and fiscal policy work themselves out in an open economy. In several of his influential collected essays as of 1968, Mundell showed how the principle of effective market classification could optimally assign monetary, fiscal, or exchange rate instruments to maintain full employment while balancing international payments. He presumed that agents in the private sector did not try to anticipate future movements in the price level, interest rates, the exchange rate, or in government policy itself.

---

*Editor's Note: One of these papers, "A Plan for a European Currency" is reproduced as an Appendix to this volume.

In addition to stationary expectations, Mundell (1961) posited that labour mobility was restricted to fairly small national, or even regional, domains, as in Western Europe or across developing countries. And these smallish domains could well experience macroeconomic shocks differentially, that is, "asymmetrically" in the jargon of the current literature, from their neighbours. In these special circumstances, Mundell illustrated the advantages of exchange rate flexibility in what has now become the standard textbook paradigm:

> Consider a simple model of two entities (regions or countries), initially in full employment and balance of payments equilibrium, and see what happens when the equilibrium is disturbed by a shift in demand from the goods in entity B to the goods in entity A. Assume that money wages and prices cannot be reduced in the short run without causing unemployment, and that monetary authorities act to prevent inflation....
>
> The existence of more than one (optimum) currency area in the world implies variable exchange rates.... If demand shifts from the products of country B to the products of Country A, a depreciation by country B or an appreciation by country A would correct the external imbalance and also relieve unemployment in country B and restrain inflation in country A. This is the most favorable case for flexible exchange rates based on national currencies. (Mundell, 1961, pp. 510-11)

True, Mundell carefully hedged his argument by giving examples of countries which were not optimum currency areas — as when the main terms of trade shocks occurred across regions within a single country — rather than between countries. And he also worried about monetary "balkanization" into numerous small currency domains which might destroy the liquidity properties of the monies involved. Nevertheless, our economics profession enthusiastically embraced the above delightfully simple paradigm, often without Mundell's own caveats. Textbooks took existing nation-states as natural currency areas, and argued that a one-size-fits-all monetary policy cannot be right when (i) labour markets are somewhat segmented internationally, and (ii) when the composition of output varies from one country to the next — leading them to experience terms-of-trade shocks differentially.

Thus, as the earlier Mundell had been commonly (and still is) interpreted, having an independent national monetary policy with exchange rate flexibility is the most efficient way to deal with asymmetric shocks. Even for fairly smallish countries, better macroeconomic control — in the

Mundell, the Euro and Optimum Currency Areas

Keynesian sense of an activist government standing ready to offset demand or supply shocks — would outweigh the greater costs of money changing as goods crossed international borders.

From this comforting postwar Keynesian perspective (to which the late Cambridge Nobel laureate, James Meade (1955), contributed), Mundell, and most other economists in the 1960s, presumed that a flexible exchange rate would be a smoothly adjusting variable for stabilizing the domestic economy. At the time, this presumption was also shared by monetarists, such as Milton Friedman (1953) or Harry Johnson (1972), who were not macro fine-tuners but who wanted domestic monetary independence in order to better secure the domestic price level. Whatever policy a central bank chose, they believed a flexible exchange rate would depreciate smoothly if the bank pursued easy money, and appreciate smoothly if the bank pursued tight money. (Because economists had very little experience, except for Canada, with floating exchange rates in the 1950s and 1960s, the great volatility in generally floating exchange rates after 1971 was unanticipated.)

Thus "optimum currency areas" appealed both to monetarists and Keynesians, although for somewhat different reasons. As such, it became enormously influential as the analytical basis for much of open-economy macroeconomics, and for scholarly doubts as to whether Western Europe — with its diverse national economies and relatively immobile labour forces — was ready for a one-size-fits-all monetary policy.

In the 1990s, the outstanding scholarly sceptic, was Barry Eichengreen, whose many articles (with several co-authors) were consolidated in his book *European Monetary Unification* (1997). He acknowledged Mundell's influence:

> The theory of optimum currency areas, initiated by Robert Mundell (1961), is the organizing framework for the analysis. In Mundell's paradigm, policymakers balance the saving in transactions costs from the creation of a single money against the consequences of diminished policy autonomy. The diminution of autonomy follows from the loss of the exchange rate and of an independent monetary policy as instruments of adjustment. That loss will be more costly when macroeconomic shocks are more "asymmetric" (for present purposes, more region- or country-specific), when monetary policy is a more powerful instrument for offsetting them, and when other adjustment mechanisms like relative wages and labor mobility are less effective. (Eichengreen, 1997, pp.1-2)

Eichengreen and Bayoumi (1993) had used an elaborate econometric analysis to show this asymmetry. "A strong distinction emerges between the supply shocks affecting the countries at the center of the European Community — Germany, France, the Netherlands and Denmark — and the very different supply shocks affecting other EC members — the United Kingdom, Italy, Spain, Portugal, Ireland and Greece" (Eichengreen, 1997, p. 104). On the basis of such apparently powerful argumentation, the British press and many economists still argue today that a one-size-fits-all monetary policy run from Frankfurt cannot be optimal for both continental Europe and Britain. After all, aren't business cycle conditions in Britain sufficiently different to warrant a separate counter-cyclical response from an independent Bank of England? But whether sophisticated or not, writers in this vein, most recently Martin Feldstein (2000) in "Europe Can't Handle the Euro", are definitely in thrall to the earlier Mundell.

The Later Mundell and International Risk Sharing

In a not-much-later incarnation, Robert Mundell jettisoned his earlier presumption of stationary expectations to focus on how future exchange rate uncertainty could disrupt the capital market by inhibiting international portfolio diversification and risk-sharing. At a 1970 Madrid conference on optimum currency areas, he presented two prescient papers on the advantages of common currencies. Perhaps in part because the conference proceedings were not published for several years, these papers have been overshadowed by his 1960s masterpieces.

The first of these papers, "Uncommon Arguments for Common Currencies", is of great intrinsic interest because very early it emphasized the forward-looking nature of the foreign exchange market, which was later to be worked out in more analytical detail by his students: see, for example, Frenkel and Mussa (1980). As such, it counters the idea that asymmetric shocks — those where an unexpected disturbance to national output affects one country differently from another — undermine the case for a common currency.

Instead, Mundell showed how having a common currency across countries can mitigate such shocks by better reserve-pooling and portfolio diversification. A country suffering an adverse shock can better share the

Mundell, the Euro and Optimum Currency Areas   *45*

loss with a trading partner because both countries hold claims on each other's output in a common currency. Whereas, under a flexible exchange rate without such portfolio diversification, a country facing an adverse shock and devaluing finds that its domestic-currency assets buy less on world markets. The cost of the shock is now more bottled up in the country where the shock originated. As Mundell later states:

> A harvest failure, strikes, or war, in one of the countries causes a loss of real income, but the use of a common currency (or foreign exchange reserves) allows the country to run down its currency holdings and cushion the impact of the loss, drawing on the resources of the other country until the cost of the adjustment has been efficiently spread over the future. If, on the other hand, the two countries use separate monies with flexible exchange rates, the whole loss has to be borne alone; the common currency cannot serve as a shock absorber for the nation as a whole except insofar as the dumping of inconvertible currencies on foreign markets attracts a speculative capital inflow in favor of the depreciating currency. (Mundell, 1973a, p.115)

Clearly, if interest-bearing bonds were to be added to Mundell's ultra simple theoretical model, which included only money and commodities, currency risk premia would arise naturally. (But embedding this risk reduction in a formal model is another paper.) Interest rates on domestic currency assets would tend to rise in those countries on the "periphery" (i.e., those that just might be forced to devalue if hit by an adverse shock) relative to interest rates in some *de facto* safe haven or country in the centre.

Today, Latin American countries on the periphery of the world dollar standard have much higher interest rates than those in the United States; and before the advent of the euro, the weak currency countries of Italy, Spain, and so on, operated with higher interest rates (see Figures 1 and 2) and shorter term finance than in Germany. The gains from proper risk-sharing through a common currency should show up as a net reduction in risk premia in interest rates for the system as a whole. And, after the advent of the euro on January 1, 1999 Figures 1 and 2 show the remarkable convergence of European interest rates at a lower average level than in the past.

An alternative way to limit this casino effect in foreign exchange markets is for governments to curtail Keynesian activism by giving each central bank a strict domestic price-level objective — where it no longer responds to output or employment fluctuations except as they might influence this

Figure 1: Short-Term Treasury Rates – EMU

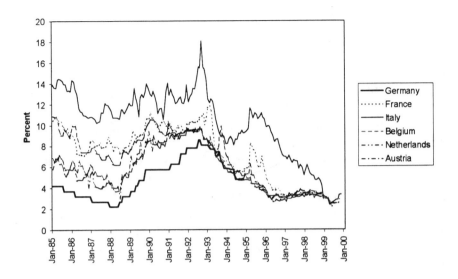

Figure 2: Ten-year Benchmark Bond Yields – EMU

inflation target. The Bank of England and the European Central Bank are more or less on such regimes. Although a big step forward in monetary management and in smoothing exchange rate movements, having separate inflation targets still does not prevent sterling's occasionally getting uncomfortably over- (or under-) valued against the euro. In May 2000, the consensus estimate seems to be that sterling is at least 20% overvalued against the euro with consequential undue stress in Britain's tradable goods sectors. Beyond inflation-targeting, the further step of Britain, Sweden, and possibly others joining the euro would seem necessary for ending intra-European exchange rate misalignments altogether.

Mundell's second Madrid paper, "A Plan for a European Currency" (reproduced as an Appendix), makes clear his early enthusiasm for the great European experiment. Until 1970, European countries all pegged uncertainly to the U.S. dollar in order to achieve a modicum of intra-European exchange stability. But the commitment to dollar parities was eroding, in large measure because the monetary anchor provided by the United States was beginning to slip. So Mundell stated:

> The only way to establish a unified money market is to kill the sporadic and unsettling speculation over currency prices that ravaged the European markets between 1967 and 1969, and permitted discounts and premia to develop on currency futures. The exchange rate should be taken out of both national and international politics within Europe.
> Rather than moving toward more flexibility in exchange rates within Europe the economic arguments suggest less flexibility and a closer integration of capital markets. These economic arguments are supported by social arguments as well. On every occasion when a social disturbance leads to the threat of a strike, and the strike to an increase in wages unjustified by increases in productivity and thence to devaluation, the national currency becomes threatened. Long-run costs for the nation as a whole are bartered away by governments for what they presume to be short-run political benefits. If instead, the European currencies were bound together, disturbances in the country would be cushioned, with the shock weakened by capital movements. (Mundell, 1973b, pp. 147 and 150)

Mundell's plan for weaning Europe from dollar dependence began by selecting one European country's currency to provide a new *numéraire* to which the others would fix their exchange rates. But European countries party to the new exchange rate agreement would send representatives to sit on the *numéraire* country's monetary board. Although the currency of any sizable European country would do, in 1970 he suggested that the pound sterling was the best choice for the *numéraire* because "Britain is the largest financial power and the pound is still a world currency" (Mundell, 1973b, p. 158).

Instead, the more stable German monetary policy, with the Deutschmark as the *numéraire* currency, became the focal point to rebuild first exchange rate stability and then monetary unity in Europe — while Britain continues to dither. With the formal advent of the euro on January 1, 1999, the forward-looking Mundell of the Madrid papers "triumphed" over his earlier Keynesian incarnation as the originator of the theory of optimum currency areas. But he is intellectual father to both sides of the debate.

Updating Mundell

From the intellectual vantage point so nicely provided by Mundell's Madrid papers, what can we say about proper exchange rate policies in the new millennium among the United States and Europe on the one hand, and then clusters of "emerging-market" economies like those in East Asia and Latin America on the other?

The traditional role of the U.S. dollar as the world's central currency — as the invoice currency for world commodity trade, as the dominant vehicle currency in the world's spot and forward foreign exchange markets, and as the official exchange reserve asset of choice — remains, and will remain, much as it was in 1970. But America's benign neglect of fluctuations in the dollar/euro exchange rate needs to be differentiated from a more purposeful policy towards East Asia and Latin America, where much greater exchange rate stability is required.

Because the euro now establishes a large zone of monetary stability in continental western Europe and its periphery, the best near-term strategy is a hands-off, *laissez-faire* policy over a wide range of values for the dollar/euro exchange rate. The dollar is no longer needed as the common monetary anchor as it was in the 1960s. Although disconcerting, the euro's fall from $1.18 in January 1999 to about $0.89 in February 2000 is not out of line with similar fluctuations in the "synthetic euro" weighted by the importance of its constituent currencies from 1980 through mid-2000 (see Figure 3). The European Central Bank and the U.S. Federal Reserve best

Mundell, the Euro and Optimum Currency Areas   *49*

Figure 3: Euro–Dollar (January 1980 – May 2000)

Euro–$ = Dollars per Synthetic Euro, derived from a weighted-average of the 11 component currencies (IMF weights).
Source: Bank of England.

intervene only if obvious panic develops, such as, if the euro started plunging instead of just drifting down. Even then, just nudging the euro back up — rather than pegging its dollar exchange rate — is all that would be appropriate.

However, economic stability in East Asia requires different and stronger medicine. Because no region-wide "Asian euro" exists or is in prospect, the dollar is the only plausible anchor for creating an East Asian zone of monetary stability in price levels and exchange rates (McKinnon, 2000). In order to prevent competitive devaluations and inflationary upheavals in the future, this zone would cover both the smaller East Asian countries that fell victim to the great 1997 currency crisis and China, which did not. And, post-crash, the evidence is very strong that an East Asian dollar standard, with the important exception of Japan, is resurrecting itself.

The advantage to Japan of being part of the dollar zone is somewhat different. Prolonged stability in the yen-dollar exchange rate is the key to quashing the *deflationary* expectations that have gripped the Japanese economy for almost a decade (McKinnon and Ohno, 1997 and forthcoming; and McKinnon, 1999).

In early May 2000, Robert Mundell embarked on a lecture tour of Brazil expounding on the virtues of a single currency for Mercosur, the South American trade group that also includes Argentina, Uruguay, and Paraguay (*Financial Times*, 2000). As a first step in the process of economic convergence, he advised the regions to link their currencies to the U.S. dollar. He said that "Interest rates would soon fall to close to U.S. levels. The big advantage is that it would lock in monetary stability and make it permanent".

Contrary to today's conventional wisdom for Latin America, Mundell did not advocate complete dollarization. Presumably a preferable "final" solution, in Mundell's view would be a "South American euro". Of course, without political unity and financial stability, the introduction of such a stand-alone regional currency is only a remote possibility.

But it is worth noting that the most systematic opposition to Mundell's view came from Brazillians quoting Mundell's earlier work. "According to Affonso Celso Pastore, a former central bank president, there is virtually no labor mobility between the Mercosur countries. As a result, the region does not constitute an optimal currency area — one of Mr. Mundell's insights" (ibid.). The contest between the two Mundells continues.

The Dollar versus the Euro

But here let us focus on the position of the real euro when most parts of the world are on some kind of dollar standard — if only putative. In judging the euro's impact on the dollar, consider two competing economic interpretations of the euro's potential future role in the world economy.

The first interpretation focuses on economic integration in goods and factor markets within Europe and with surrounding countries: an extended optimum currency area. Because of the EU's huge economic size and far-reaching trade connections, this interpretation suggests a wider influence for the euro well beyond the current political borders of the European Union. The EU countries will constitute an economic mass nearly as large as that of the United States itself, and European exports to the rest of the world (net of what are currently counted as intra-European exports) will be similar in magnitude to American exports. Many Eastern European countries will opt

Mundell, the Euro and Optimum Currency Areas   *51*

to peg to the euro because they are so open to EU trade — as are many former European colonies in Africa. For both types of countries, the new euro could well dominate as an intervention and reserve currency.

The second interpretation focuses on the need for international money *beyond* that associated with unusually close trade linkages. The world economy itself needs a unit of account, means of payment, and store of value for both governments and private firms. In the absence of a generally accepted metallic money such as gold or even a dominant country like the United States, one of the national currencies would still be selected by habit or custom. Once selected, however, this national currency's role as international money becomes a natural monopoly. That is, the scope for more than one national currency to serve in a dual role as international and domestic money is limited.

In the aftermath of World War II, the United States provided the essential funding for the International Monetary Fund, the Marshall Plan, and the Dodge Plan, which jointly restored exchange and price-level stability among the industrial countries while replenishing official exchange reserves (McKinnon, 1996). The world's only capital market without exchange controls was the American. Thus, the U.S. dollar became the dominant international vehicle currency for private transacting as well as the reserve currency for official interventions.

Even when the American money manager, the Federal Reserve System, was doing quite badly, as from the inflationary 1970s into the early 1980s, the dollar-based system proved surprisingly resilient. Although many other countries had by then opened their financial markets, the dollar was not significantly displaced as international money. Now that American monetary policy has been quite stable for more than a decade, could the momentous advent of the euro — with an open European capital market — displace the dollar?

The Role of an International Vehicle Currency

Consider first a world of "N" national currencies without official interventions or foreign exchange targeting by governments. In organizing private interbank markets for foreign exchange, great savings in transactions costs can be had if just one national currency, the Nth, is chosen as the vehicle currency. Then all foreign exchange quotations, bids and offers, at all terms to maturity can take place against this one vehicle currency. The number of active markets can be reduced from N(N-1)/2 to just N-1. In a world of more than 150 national currencies, this is a tremendous economy of markets for the large commercial banks that make the foreign exchange market. The dollar's interbank predominance (being on one side of almost 90% of interbank transactions) allows banks to cover both their forward exchange and options exposures much more efficiently.

Trade in primary commodities shows a similar pattern of using one national money as the main currency of invoice. Exports of homogeneous primary products such as oil, wheat, copper, and so on, all tend to be invoiced in dollars with worldwide price formation in a centralized exchange. Spot trading, but particularly forward contracting, is concentrated at these centralized exchanges — which are usually in American cities such as Chicago and New York, although dollar-denominated commodity exchanges do exist in London and elsewhere. In periods of reasonable confidence in American monetary policy, these *dollar* commodity prices are relatively invariant to fluctuations in the dollar's exchange rate. In contrast, if any other country allows its exchange rate to fluctuate against the dollar, its domestic currency prices of primary commodities will vary in proportion, unless its trade is restricted.

Invoicing patterns for exports of manufactured goods are more complex. Major industrial countries with strong currencies tend to invoice their exports in their home currencies. More than 75% of German exports were invoiced in D-marks, more than 50% of French exports invoiced in francs, and so on. With the advent of EMU, continental European countries will begin invoicing their net exports outside the European Union mainly in euros.

However, Japan invoices about 36% of its exports in its own currency. This is low by the standards of other large industrial countries, in part because the United States is its main export market. On the import side, about 70% of goods coming into Japan are invoiced in dollars, in part because Japan is such a heavy importer of primary products and manufactures from the United States. Thus, Japan suffers high variation in domestic yen prices, that is, "pass-through" is high, when the yen-dollar exchange rate fluctuates.

At the other extreme, the U.S. price level is fairly immune to fluctuations in the dollar's exchange rate against other currencies because *both* its exports and imports are largely invoiced in dollars: 98% of American exports of primary products and manufactures are dollar invoiced and an amazing

Mundell, the Euro and Optimum Currency Areas   *53*

88% or so of American imports. (For example, almost all of Japan's exports to the United States are dollar invoiced.) In addition, for trade not directly involving the United States, the dollar is heavily used as an invoice currency for manufactured (and, of course, primary) exports from developing and transitional economies in Asia, Latin America, and elsewhere.

Here then lies an important distinction between Euroland and East Asia. Euroland is naturally more insular in a monetary sense. It is a large integrated economy that uses its own currency for invoicing much of its foreign trade. Fluctuations in the euro-dollar exchange rate have little impact on Europe-wide price indexes; and thus, over moderate ranges, can be more or less ignored. In contrast, the price levels of all East Asian countries, including Japan's, are much more affected by fluctuations in their separate exchange rates against the region's dominant trading currency, the U.S. dollar. Even more so does the dollar dominate trade in Latin America.

Once private interbank foreign exchange and commodity markets are set up with the dollar as the vehicle and invoice currency, official interventions follow the same pattern. Governments pursue their exchange rate objectives more conveniently by intervening only in dollars (at different terms to maturity) against their domestic monies. Using only one currency for intervention prevents inconsistency in the setting of cross rates with other foreign monies.

This pattern of official intervention determines the pattern of official holdings of foreign exchange. Apart from gold, about 70% of official reserves held outside Europe are dollar denominated. True, the desire for safety through portfolio diversification is important. But this cuts against the convenience of holding reserves in the intervention currency, with its relative stability in real purchasing power measured against internationally traded goods. Thus governments outside Europe have preferred to hold dollars — mainly U.S. Treasury bonds. Certainly, most of these governments will want to hold euros to replace their Deutschmarks, franc, and sterling assets as these national European currencies disappear. But it seems unlikely that any *official* demand to hold euro assets will be much greater than the former demand for reserve holdings in Europe's legacy currencies.

There is the further problem of what the benchmark euro asset will be. The EU central government itself does not have significant debt outstanding like the huge stock of U.S. Treasuries. In Europe, government debt is lodged with the old national, now middle-level, governments who no longer control their own central banks. Now, default risk is not insignificant. In comparison to U.S. Treasuries, a position in euro-denominated bonds will involve some (possibly minor) default risk which differs by country. Although both U.S. Treasuries and European government bonds now denominated in euros will be subject to (differing) currency risk — that is, concern for inflation and devaluation — European bonds will probably remain marginally less attractive to foreign governments as official reserve assets.

Portfolio Diversification, Falling Risk Premia, and the "Weak" Euro

But *within* Euroland private euro-denominated bond issues are now growing explosively. For the first half of 1999, Table 1 shows overall euro bond issues growing by 80% compared with bond issues in the old legacy currencies during the first six months of 1998. Most strikingly, issues of euro-denominated *corporate* bonds are running at a rate almost four times as high in 1999 compared to 1998. Why the startling difference?

In the pre-euro regime when the Deutschmark was king, corporations in European countries on the German periphery, such as Italy, Portugal and Spain, suffered currency risk relative to German issuers of mark-denominated bonds because of the existence of the lire, escudo, and peseta. The resulting risk premia, that is, higher interest rates particularly at longer term, kept finance short term and largely bank based. In 1999, the extinction of these risky currencies has allowed previously hobbled Italian, Portuguese, Spanish (and even French?) firms to lengthen the term structure of their debts by issuing euro-denominated bonds at lower interest rates while escaping from the clutches of their bankers. European banks, in turn, are madly consolidating, although unfortunately only at the national level.

On the demand side, European insurance companies and pension funds had been confined to keeping the bulk of their assets denominated in domestic currency in order to better match their liabilities. But with the move to a common, and for the peripheral countries, a stronger currency, they are free to diversify and acquire assets on a Europe-wide basis — from foreigners who are willing to sell euro-denominated bonds. Thus is the term structure of corporate finance in Europe being lengthened with the lower interest rates reflecting lowered overall portfolio risk. This broader risk-sharing, and

Table 1: European Bond Issues, 1999 versus 1998

Volume of euro-denominated international bonds, by issuer type
1/1–30/6/1999

	Total		
	Amt. m (US$)	*%*	*Iss.*
Banks/Finance	240,209.117	66.15	597
Corporate	79,012.498	21.76	166
Utilities	16,771.171	4.62	33
Sovereign	16,130.135	4.44	38
Supranational	7,012.887	1.93	31
Others	4,005.959	1.10	30
Local authority	4,005.959	1.10	30
Total	363,141.767	100.00	895

Volume of international bonds issued in legacy currencies
(including ecu and euro), by issuer type
1/1–30/6/1998

	Total		
	Amt. m (US$)	*%*	*Iss.*
Banks/Finance	131,561.740	65.85	548
Sovereign	28,462.517	14.25	49
Corporate	20,263.587	10.14	97
Supranational	11,595.437	5.80	56
Utilities	6,889.331	3.45	16
Others	1,023.143	0.51	6
Local authority	1,023.143	0.51	6
Total	199,779.755	100.00	772

Source: Capital Data, Aldwych House, London, U.K.

thus risk reduction, in European capital markets — by eliminating fluctuating relative currency values — is precisely what the forward-looking Mundell of the Madrid papers (1973a,b) had in mind.

Can the rapid development of a broad and deep capital market in euro-denominated assets "explain" the surprising weakness of the euro since

January 1, 1999? (Although the euro is not so weak when considered in proper historical perspective, as per Figure 3.) Foreign borrowers, for example, American or those from developing countries, may now be tapping this large newly integrated pool of euro-denominated capital on greater scale than had previously been expected. The resulting incipient capital outflow from Euroland has become greater than its (large) current account surplus. But this one-time stock adjustment from the improved conditions in the European financial markets should not persist, and is not something to worry about.

Nevertheless, on the broader global stage, the dollar's continued vehicle-currency role is unlikely to be displaced by the extended currency-area role for the new euro — and the growing net creditor status of Euroland as a whole. Even if the dollar's use as an international vehicle currency outside Europe is largely unaltered by the euro's advent, eliminating currency risk within the greater European economy is a remarkable benefit, as Mundell correctly foresaw in his second incarnation.

References

Eichengreen, B. (1997), *European Monetary Unification: Theory, Practice, and Analysis* (Cambridge, MA: MIT Press).

Eichengreen, B. and T. Bayoumi (1993), "Shocking Aspects of European Monetary Unification", in F. Torres and F. Giavazzi (eds.), *Adjustment and Growth in the European Monetary Union* (New York: Cambridge University Press), reprinted in Eichengreen, *European Monetary Unification*, 73-109.

Feldstein, M. (2000), "Europe Can't Handle the Euro", *Wall Street Journal*, February 8.

Financial Times (2000), "'Father of the Euro' Stirs up Currency Debate in South American Family", May 9, p. 6.

Frenkel, J. and M. Mussa (1980), "The Efficiency of the Foreign Exchange Market and Measures of Turbulence", *American Economic Review* 70(2), 374-381.

Friedman, M. (1953), "The Case for Flexible Exchange Rates", in *Essays in Positive Economics* (Chicago: University of Chicago Press), 157-203.

Johnson, H. (1972), "The Case for Flexible Exchange Rates, 1969", in *Further Essays in Monetary Economics* (Winchester: Allen & Unwin), 198-222.

McKinnon, R.I. (1996), *The Rules of the Game: International Money and Exchange Rates* (Cambridge, MA: MIT Press).

_____ (1999), "McKinnon on Japan: Wading in the Yen Trap", *The Economist,* July 24, 83-86.

_____ (2000), "The East Asian Dollar Standard, Life after Death", *Economic Notes* 29 (February), 31-82.

McKinnon, R.I. and K. Ohno (1997), *Dollar and Yen: Resolving Economic Conflict between the United States and Japan* (Cambridge, MA: MIT Press).

_____ (forthcoming), "The Foreign Exchange Origins of Japan's Economic Slump and Low Interest Liquidity Trap", *The World Economy.*

Meade, J.E. (1955), "The Case for Variable Exchange Rates", *Three Banks Review* (27 September), 3-27.

Mundell, R.A. (1961), "A Theory of Optimum Currency Areas", *American Economic Review* 51 (November), 509-517.

_____ (1963), "Capital Mobility and Stabilization Policy under Fixed and Flexible Exchange Rates", *Canadian Journal of Economics and Political Science* 29 (November), 475-485.

_____ (1968), *International Economics* (New York: Macmillan).

_____ (1973a), "Uncommon Arguments for Common Currencies", in H.G. Johnson and A.K. Swoboda, *The Economics of Common Currencies* (London: Allen & Unwin), 114-132.

_____ (1973b), "A Plan for a European Currency", in H.G. Johnson and A.K. Swoboda, *The Economics of Common Currencies* (London: Allen & Unwin), 143-172.

The New Economy and the Exchange Rate Regime

Richard G. Harris

Introduction

Robert Mundell changed the intellectual landscape of international economics forever, and his receipt of the 1999 Nobel Prize in Economics was long overdue. Many of his contributions to the field were motivated by his perspective on the international economy that came from his early life and education in Canada. That perspective is one in which the "open economy" is given prominence both analytically and in the policy framework. In this paper I pursue an issue that Mundell has raised at numerous times in his criticism of flexible exchange rate regimes, and Canada's exchange rate regime in particular. Mundell has argued in public debate that Canadian living standards can only achieve American levels under a permanently fixed exchange rate between Canada and U.S. dollars.[1] This position is somewhat

---

I am indebted to conference participants for comments on an earlier draft.

[1] It would be impossible to cite the numerous speeches and press reports in which he has made this point. In the Canadian exchange rate debate his 1990 paper (Mundell, 1990) subsequently published in French in 1991, made the point clearly.

59

at odds with traditional open economy macroeconomic theory which takes productivity as exogenous relative to either the nominal exchange rate or the exchange rate regime.

The productivity issue has become central to the debate within Canada on the causes and consequences of the significant real depreciation of the Canadian dollar over the 1990s. Courchene and Harris (1999a,b) and Grubel (1999), among others, have argued that the depreciation contributed to the well-documented widening productivity gap between Canada and the United States. Comments on the other side of the ledger, including statements by the Governor of the Bank of Canada, argue that Canada's flexible exchange rate served as an important *buffer* to those external shocks which are asymmetric relative to those in the United States. In the Bank of Canada's own review of the evidence (see Lafrance and Schembri, 2000), the claim is that there is no evidence to suggest a link running from exchange rate depreciation to a widening productivity gap. Furthermore John Murray (2000) has argued that Canadian dollar real depreciation was an equilibrium response to the decline in the terms of trade resulting from falling commodity prices which, in turn, occurred in the wake of the Asian crisis.

It is not my intent to review all these arguments here.[2] Rather, this paper will address two issues which are central to the productivity question. First, I will argue that there are good reasons to treat productivity as endogenous within a macroeconomic framework in which the exchange rate regime is *either* fixed or floating. The motivation for these observations is drawn from a reading of both the new endogenous growth theory, and selected recent evidence specific to the determinants of Canadian productivity. Second, I will argue that the Canada-U.S. experience of the 1990s may typify a more pervasive problem with floating rates, namely that associated with an economy undergoing a major and permanent structural transition. The emerging "new economy" paradigm in the United States suggests that we are in the midst of a major technological transition being driven by a convergence of computer technology, the Internet, and a wide range of innovations in information technology (IT). The acceleration in the U.S. productivity data after 1995 is the principal macro evidence supporting the hypothesis that a major new general purpose technology (GPT) (the IT revolution of the new

---

[2]For a reasonably exhaustive discussion of these issues see Courchene and Harris (1999a) and references, and the fall 1999 issue of *Canadian Business Economics*.

economy) is driving economic activity in the United States.[3] Canada on the other hand has lagged in these areas and this in part may explain the poorer productivity performance in Canada.[4] I will argue in this paper that in the face of dual shocks — (i) a decline in old economy or in resource prices and (ii) the arrival of a new major GPT — an exchange rate regime which *buffers* the old economy by an accommodating depreciation may lead to a slower rate of economic growth and a permanently lower level of real income relative to a non-buffered exchange rate path.

The Exchange Rate and Endogenous Productivity Growth

In the last two decades, but most notably in the 1990s, a major change in macroeconomic theory was the view promoted within endogenous growth theory that over the longer term productivity growth is endogenously determined, and affected by economic policy including, but not limited to, macroeconomic policy.[5] The open economy macro theory that is used in discussions of fixed versus flexible exchange rates, and empirical studies of exchange rates, remains largely untouched by this paradigm change. The standard textbook discussion of the link between the real exchange rate and productivity is based on the Balassa-Samuelson model which takes productivity changes as exogenous. In the Balassa-Samuelson model an

---

[3]Robert Gordon (1999) surveys this evidence as of mid-1999, and is a well-known critic of the New Economy hypothesis. As of mid-2000 the acceleration in the growth of U.S. labour productivity remains intact.

[4]For a discussion of the Canadian productivity growth and levels, in particular in comparison with the United States, a good source and overview is the selection of papers on the Web site of the Canadian Centre for the Study of Living Standards at <www.csls.ca>. In particular, the manufacturing data are reviewed in the papers from the conference on the Canada-U.S. Manufacturing Productivity Gap.

[5]The endogenous growth framework is clearly laid out in Aghion and Howitt (1999); Grossman and Helpman (1991); and Romer (1990).

The New Economy and the Exchange Rate Regime

exogenous increase in the home country's productivity in the tradables sector, holding productivity in non-tradables constant, will lead to an appreciation of the real exchange rate, or a fall in the relative price of tradables relative to non-tradables. The model is silent, however, on the source of the productivity changes.[6] This lack of integration of the exchange rate literature with endogenous growth theory is a serious deficiency in the literature and one that clearly needs to be addressed.

Economists when discussing exchange rate regimes, and issues such as monetary union and dollarization, will almost always assume long-run separation of real from monetary phenomena. That is they assume that for time horizons greater than the typical business cycle (the "long run" which separates business cycle theory from growth theory) monetary and exchange rate policy does not impact on long-run economic growth. There are at least three reasons this view should be viewed sceptically.

First, in the closed-economy, business-cycle literature, the separation of the cycle from growth is of course at the heart of much of the recent research. The "new view" is that such a separation is infeasible. There is a substantial theoretical and empirical literature which treats productivity as subject to cyclical influences driven by either demand or supply shocks. Reorganizations, cleansing recessions, and Verdoon effects are all reasons that are cited as to why cycle and productivity growth cannot be separated.[7] If one accepts these arguments as valid in closed economies, then one certainly cannot ignore them in open economies. In the case of the open economy the movement in the real exchange rate would logically be one price which might have consequences for the determinants of productivity growth.

Second, the link between the nominal exchange rate and real variables, including the real exchange rate, remains one of the more well-documented facts in international economics. The conventional assumption of the separation of long run real from monetary phenomena dictates that the real exchange rate be treated as a relative price whose value in the long run is

---

[6]In the Canadian context, the Balassa-Samuelson explanation for the real depreciation of the Canadian dollar would have to rely either (a) on a fall in productivity in Canada relative to the United States in tradables, or (b) on an increase in the relative productivity of services (non-tradables) in Canada relative to the United States.

[7]Some of the recent literature includes Hall (1991); Burnside and Hammour (1992); and Saint-Paul (1993).

dictated by purely real factors. On the other hand, virtually any acceptable theory of the medium-run macroeconomy assumes some form of nominal rigidities, either in wages or prices, which in turn provide a reason that nominal exchange rate changes can have real relative price consequences. Modern theories of exchange rate pass-through, for example, specifically rely on such rigidities whose time duration can be considerable. Moreover, the evidence is that productivity growth can accelerate and decelerate quite rapidly. Thus, the central empirical question is what are the relevant speeds of adjustment in productivity drivers and the real exchange rate. There is no evidence which either proves, or even suggests, that productivity drivers such as investment (or even outcomes as measured in productivity statistics) are necessarily slow to adjust relative to movements in nominal prices and wages.

Third, the question of causality between exchange rates and productivity growth is crucial. There are a couple of pieces of evidence on this issue. Strauss (1999) finds, in an examination of a cross-country VAR study on real exchange rates and productivity growth, evidence of causality running from exchange rates to tradables productivity growth, contrary to Balassa-Samuelson. Second, the extensive literature on purchasing power parity (PPP) continues to point to strong evidence of lengthy periods of misalignment but with long-term mean reversion of nominal exchange rates toward their PPP values with convergence periods averaging around five years.[8] At the same time the evidence on wage and price rigidity indicates similar sorts of horizons at which wages and prices adjust. In addition, productivity growth is both highly volatile and remarkably non-persistent. We have numerous examples of countries which have gone from low to high rates of productivity growth (Ireland) over the course of a few years, and vice versa (Japan). Putting these facts together, it is at least questionable to assume that productivity changes are inherently slow moving long-term variables relative to real exchange rates, prices, or wages. An alternative framework in which all are viewed as endogenous is equally plausible on both theoretical and empirical grounds.

---

[8]Lothian's work (1997) is a recent example of econometric research that has found this to be a robust empirical characterization of medium-term exchange rate trends.

The Exchange Rate and Endogenous Productivity Theory

There is a large set of theories which generate endogenous productivity growth. These run the gamut from A-K models, R&D or innovation-led growth models, Schumpeterian theories of entry and exit dynamics, organizational failures and reorganizations, x-inefficiency, agglomeration of economic activity in cities or regions, and large-scale technological change induced by a general and widely used innovation referred to as a General Purpose Technology.[9] Most of these theories have been constructed for the purposes of explaining long-run economic growth. A few have been extended to business-cycle models, both real and monetary. Virtually none are in the context of an open economy framework in which the exchange rate is an important endogenous macro variable. It should be fairly straightforward for the next generation of open economy theorists to develop such models. At the partial equilibrium level in which major nominal variables such as wages are treated as fixed, this is straightforward. In these models exchange rate changes are very similar to changes in tariffs and export subsidies (an exchange rate depreciation is similar to a tariff increase for an import competing industry). Moreover, there is an extensive partial equilibrium literature on both hysteresis in trade and exchange rate pass-through which could easily be adapted to this problem. More difficult will be a full dynamic general equilibrium treatment of the problem. These models have the usual problem of (a) specifying what determines nominal exchange rates and (b) specifying the nature of the nominal rigidities which translate nominal exchange rate changes into real exchange rate changes.

In either a partial or general equilibrium framework, however, there are certain factors that are likely to prove most interesting in the context of the exchange rate-productivity link. The Canadian productivity debate points to the following set of potential factors.

---

[9]See Helpman (1999) on the GPT concept.

The Costs of Innovation and Technology

One class of theories focuses on those direct factor costs which occur at the level of the firm such that an exchange rate change has an impact on the profit maximizing level of productivity-improving investments. For example:

• an increase in the cost of new imported capital goods reduces the rate at which new technology is installed or investments in innovation occur;

• exchange rate uncertainty can increase the cost of capital by raising the option value of "waiting" for an irreversible capital installation;

• a temporary exchange rate depreciation may have an intertemporal substitution effect on a profit-maximizing firm which reduces the return on productivity enhancing activities and raises the return on short-run output increases.

Industry Dynamics

There are many studies which have identified firm level heterogeneity and entry and exit as a major source of productivity growth (40% to 50% of all productivity growth in some industries, as summarized, for example, by Foster, Haltwianger and Krizan, 1998). A large and unanticipated exchange rate depreciation can have consequences for both entry and exit of firms via a variety of channels:

• It can impact the relative profitability of old versus new firms; old firms have sunk costs and an exchange rate depreciation will tend to reduce their rate of exit while at the same time it raises the cost of entry (due to investments in technology required). This can slow the overall rate of industry productivity growth.[10] A major piece of evidence in this regard in the Canada/U.S. case are the differences between the size distribution of firms in Canada and the United States, with Canada sustaining a much larger fraction of small firms (see Daly, Helfinger and Sharwood,

---

[10]Grubel (1999) has raised this argument specifically in the case of the resource sectors in Canada.

2001). One possible explanation for this is that rates of exit for small firms who are typically less productive than large firms, may not have been as large in Canada as the United States due to exchange rate sheltering effects.

- Grubel (1999) has noted that previously marginal entrants in contestable industries (industries with low entry costs) may now find it profitable to enter, driving down productivity growth in the industry as a whole as the output share of the low productivity group increases.

- Entrepreneurship and the supply of human capital will respond to the depreciation. A real depreciation can reduce the returns to skilled labour via Stolper-Samuelson effects (assuming the tradables sector is human capital intensive), and it can induce entrepreneurial and skilled labour out-migration in response to exchange-rate-induced real income decreases.

Managerial Theories of the Firm

There is a class of theories on the firm based on imperfect monitoring and principal agent problems that posit that managerial discretion will lead to management utility maximization rather than profit maximization. In this case managers may be less motivated to reduce costs, innovate, and restructure if exchange rate depreciations provide cost-sheltering effects. This model is very close to the "lazy manufacturers hypothesis" which has been discussed in the Canadian debate by McCallum (1999) or the class of theories described by the x-inefficiency hypothesis.

Strategic Theories (Imperfect Competition) in Export and Import Markets

Strategic trade theory of the 1980s emphasized the role of international R&D competition in oligopolistic markets in a class of theories due to Brander and Spencer based on strategic pre-emption.[11] In these models export subsidies

---

[11]These are reviewed in the survey by Brander (1997).

or taxes can have an impact on the international distribution of R&D depending on the nature of the strategic competition between foreign and domestic firms. For similar reasons an exchange rate depreciation with some nominal rigidities in domestic factor costs can have similar effects. Consider for example the two firm-two country standard Brander-Spencer model for third country export markets using R&D investments as a way to build market shares. If R&D investments are *strategic substitutes*, a home currency depreciation will cut the home country R&D expenditure and raise the foreign R&D (home depreciation is equivalent to an export subsidy). In more complicated models with strategic entry deterrence one could also get an impact on the extent of entry deterring investments due to an exchange rate effect which affects a foreign and domestic firm differently. As these investments (such as spare capacity) would impact on productivity this also provides a link between the exchange rate and productivity although the qualitative nature of the result is sensitive to the specific model used.

Structural Transitions and Exchange Rate Buffering

It is clear that there are a number of potential theoretically sound micro-economic links running from real exchange rate change to endogenously generated productivity growth. These models, however, miss one important macro-economic aspect of the exchange rate. This is the impact an exchange rate change has on relative demands across sectors and the labour market responses to the exchange rate. In traditional optimal currency area theory the interaction between asymmetric intersectoral shocks and the exchange rate response in the face of some labour market rigidities was the core of the analysis.[12] In this section I extend the traditional optimal currency area model to one in which productivity growth is endogenous and driven by the arrival of a major new technology or GPT. This can be thought of as a model of structural transition from an old economy to new economy due to the arrival

---

[12]I use the term optimal currency area literature to refer to the generic literature on fixed versus flexible rates which emphasizes asymmetric sectoral shocks. In some cases these sectors are geographically distinguished while in other models this is less important than other sectoral differences.

The New Economy and the Exchange Rate Regime

of a major GPT.[13] The old economy is characterized by reduced growth opportunities and labour market rigidities. The new economy has major growth opportunities and flexible labour markets.

The nature of this transition is critically dependent upon whether or not an exchange rate depreciation, which buffers the old economy, delays the arrival of the new economy either temporarily or permanently. Buffering in effect results in a slowdown in creative destruction within the old economy. As noted in the introduction, a standard defence of the Canadian dollar depreciation of the 1990s was that it buffered the Canadian economy against commodity price declines. In the Canadian context the "old economy" may be interpreted as the resource sectors. The general argument may be of relevance to other non-resource-based industrial economies where there is a concentration of employment and output in old economy industries. For example, the old economy might be traditional heavy manufacturing industries in which the economy was initially relatively heavily specialized. The external shock to the old economy in this case might be a large-scale increase in global excess capacity due to the emergence of new global competition from newly industrializing countries. In either interpretation of the old economy there is an underlying assumption that both shocks are truly permanent, but may mistakenly be interpreted by both markets and policy-makers as temporary.

The model is one of a small open economy in which the old and new economies produce different outputs, and have segmented or sector-specific labour markets.[14] The old economy (or natural resources) is indexed with R, and the new economy (or Software) indexed with an S. Both goods are traded at fixed world prices and the sole factor of production is labour which is specific to each sector in the short run. The economy is faced with two sources of permanent structural change. It is simultaneously hit with (a) the arrival of a major new GPT which opens new opportunities for productivity

---

[13]My view of the GPT would fit with any number of definitions all of which revolve around economy-wide technological change based on a common but critical new technology. The volume edited by Helpman (1999) provides an historical and analytical overview of GPTs.

[14]The model bears some resemblance to the old Dutch disease models of the 1970s and early 1980s. In that case the "favourable shock" was an increase in resource prices which led to a real exchange rate appreciation and a subsequent decline in manufacturing exports.

growth, and (b) a price decline for the output produced in the old economy. It is assumed that there are limited opportunities for productivity growth in the old economy.

Labour market rigidities are present only in the old economy; these are modelled as a rigid nominal wage. Labour market equilibrium occurs in the old economy via changes in unemployment; these rigidities also serve as the rationale for the exchange rate to buffer old economy price declines — that is, to prevent increases in unemployment. Nominal wages are fully flexible in the new economy and adjust to equate labour demand to labour supply which is specific to each sector in the short run. In the short run, labour supply is inelastic and specific to each sector. Over time labour is reallocated across sectors as discussed below.

What is unique to this model is the nature of the productivity dynamics, which are endogenous and reflect three basic mechanisms:

- the presence of the new GPT which creates opportunities for significant productivity increases;

- the existence of scale effects in the new sectors such that productivity growth accelerates with larger output scales in the new economy due to learning-by-doing effects or internal spillovers;

- the direct cost effects of productivity improvements which depend on imported technology and capital; exchange rate depreciation which raises the cost of these investments may lower productivity growth.[15]

The notation used is outlined as follows:

---

[15]The last assumption hinges upon a presumption that productivity investments are to a significant degree imported. For many small open economies who buy technology and capital equipment, this is a reasonable assumption. Lafrance and Schembri (2000) show that the Canadian dollar depreciation of the 1990s has been coincident with a substantial increase in the relative factor price of capital to labour in Canada when compared to the same factor price trend in the United States. Also during the same period a large gap developed between the levels of investment in machinery and equipment in Canada and the United States, no doubt some of which can be explained by the difference in relative factor costs in the two countries.

The New Economy and the Exchange Rate Regime

L_i the labour force in sector i (old economy R, and new economy S)

L   the total labour force (assumed constant)

E_i employment in sector i

w_i nominal wage in sector i

A   productivity level in the new economy sector

A*   level of productivity attainable with new GPT

m   natural employment rate in the old economy

F_i production functions of each sector

E   the domestic currency price of a unit of foreign exchange

p^*_R, p^*_S the foreign currency prices of R and S sector goods

$Y_R = F_R(E_R)$; $Y_S = AF_S(E_S)$ production functions

The wage rate in the old economy, w_R is treated as constant. Given the price of output, the nominal exchange rate and the wage rate, employment in the old economy, E_R adjusts so that all firms are on the labour demand curve. The wage in the S sector adjusts so that all labour in that sector is fully employed, hence $E_S=L_S$. Hence in the short and long run labour market equilibrium implies that the following conditions hold.

$$w_S = Ep^*_S AF_S'(L_S)$$

$$w_R = Ep^*_R F_R'(E_R)$$

$$L = L_S + L_R, \ E_R \leq L_R$$

Dynamics

There are two basic dynamics equations which govern the evolution of the economy over the transition. One, the productivity dynamics which reflect the endogenous evolution of productivity in the new economy. Two, the labour force reallocation dynamics which describe how labour moves between the new and old economies.

Productivity Dynamics:

$$\dot{A} = \phi(L_S, A/A^*, E)$$

$$\phi_1 > 0, \ \phi_2 < 0, \ \phi_3 < 0$$

New economy productivity growth is affected by the size of the labour force in the new economy (positive), the potential gap between current new economy productivity and its ultimate potential level A* (positive), and finally by the nominal cost of imported technology and capital as effected by the exchange rate E (negative).

Labour Market Dynamics:

$$\dot{L}_R = -\dot{L}_S = \alpha[E_R/L_R - m] - \gamma[w_S - w_R]$$

The total labour force is constant so that growth in the labour force in the new economy equals the decline in the old economy labour force. There are two factors which affect the rate at which labour moves from one sector to another. First, following natural rate theory the extent to which the current employment rate (and hence unemployment rate) differs from the natural rate. A higher than natural rate of employment will tend to attract labour. Labour market rigidities are reflected in both the natural rate of employment, denoted by the parameter m, with more rigid labour markets having a higher m. The speed of adjustment is the parameter α; a lower value of α which reflects the rate at which excess unemployment induces labour to reallocate to the new economy. I treat both parameters as constant for the purposes of

The New Economy and the Exchange Rate Regime

this paper.[16] Second, labour force reallocation is affected by the wage gap between the old and new economies.

It is important to note that implicit in this model are a set of inherent timing assumptions. The model assumes that productivity and sectoral reallocation are medium-run dynamic variables. Note that productivity change and labour force dynamics are on the same time scale, while labour market rigidities in the old economy are on a much slower time scale. For simplicity, the old economy nominal wage is treated as constant. This last assumption is extreme but appears to capture the stylized characteristic of labour markets in declining industries. A complete treatment of asset and exchange rate markets would complicate the analysis considerably. For the purposes of this paper the nominal exchange rate will be treated as a constant over the transition period as will the prices of the output of both sectors.

The stationary loci for L_R will be denoted as bb' and the stationary loci for A will be denoted as aa'. I will illustrate the model dynamics in phase-plane diagrams in L_R and A space.

Two possible exchange rate regimes are modeled in the face of changes in p_R^* and A^* as follows:

- A *fixed exchange rate regime*, i.e., E constant

- A *buffered exchange rate*, i.e., E is assumed to be targeted such as to keep Ep_R^* constant — the nominal exchange rate depreciates to offset the external commodity price decrease.

Obviously this is a bit of a short hand for a more complicated treatment of asset markets with exchange rate and current account dynamics. The fixed exchange rate can be thought of as resulting from some credible fixed exchange rate policy which assumes the authorities can successfully hold a nominal fix in the event of the two shocks being contemplated. A buffered exchange rate regime reflects either an active policy of targeting the exchange rate to old economy prices, or alternatively assumes that market

---

[16]One could imagine either of these parameters would be affected by labour market policies, such as changes in the Employment Insurance system, for example.

forces result in the exchange rate tracking old economy prices.[17] In either event the effect is to "buffer" employment in the old economy. By keeping the nominal value of the marginal product constant at the initial level of employment, the fall in old economy prices does not result in an increase in unemployment which would otherwise occur. Under a fixed exchange rate when p_R* falls there is an immediate reduction in employment and an increase in unemployment in the old economy.

A Special Case Model. To illustrate the central workings of this model I consider a special case of the dynamics elaborated above. This assumes

- There are no wage gap effects on sectoral reallocation dynamics — so $\gamma=0$ (hence bb' vertical). In the case that γ is small the bb' locus will be negatively sloped but fairly steep.

- Productivity growth is governed by additive spillovers and a convergence effect.

$$\dot{A} = a(L_S - L_c) + b\frac{(A^* - A)}{A^*}$$

The impact of these two assumptions is to simplify fairly starkly the dynamic effects at work on the model. In the case of the labour market, only divergences from the natural rate of unemployment induce labour force re-allocations. In the case of productivity, additivity in the convergence and scale effects eliminates the possibility of multiple equilibria due to strategic complementarities between the two effects. L_c is a critical size parameter in the new economy productivity dynamics such that for a labour force smaller than L_c there is a tendency for productivity to fall, holding the convergence effect constant.

This model is depicted in Figure 1 in A-L_R space. The stationary productivity locus is downward sloping reflecting a trade-off between a larger old economy, which reduces productivity growth in the new economy,

---

[17]Bill Scarth pointed out to me that the buffered exchange rate policy is in fact equivalent to price level targeting. A fully buffered exchange rate depreciation leaves the short-run price level constant while a fixed exchange rate results in a one-shot deflation in response to the fall in commodity prices.

The New Economy and the Exchange Rate Regime

Figure 1: Unbuffered Old Economy Price Decline

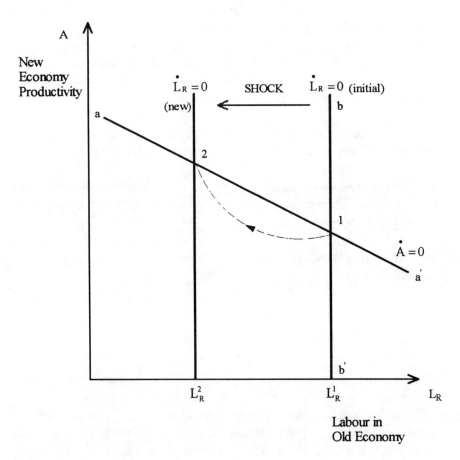

and a stronger convergence effect which results from the extent to which the current level of new economy productivity falls short of its potential with the current GPT. The arrival of a new GPT shifts the aa' locus up with an increase in A*. The stationary loci for the labour supply in the old economy is a vertical line for a given level of L_R, which corresponds to the natural level of employment in the old economy. The dynamics of this model are such that the stationary equilibrium are globally stable. For levels of old economy labour supply above the "natural level", there is excess supply and thus a tendency for labour to move out of the old economy and into the new. For productivity levels above the aa' locus, productivity tends to decline.

A fall in the price of the old economy output, p_R^* which is not buffered by a nominal exchange rate depreciation, results in a reduction in the steady state *level* of employment in the old economy, and thus a reduction in the natural level of the labour supply in the old economy. The economy moves from the equilibrium denoted by 1 to the new equilibrium denoted by 2. As the old economy contracts and new economy expands, productivity begins to increase. As a result, total output will also increase. The lack of buffering has costs, however, in terms of increased transitional unemployment. In Figure 2 the buffered versus non-buffered paths with a shock at time t_o are depicted. The fully buffered shock holds employment in the old economy constant and thus also in the new economy.

What makes the new economy "new" of course is the arrival of a new GPT which increases A^*. In Figure 3, the dynamics GPT shock is illustrated for a case with a small but positive wage response coefficient. The initial equilibrium is 1 and the arrival of GPT shifts aa' vertically. Productivity

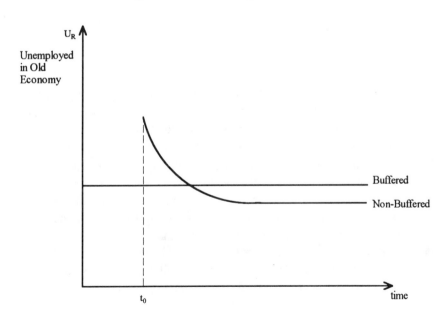

Figure 2: Unemployment Consequences of Exchange Rate Buffering

Figure 3: A GPT Arrival under Fixed Exchange Rates

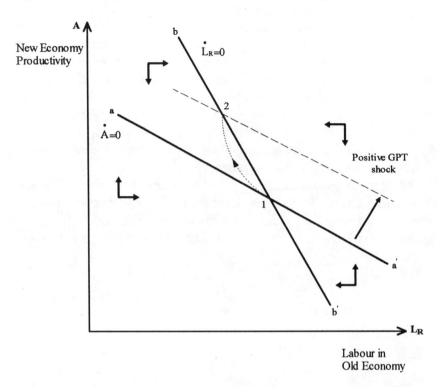

immediately begins to increase and employment in the new economy expands, until a new stationary point is reached. This is all done without an exchange rate change since p_R^* is assumed to be constant.

We now get to the central case of interest — a structural transition with the arrival of both a new economy GPT and an old economy price decline. The joint coincidence of these two events and the exchange rate response have important consequences for long-term economic growth. The relevant diagram is Figure 4, drawn for the case of inelastic wage response. The initial equilibrium is I. In a non-buffered case the GPT shock shifts aa' up and the old economy shock shifts the vertical bb' locus to the left at the new value L_R^2. In the absence of buffering the new equilibrium occurs at point N. The dynamics are an increase in productivity and a reduction in employment in the old economy. In this case, however, there is an added impetus to

Figure 4: A Structural Transition

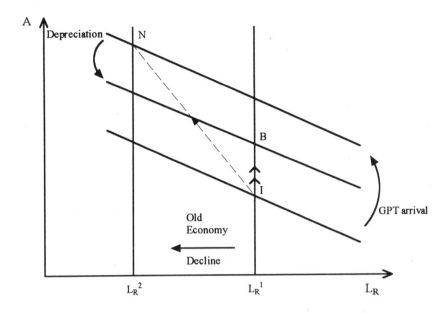

growth. The decline in the old economy boosts employment in the new economy which further increases productivity growth there. As labour is reallocated from the old to new economy, total output increases at an accelerating rate as the new economy expands. Moreover, there is a third effect at work. Because the new economy is assumed to have flexible labour markets, as the labour force reallocates itself from the old to the new *total* unemployment falls, even though the natural rate of unemployment is assumed to be unchanged in the old economy.

Now consider the impact of exchange rate buffering in this case. The buffering has two impact consequences. As noted previously it stabilizes employment in the old economy and thus total unemployment and the size of the new economy. The long-term impact on relative sectoral size will be dependent upon the sectoral wage response coefficient γ. If this value is zero there is no long-run impact with buffering on sector sizes. Second, buffering is accomplished by depreciating the nominal exchange rate. In the presence of a cost of productivity improvements effect, this will tend to slow the rate at which investments in productivity improvements are made, thus shifting the aa' locus down. It may not shift back to its initial position but as depicted

The New Economy and the Exchange Rate Regime

will fall somewhere below the GPT induced shift. In Figure 4 this is depicted as a transition from the initial point I to the final point N. The old economy is larger and the new economy is less productive than in the absence of buffering.

Implications for Fixed versus Flexible Exchange-Rate Regimes

The implication of the above analysis of exchange rate buffering during structural transitions carries implications for exchange rate regime choice. As is well documented, exchange rate misalignment under flexible rates tends to be persistent and defies easy generalization as to its causes. The literature thus far has mainly viewed misalignment against a backdrop of longer term trends in both economic structure and growth rates. The degree of misalignment, however, is endogenous in the long run as it is dependent upon the structure and circumstances an economy finds itself in. The recent decade and the current period may be relatively unique in that a period of larger scale technological change is occurring globally due to the arrival of what has become known as the new economy — a particular bunching of innovations in computing and communications technology which is the new general purpose technology. As with other GPTs, creative destruction is an important feature of this process. A structural shift appears as a negative shock to the old economy. If under flexible rates such a shock tends to produce persistent exchange rate depreciation in small open economies that import technology this may tend to delay both technological adoption and sectoral labour force reallocation towards the new economy. What thus initially appears to be a misalignment in the exchange rate endogenously becomes an equilibrium exchange rate due to reduced productivity growth induced by initial depreciation. The "misalignment" is temporary but the real depreciation is permanent.

A fixed rate avoids this problem by essentially transmitting the full relative price shocks which are induced by the joint arrival of the new economy and the decline of the old. It does this at the cost of the structural adjustments induced within the economy.

Even if one agrees with this analysis, it can be argued that it does not offer a permanent indictment of flexible exchange rate regimes. The arrival of major GPTs are relatively rare events, and thus the buffering benefits of flexible exchange rates would remain even after the new GPT had been fully adjusted to in the very long run. In the absence of other reasons to fix exchange rates the "productivity case" based on large-scale structural change appears to be a "one-off" case. There are two responses to this argument.

First, from what we know of previous major GPTs the period of structural change is fairly long lived — often in the range of a few decades. The case of electrification, for example, is often cited to have taken upwards of 30 years.[18] Thus structural change occurs at frequencies often associated with Solow growth transitions, rather than business-cycle shocks. Under these circumstances a misaligned exchange rate could seriously delay a transition by as much as a decade or more by providing inappropriate price signals in highly open economies. Fixed rates to the extent they would eliminate such confusion could avoid these problems.

Second, there is the possibility that the argument pertains to any shock which is relatively permanent. The buffering argument is based on the notion that the asymmetric shocks faced by the economy are largely temporary against the backdrop of the longer term highly persistent trends. As is well known there is considerable debate as to this empirical characterization of the growth process. An alternative view is that economies are hit by unpredictable but largely permanent shocks, or a series of overlapping structural changes. If one accepts this view each attempt to buffer a shock is largely in vain. This applies not only to exchange rate buffering but to all economic policies which attempt to slow down the response to structural change. Flexible exchange rates will not work well if they produce trend movements in real exchange rates which always appear to be responding to the last shock.

Of course not all exchange rate misalignments are undervaluations. By definition some exchange rates are overvalued if others are undervalued, however this benchmarking is done. A country that faces an overvalued exchange rate during a major GPT arrival will tend to lose competitiveness in the traditional sectors. This would imply a faster than otherwise process of creative destruction in that economy, and thus higher rates of productivity growth and faster reductions in the rate of unemployment than would occur under fixed exchange rates. This would seem to be nothing but good news on

---

[18]The collection of papers in Helpman (1999) reviews the historical evidence on major GPTs.

The New Economy and the Exchange Rate Regime

the productivity front. Exchange rate misalignment thus essentially redistributes growth internationally in parallel with the process of creative destruction. This argument applies with equal force to large economies as it does to small. For example a persistently weak euro against the U.S. dollar in current circumstances, for example, might lead to lower rates of European productivity growth relative to that of the United States.

Misalignments also re-distribute export growth across countries. The traditional misalignment literature of the 1980s was concerned with the loss of export markets to countries with persistently overvalued exchange rates and the longer run current account adjustment this might require.[19] Obviously this must be a factor in a full evaluation of fixed versus flexible rates during structural transitions. In the old-new economy context the composition of exports will shift as will the volume of exports in response to exchange rate misalignment. A country with an undervalued exchange rate will tend to reinforce its comparative advantage in the old economy, and conversely for countries with overvalued exchange rates. In reality the new economy involves new goods and services whose prices are highly unpredictable. The concept of a "terms of trade" between old and new goods is thus fraught with uncertainty. It is conceivable that the relative prices might evolve in a manner such as to support what appeared to be initially an incorrectly valued currency.[20] If the value of new economy exports turns out to be sufficiently large such as to produce a sustainable current account balance then what was perceived to be a misalignment may turn out to be ultimately an equilibrium exchange rate. Of course this may not occur. The exchange rate misalignment may be such as to produce an unsustainable current account deficit in the overvalued new economy leader, with the subsequent adjustment problems. Under a fixed exchange rate regime none of this could occur.

---

[19]The literature on misalignment and trade hysteresis is reviewed in Harris (1993).

[20]Asymmetric income effects with technological change can also lead to similar consequences. If new economy goods have income elasticities of demand greater than unity and old economy goods less than unity then economies specialized in new economy production will tend to have a higher rate of growth in external demand or equivalently improving terms of trade.

Conclusion: Optimal Currency Area Theory

In line with Mundell's (1961) optimal currency area theory it is natural to ask whether these arguments amend the cost-benefit calculation of optimal currency area groupings. Would it suggest, for example, that countries that trade with each other a great deal should worry more about the exchange rate consequences of the timing of large-scale structural transitions of one region relative to another? Moreover, do they suggest anything about the benefits of an optimal currency area when trade volumes and factor flows are substantial? A full theoretical analysis of this needs to be worked out but I think this paper suggests an answer in the affirmative. For countries that trade regularly with each other due to geographic proximity, major structural change is likely to be both transmitted and accommodated through trade flows and factor movements. There is a large body of evidence that suggests that the international transfer of technology is closely linked to trade flows and investment flows.[21] During a period of major technological change the forces which produce both the adoption of new technology and the obsolescence of the old will tend to be concentrated at similar times and in similar sectors for economies that are closely integrated. During these periods exchange rate misalignment between such countries could induce asymmetry in the structural adjustment pattern which would tend to bias growth against one country and in favour of the other, with the new sectors expanding at faster rates in one country, and mobile factors shifting towards those sectors from both countries. A common currency would eliminate the exchange rate misalignment problem during such a period, equalizing the growth potential across all members of the currency area. This argument would clearly not be as strong if economic integration was relatively weak.

In one sense this argument is just an extension of the "common shock" case for currency unions. In this case a common GPT has hit both countries. With large trade volumes and substantial factor mobility between regions there is no particular case for using an exchange rate change to buffer adjustment in one country relative to another and moreover the consequences of attempting to do so could be harmful. In the Canada-U.S. context it would suggest yet another reason as to why Canada's floating rate regime should

---

[21]For a discussion of these issues and a review of the evidence see Harris (2000).

The New Economy and the Exchange Rate Regime

be re-examined. The asymmetry in this case clearly works against Canada which is both small and well endowed with old economy natural resources. This is yet another argument that supports Robert Mundell's contention that Canadian-U.S. living standards are unlikely to converge until Canada either fixes its exchange rate against the U.S. dollar or enters a monetary union with the United States.

References

Aghion, P. and P. Howitt (1999), *Endogenous Growth Theory* (Cambridge, MA: MIT Press).

Brander, J. (1997), "Strategic Trade Theory", in G. Grossman and K. Rogoff (eds.), *Handbook of International Economics*, Vol. 3 (Amsterdam: North-Holland).

Burnside, C. and M. Hammour (1992), "The Cleansing Effect of Recession", unpublished paper (Cambridge, MA: Massachusetts Institute of Technology).

Courchene, T.J. and R.G. Harris (1999a), *From Fixing to Monetary Union: Options for North American Currency Integration*, Commentary No. 127 (Toronto: C.D. Howe Institute).

_____ (1999b), "Canada and a North American Monetary Union", *Canadian Business Economics* 7(4), 5-14.

Daly, D., M. Helfinger and G. Sharwood (2001), "Small Business in Canada-U.S. Manufacturing Productivity and Cost Comparisons", in J. Bernstein, R.G. Harris and A. Sharpe (eds.), *The Canada-U.S. Manufacturing Productivity Gap*, forthcoming, and available at <http://www.csls.ca>.

Foster, L., J. Haltwianger and C.J. Krizan (1998), "Aggregate Productivity Growth: Lessons from Microeconomic Evidence", NBER Working Paper No. W6803 (Cambridge, MA: National Bureau of Economic Research).

Gordon, R.J. (1999), "Has the 'New Economy' Rendered the Productivity Slowdown Obsolete?" Northwestern University and NBER available on the Web at <http://faculty-web.at.nwu.edu/economics/gordon>.

Grossman, G. and E. Helpman (1991), *Innovation and Growth in the Global Economy* (Cambridge, MA: MIT Press).

Grubel, H.G. (1999), *The Case for the Amero: The Merit of Creating a North American Monetary Union* (Vancouver: Fraser Institute).

Hall, R.E. (1991), "Recessions as Reorganizations", *NBER Macroeconomics Annual* (Cambridge, MA: National Bureau of Economic Research).

Harris, R.G. (1993), "Exchange Rates and Hysteresis in Trade", in J. Murray (ed.), *The Exchange Rate and the Economy* (Ottawa: Bank of Canada).

_____ (2000), "Determinants of Canadian Productivity Growth: Issues and Prospects", Industry Canada Occasional Papers, available at <www.strategis.ca>.

Helpman, E. (1999), *General Purpose Technologies* (Cambridge, MA: MIT Press).

Lafrance, R. and L. Schembri (2000), "The Exchange Rate, Productivity and the Standard of Living", *Bank of Canada Review* (Winter 1999/2000), 17-28.

Lothian, J.R. (1997), "Multi-Country Evidence on the Behaviour of Purchasing Power Parity under the Current Float", *Journal of International Money and Finance* 16, 19-35.

McCallum, J. (1999), *Canada, the Euro and Exchange Rate Fixity*, a paper in the Current Analysis series (Toronto: Royal Bank of Canada).

Mundell, R.A. (1961), "A Theory of Optimum Currency Area", *American Economic Review* 51(4), 657-665.

_____ (1990), "The Overvalued Canadian Dollar", paper prepared for the first meeting of the Canadian Monetary Policy Review Board, McGill University, Montreal, (April 4-5) (mimeo) or "De la surévaluation du dollar canadien", *Actualité économique* 67 (March 1991), 5-36.

Murray, J. (2000), "Why Canada Needs a Flexible Exchange Rate", *North American Journal of Economics and Finance* 11(1), 41-60.

Romer, P.-M. (1990), "Endogenous Technological Change", *Journal of Political Economy* 98(5), S71-102.

Saint-Paul, G. (1993), "Productivity Growth and the Structure of the Business Cycle", *European Economic Review* 37, 861-883.

Strauss, J. (1999), "Productivity Differentials, the Relative Price of Non-Tradables and Real Exchange Rates", *Journal of International Money and Finance* 18, 383-409.

The New Economy and the Exchange Rate Regime

Money, Markets and Mobility

Part III:

Optimum Currency Areas:
Empirical Perspectives

Exchange Rate Flexibility and Monetary Policy Choice for Emerging Market Economies

Michael B. Devereux and Philip R. Lane

Introduction

The experience of emerging market economies over the past decade has led to a re-evaluation of the choice over monetary policy stance. One part of this debate has been conducted at the level of choosing between fixed and flexible exchange rate regimes. The path-breaking work of Robert Mundell has given the profession a powerful tool with which to evaluate the costs and benefits of alternative exchange rate regimes. According to the Mundell-Fleming model, if the economy is subject to foreign disturbances such as real interest rate or demand shocks, it is better to let the exchange rate adjust so as to cushion the effect of this shock. In the crises of the 1990s, all of the worst hit countries were attempting to peg or stabilize their exchange rates in the pre-crisis period. Most commentators have suggested that the implication of the Asian and Mexican crises was to completely undermine the case for pegged exchange rates in emerging markets (see, e.g., Sachs, 1998). The evidence seemed to suggest that the stability of exchange rates led to the over-accumulation of un-hedged, foreign currency debt, which partly gave rise to the conditions that led to the financial crises.

But a recent series of papers have questioned the wisdom of floating exchange rates for emerging markets. Some writers such as Calvo (1999a,b) argue that exchange rate flexibility gives too much discretion to the monetary authority, and especially in Latin America, discretionary monetary policy has typically led to damaging episodes of inflation. The best option, under this view, is to remove discretion entirely by choosing a currency board, or outright dollarization. Other authors have focused on issues of "financial fragility" in emerging markets to argue that volatility in exchange rates may be particularly damaging in ways that would not occur in developed economies (Eichengreen and Hausmann, 1999; Aghion, Bachetta and Banerjee, 2000; Krugman, 1999). The particular explanations vary between these authors, but the essential message is that the combination of financial market vulnerability and a high exposure to exchange rate changes via foreign currency liabilities make emerging markets very reluctant to allow exchange rates to fluctuate freely. Typically emerging market firms face a currency mismatch, having most of their liabilities denominated in foreign currency, such as U.S. dollars, but assets mostly concentrated in local currency. Fluctuations in the exchange rate may therefore cause wide fluctuations in net worth for these firms. In the presence of imperfections in financial markets, in which net worth plays a key role in the tightness of financial market constraints, in the manner suggested by Bernanke, Gertler and Gilchrist (1999), for instance, exchange rate fluctuations may be very damaging.

This paper makes a contribution to the debate on monetary policy in emerging markets in two ways. First, in the next section, we present some preliminary empirical evidence that suggests that countries which have greater financial market linkages tend to display less bilateral exchange rate volatility. This broadly supports the view that exchange rate fluctuations may have negative effects working through financial markets.

In the second part of the paper, we develop a theoretical model to investigate the effects of alternative monetary policies that place greater or lesser emphasis on exchange rate stability. We agree with the view of Mishkin and Savastano (2000) that the debate needs to be broadened beyond the question of "fixed versus floating" to that of a wider discussion about the appropriate monetary policy rules that an emerging market economy should follow. Thus, while a fixed exchange rate regime represents a clear and coherent monetary policy rule, "floating exchange rates" do not represent a rule at all, but are consistent with a large set of alternative monetary policies, some of which are obviously more desirable than others. Thus, the appropriate way to conduct the debate is to ask to what extent should an optimal monetary policy in an emerging market economy attempt to achieve exchange rate stability, and more generally, what should monetary policy target. Following from the experience and research on monetary policies in the developed world, it has been suggested that monetary authorities in emerging markets should follow an inflation targeting policy. In the study below, we will compare a range of alternative monetary rules for an emerging market, including inflation targeting, price stability, and fixed exchange rates. At issue is which of these rules has the best overall characteristics.

Our simulation results come from a "dynamic general equilibrium" model which is part of a wider study of financial markets and exchange rate/monetary policies in emerging markets (Devereux and Lane, 2000). In the present paper, we investigate the desirable monetary policy response to a foreign interest rate or "risk premium" shock in an emerging market.

The theoretical model is extended in ways that allows us to investigate how financial market distortions affect the optimal monetary rule for an emerging market economy. Does the presence of un-hedged foreign currency denominated liabilities and net worth constraints on emerging market firms eliminate the potential benefits of exchange rate flexibility, or at the very least suggest that emerging market monetary authorities might want to shape monetary policy rules towards reducing overall exchange rate flexibility?

We conduct this investigation by introducing financial market frictions into our prototype model of an emerging market. Following the method of Bernanke, Gertler and Gilchrist (1999), we assume that investment in the emerging market is constrained by net worth considerations, and that all international borrowing must be done in foreign currency. This leaves firms exposed to "balance sheet risk" in response to exchange rate changes. In principle, this might introduce an argument for more exchange rate stability than one would expect in the frictionless financial market model.

The results of our theoretical investigation indicate that there is little case for monetary policies which attempt to minimize exchange rate volatility in emerging markets. In fact, the optimal monetary policy suggests that more exchange rate variability than is allowed by some typical monetary policy operating rules would be desirable. Moreover, this holds true despite the presence of financial market distortions. In fact, with financial market distortions driven by lending constraints as described above, the model surprisingly indicates that the real exchange rate should be allowed to move by more than would be the case in the absence of these distortions. Thus, while there may be evidence that many emerging markets do wish to limit their exposure to exchange rate variance, and that this is linked to financial market vulnerability, the types of financing restrictions that have been identified in previous literature do not provide much theoretical support for this behaviour.

Discussion and Empirical Evidence

How much should developing economies attempt to ensure exchange rate stability? A traditional answer to this question was that developing economies should peg their exchange rates to the currency of a large trading partner. With heavy reliance on export markets, and little market power in setting prices, there was little role for exchange rate adjustment in such economies. High exchange rate variability could be disruptive to exporters and might reduce trade volume. In addition, the reluctance to allow exchange rate movements was related to the popular argument that in developing countries devaluation could not work as a macroeconomic tool, but may in fact lead to a contraction in gross domestic product (GDP) (Agenor and Montiel, 1998). Finally, from the viewpoint of macroeconomic discipline, a fixed exchange rate could bring benefits by helping to achieve low and stable rates of inflation.

But with the opening up of emerging markets to capital flows in the 1980s and 1990s, the sustainability of fixed exchange rates came under threat. It becomes increasingly difficult to manage the exchange rate in an environment of very volatile capital flows. Central banks that may have followed multiple objectives for monetary policy in absence of liberalized capital markets will find their room for manoeuvre severely circumscribed once capital flows can take place more freely.

The high incidence of both currency crises and banking crises in emerging markets over the last 20 years suggests that the costs of following a non-credible pegged exchange rate regime may be very high. By contrast, exchange rate flexibility itself may be a desirable way to limit the dangers of capital flows, as we have suggested above. In face of this, many emerging market economies have moved away from explicit policies of pegged exchange rates. For instance, in 1975, 87% of developing countries followed some type of exchange rate peg, but this had fallen to less than 50% by 1996

(Caramazza and Aziz, 1998). Since the financial crises of 1997–1999, this proportion has dropped even further.

But some writers have noted recently that the *de jure* exchange rate regime as reported to the International Monetary Fund (IMF) may be quite different from the *de facto* flexibility allowed by monetary authorities in exchange rate movements. Calvo and Reinhardt (2000) note that many countries officially classified as operating under floating exchange rates have much less variability in their effective exchange rates than the United States or Japan, for instance, while being subjected to higher volatility in shocks to their terms of trade and other macroeconomic variables. They argue that there seems to be a pervasive "fear of floating" among many developed and developing countries.

The explanation for the lack of willingness to allow the exchange rate to fluctuate is likely to be different for developing and developed economies. For emerging markets, Eichengreen and Hausmann (1999) have suggested the exchange rate volatility is costly due to the "original sin hypothesis", meaning that these countries cannot borrow or lend in their own currencies, and have poorly developed domestic financial markets in which domestic currency government or corporate securities may be traded. This phenomenon of missing markets in domestic currency instruments leads many emerging market economies to be "dollarized" to the extent that their financial systems and corporate balance sheets are highly exposed to exchange rate fluctuations. A natural response is to attempt to limit exchange rate volatility against the principal currency in which both external and internal liabilities are denominated.

To test this hypothesis, we conduct a simple regression analysis. In work in progress (Devereux and Lane, 2000), we are investigating the determinants of bilateral exchange rate volatility. Here, we report some initial findings. The basic regression specification is

$$VER_{ij} = \alpha + \gamma * FINANCE_{ij} + \varepsilon_{ij}$$

where VER_{ij} is a measure of bilateral exchange rate volatility between countries i and j and $FINANCE_{ij}$ is the stock of liabilities owed by country i to country j, as a percentage of country i's gross national product (GNP). The prediction is that $\gamma < 0$: reduced bilateral exchange rate volatility with respect to major creditor countries.

Exchange rate volatility is measured as the standard deviation of the log first difference of the bilateral exchange rate on quarterly data over 1974.1

Exchange Rates in Emerging Markets

to 1998.4. We look at both nominal and consumer price index (CPI)-based real exchange rates, with these data taken from the IMF's *International Financial Statistics* CD-ROM. The measure of bilateral financial liabilities is taken from the IMF's *Comprehensive Portfolio Investment Survey* which has been recently published and is a snapshot of end-1997 portfolio equity and long-term debt positions. We currently have data on 49 countries. In our initial work, we focus on bilateral exchange rate volatility vis-à-vis the United States, United Kingdom, Japan and France.

Table 1 presents the results. Although the overall explanatory power varies, we generally find a significant negative relationship between the scale of financial liabilities and the level of exchange rate volatility. This is in line with the notion that such financial linkages provide an additional motivation to avoid instability in the bilateral exchange rate. The results are generally stronger for the nominal exchange rate than the real exchange rate, so avoiding nominal volatility appears especially important.

Of course, these are preliminary findings. In particular, in work in progress, we are attempting to control for other determinants of bilateral exchange rate volatility such as trade linkages and to address the potential endogeneity of both financial and trade linkages to the exchange rate regime. Moreover, we expect the importance of external liabilities in determining monetary and exchange rate policies to vary according to the level of domestic financial development, so it will be important to investigate interaction effects.

We now move on to discuss a theoretical framework for evaluating monetary policy and exchange rate stability in an emerging market.

Monetary Policy in a Small Open Economy

Outline of the Model

Here we describe a dynamic model of a small open economy which may be used as a vehicle for discussing some of the questions concerning monetary policy choice for small, emerging market economies. The structure is a relatively standard two-sector "dependent economy" model, with production taking place in a domestic non-traded good, and an export good, the price of

Table 1: Bilateral Exchange Rate Volatility and Financial Linkages

		Finance	*R2*	*N*
USA	NER	0.001 (.035)	0.012	49
	RER	-6.3 (-1.2)	0.001	49
UK	NER	-0.67 (-2.48)	0.071	49
	RER	-29.6 (-1.84)	0.022	49
JAP	NER	-0.86 (-2.67)	0.109	49
	RER	-41.4 (-1.67)	0.038	49
FRA	NER	-2.52 (-4.15)	0.14	49
	RER	-72.1 (-2.06)	0.02	49
POOL	NER	-0.23 (-3.3)	0.035	196
	RER	-10.7 (-1.74)	0.01	196

Note: Heteroskedasticity-corrected t-statistics in parentheses. NER is nominal exchange rate and RER is real exchange rate. Pooled regressions include dummies for United States, United Kingdom, Japan and France.

which is fixed on world markets. Three central aspects of the model are (i) the existence of nominal rigidities, (ii) the presence of lending constraints on investment financing, and (iii) the requirement that all foreign liabilities be denominated in foreign currency. The first feature is, of course, necessary to motivate a role for the exchange rate regime at all. The specific assumption made is that the prices of non-traded goods are set by individual firms and adjust only over time. The specification of price-setting follows Calvo (1983) and Yun (1996). With respect to the lending constraints on

Exchange Rates in Emerging Markets

foreign investment we follow the model of Bernanke, Gertler and Gilchrist (1999), which assumes that entrepreneurs undertake investment projects with returns that can be observed by lenders only at a cost. This leads entrepreneurs to face higher costs of external financing of investment relative to internal financing, and as a result investment depends on entrepreneurial net worth. The final feature of the model is based on the observation by Eichengreen and Hausmann (1999), among many others, noting that emerging market economies have almost no ability to issue debt denominated in local currency. For instance, almost all the debt issued by East Asian countries during the period of rapid inflows in the early 1990s was denominated in U.S. dollars.

The specific details of the model are presented in the Appendix. Here we highlight the important general aspects of the structure. There are four sets of actors; consumers, production firms, entrepreneurs, and the monetary authority. In addition, of course, there is a "foreign" sector where prices of export and import goods are set, and where lending rates are determined.

Consumers consume domestic non-traded goods and an imported foreign good. They receive wage income from firms, and may borrow or lend freely in international capital markets at exogenous foreign nominal interest rates. In addition, they hold domestic money balances. While it would be possible to extend the model so that consumers face the same constraints on foreign lending as do domestic entrepreneurs, this would probably have little impact on the results. The assumption of full capital market access on the part of consumers ensures that uncovered interest rate parity will hold within the model.

Production firms in the traded (export) sector are competitive. Output in the traded sector requires labour and capital. Output in the non-traded sector is differentiated, with production of individual goods being carried out by monopolistic competitive firms who set prices in advance. Production in the non-traded sector requires labour and "land", which is assumed to be in fixed supply for the economy as a whole.

Production of capital goods (for use in the export sector) is also carried out by competitive firms, who combine both traded and non-traded goods in production to supply unfinished capital goods. There are adjustment costs of investment, so that the marginal return to investment in terms of capital goods is declining in the amount of investment undertaken, relative to the current capital stock. The unfinished capital goods are sold to individual entrepreneurs, who turn them into finished capital goods according to their idiosyncratic private information technologies. Finished capital goods are then rented to firms in the traded goods sector.

The details of the entrepreneurial sector are as follows. Entrepreneurs are risk neutral, and finance investment from their current net worth, and new foreign currency borrowing from lenders abroad. Entrepreneur's net worth accumulates through returns on previous investments. Letting net worth of an individual entrepreneur j at the end of time t be N_{t+1}^j denominated in domestic currency, the entrepreneurs balance sheet implies that

$$P_t K_{t+1}^j q_t = N_{t+1}^j + S_t D_{t+1}^j \qquad (1)$$

Here P_t is the price of the composite CPI good in the economy, K_{t+1}^j is the capital acquired by entrepreneur j, and D_{t+1}^j is the debt issued by entrepreneur j.

The borrowing of entrepreneurs is governed by an optimal contract offered by risk-neutral foreign lenders. The contract structure follows closely that of Bernanke, Gertler and Gilchrist (1999). Entrepreneurs may monitor the individual projects of borrowers at a cost. The optimal incentive-compatible contract is a debt contract. Monitoring only occurs when project returns are below a certain threshold. The contract is such that there is an "external finance premium" on each entrepreneur, meaning that the required rate of return on borrowed funds exceeds the world opportunity cost of funds. Moreover, the external finance premium depends negatively on the entrepreneur's net worth, relative to the value of capital purchases.

Let R_{t+1}^k be the expected real return on domestic investment, and R_{t+1}^* be the expected real cost of funds borrowed from abroad. Then the external finance premium implies that:

$$R_{t+1}^k = R_{t+1}^* \psi \left(\frac{N_{t+1}}{q_t P_t K_{t+1}} \right) \qquad (2)$$

where $\psi'(.) < 0$. Thus, the external finance premium is lower, the greater is entrepreneurial net worth, relative to the cost of capital.

Entrepreneurial net worth is determined by the return on investment. Assuming that entrepreneurs save a given fraction ζ of their returns, we may write

$$N_{t+1} = \zeta (R_t^k P_t q_{t-1} K_t - (1 + i_t^*) S_t D_t - BC_t) \qquad (3)$$

Exchange Rates in Emerging Markets

where i_t^* is the foreign nominal interest rate, and BC_t is the net cost of monitoring incurred by the lenders (see Appendix for details). The important feature of equation (3) is that it depends negatively on the current exchange rate. An unanticipated devaluation will reduce net worth of the entrepreneurial sector. Given (2) this will raise the external finance premium, and reduce investment. This introduces a non-standard mechanism for the effects of exchange rate shocks. As stressed by Krugman (1999), when emerging market firms have outstanding foreign currency liabilities, movements in the exchange rate can impinge directly on their investment opportunities by affecting the strength of their balance sheets.

Monetary Rules

The next critical feature of the model is the stance of the monetary authorities. We wish to explore a set of alternative monetary policy rules that emerging markets might follow. A fixed exchange rate is a simple and coherent rule. But the alternatives allow a wide variety of monetary policies. To fix ideas, we explore the implications of five different monetary policy rules, listed as follows:

1. *Fixed Exchange Rate*. We assume that the fixed exchange rate is fully credible and sustainable. Our aim is to evaluate the properties of robust alternative monetary policy rules for emerging market economies. It seems clear that the performance of weak pegs has been uniformly bad. Therefore, a durable fixed exchange rate has to be associated with rigorous monetary and fiscal discipline. Therefore we might think of this regime as a currency board or a policy of dollarization.

2. *Monetary-Growth Rule*. In this case, the monetary authority sets a constant growth rate of money, and interest rates are determined freely.

3. *Price-Stability Rule*. Under this rule, the monetary authority maintains a constant growth rate of the consumer price index. This is a much tighter policy than what is typically known as "inflation targeting".

4. *Taylor Rule*. Under this policy, the monetary authority sets the short-term interest rate to target the rate of domestic CPI inflation and the deviation of domestic output from its "target level", following the rule put forth by Taylor (1993). Thus, interest rates are set so that

$$i_{t+1} = \varphi_1 \pi_t + \varphi_2 y_t$$

where π_t is the domestic CPI inflation rate, and y_t is the deviation of domestic output from its natural level. Following Taylor (1993), we let $\varphi_1 = 1.5$ and $\varphi_2 = 0.5$.

The Taylor rule may be thought of as being close to an "inflation targeting" rule, although in some key respects it differs from the popular definitions of inflation targeting as in Svensson (1999), for instance.

5. *Optimal Monetary Policy Rule.* Under this rule, the monetary authority follows a policy of adjusting either money or interest rates to ensure that the domestic price of non-traded goods equals marginal cost. This policy follows the suggestion of King and Wolman (1999). The rule in fact ensures that the response of the economy to shocks replicates that of a fully flexible price economy. While this is an unrealistic candidate for a monetary policy rule, it offers a useful and interesting benchmark against which to compare the other rules. Moreover, in the absence of external financial constraints, this is the welfare optimizing monetary policy stance for the monetary authority to follow.[1]

Capital Market Shocks

We will illustrate the workings of the model by examining the behaviour of the small economy when subjected to capital market shocks. As discussed by Calvo (1999a), the most obvious macroeconomic characteristic of emerging market economies in the 1990s was the high volatility in capital flows. Periods of very large capital inflows and current account deficits are followed by abrupt "capital market reversals" and current account surpluses. Figure 1 illustrates the case of Thailand after the middle of 1997. From being in a position of a current account deficit of around 8% of GDP in 1996 and early 1997, Thailand underwent a dramatic transformation towards a current account surplus of over 10% of GDP within a 6–8 month period. This reversal in the current account was associated with a 50% real exchange rate depreciation, a 16% fall in real GDP, and a 19% fall in real private consumption.

---

[1]The model economy has two goods-market deviations from the first-best; sticky prices and imperfect competition. The welfare costs of imperfect competition may be eliminated by a production subsidy to firms. This leaves price stickiness as the only welfare loss. Therefore, a monetary policy which replicates the flexible price economy is fully optimal.

Exchange Rates in Emerging Markets

Figure 1a: Thailand: GDP and Private Consumption

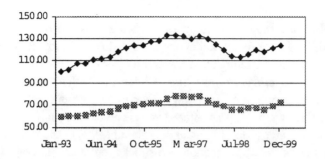

Figure 1b: Thailand: CA/GDP

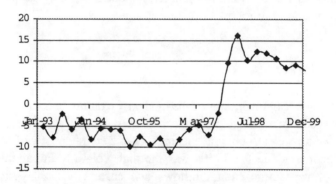

Figure 1c: Thailand: Real Exchange Rate

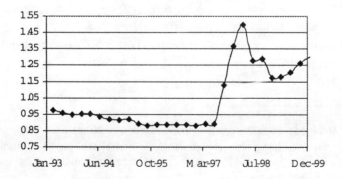

Figure 1d: Thailand: Six-Month Government Bond Yield

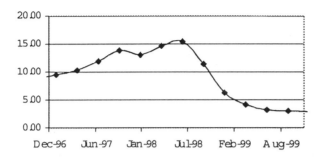

A large research literature has developed in an attempt to understand the determinants of the Asian crisis and more generally the source of capital market volatility for emerging markets. For our purposes, we wish only to model the effects of capital market shocks. An imperfect but appealingly simple way to describe a capital market shock within the structure of our small economy model is by an exogenous rise in the "risk-premium" on foreign lending. Effectively, this is equivalent to a rise in the foreign interest rate, i_t^*. As described more fully in the Appendix, a capital market shock is then modelled as

$$i_t^* = \hat{i}_t^* + u_t$$

where $\hat{i}_t^*$ is the foreign nominal interest rate, and $u_t = \rho u_{t-1} + \varepsilon_t$ is a "risk-premium" shock, with $0 \leq \rho \leq 1$, and $\varepsilon_t \sim IID(0,\sigma_\varepsilon^2)$. Since the foreign interest rate is exogenous in any case, there is effectively no distinction in the model between a risk premium shock and a shock to the foreign interest rate itself. Figure 1 shows that interest rates on government guaranteed bonds in Thailand rose by about 500 basis points in the immediate aftermath of the capital market crisis.

Solution and Calibration

How does a capital market shock impact on the small economy? The model is calibrated and simulated using standard parameter value assumptions. The Appendix describes this process in more detail. The most critical assumptions relate to the size of the non-traded goods sector, and the factor intensity of the different sectors. We assume that the non-traded goods sector accounts for 55% of total GDP, and that non-traded goods are more labour-intensive than the export good. This seems reasonably accurate as a description of emerging markets (see Devereux and Cook, 2000).

The Frictionless Financial Market Case

We first describe the characteristics of the model in the absence of lending constraints on entrepreneurial investment. Thus, in equation (2) above, $\psi(.) = 1$. Simulations from the model are described in Figures 2a–2d. The experiment described in these Figures is a five-percentage point increase in the risk premium facing the emerging market economy that persists with AR(1) coefficient of 0.25. This is roughly consistent with the picture for Thailand in Figure 1.

Each figure shows the response of the economy for each of the five different monetary policy rules. The figures show a quite consistent pattern of response to the risk premium shock across all monetary rules. In each case, there is a real exchange rate depreciation, a fall in private consumption, and an increase in the trade balance surplus. But the nature of the immediate response of GDP depends on the monetary rule. For the money-targeting rule and the optimal monetary policy, GDP rises. For a fixed exchange rate regime, a Taylor rule, and a price stability rule, GDP falls. Note that the response of GDP to the risk premium shock is the value-weighted sum of the response of output in the non-trade sector and the traded sector. For all monetary rules, output in the traded sector expands (as the economy shifts resources out of non-traded goods to generate a rise in net exports), while output in the non-traded sector contracts. But the effect on total GDP does depend on the rule.

In comparing the rules, we see that the fixed exchange rate rule does significantly worse in the sense that (i) the fall in consumption and output is greater than for all other rules and (ii) the increase in the trade balance surplus exceeds all other rules. At the same time, the real exchange rate depreciation is significantly less under fixed exchange rates than under all other rules. Under fixed exchange rates, a rise in the foreign risk premium leads to an immediate rise in domestic nominal interest rates. With sluggish prices in the non-traded sector and no movement in the exchange rate, this generates a real interest rate increase by almost as much. The result is a large

Figure 2a: Output

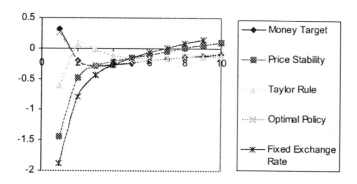

Figure 2b: Consumption

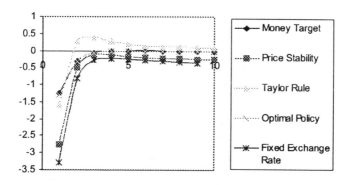

Figure 2c: Real Exchange Rate

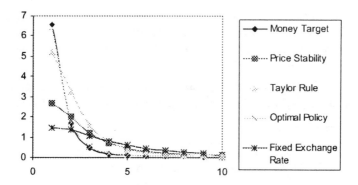

Figure 2d: Trade Balance

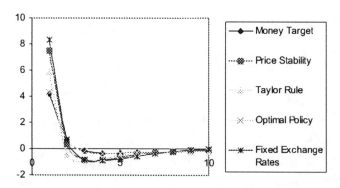

fall in domestic consumption and investment, which is felt in a large drop in the production of non-traded goods. As demand for labour in the non-traded sector falls, nominal wages fall, and the traded sector expands. The combination of a traded sector expansion and a drop in domestic absorption leads to a trade balance improvement.

By contrast, under a monetary rule that allows the exchange rate to adjust, for instance the money-targeting rule, the risk premium shock leads to an immediate depreciation on the nominal exchange rate. This cushions the impact of the shock on the nominal and real interest rate (as there is expected nominal and real exchange rate appreciation). As a result, the fall in domestic consumption, investment, and demand for non-traded goods is much less. This translates into a smaller improvement in the current account and, for the money targeting rule and the optimal monetary policy rule, the expansion in traded sector output offsets the decline in non-traded goods output so, overall, GDP rises.

Figure 2 may also be used to compare across the different rules that allow exchange rate adjustment. The price stability rule accommodates real exchange rate depreciation, but only to the extent that the non-traded goods price index is reduced, to allow a stable overall level of the CPI.[2] The result is a much smaller real exchange rate depreciation than the other flexible exchange rate rules, which implies a larger fall in output and consumption,

---

[2]Note that under the Calvo (1983) price setting structure, the contemporaneous price index for non-traded goods is not predetermined, but follows a partial adjustment process. Thus, the non-traded goods price index does move partially even in the period of the shock.

and a larger increase in the trade balance surplus. It is notable that Figure 2 indicates relatively little difference between a price stability rule and a fixed exchange rate rule. The movement in consumption, output, and the real exchange rate are all of quite similar magnitude for the three rules.

The Taylor rule has an intermediate effect between the money-targeting rule and the price-stability rule. Interest rates rise due to a rise in inflation, but fall in response to a fall in output. The increase in the real interest rate is between that of the other two rules. As a consequence, consumption falls by more than the money-targeting rule, but less than the price-stability rule. Output also falls, but by less than the price-stability rule. As to be expected, the real exchange rate depreciation is then less than under money targeting, but greater than under price stability.

In comparing alternative monetary rules, we may conclude that the monetary-targeting rule is preferable to all the others, including a fixed exchange rate. This is because the money-targeting rule very closely approximates the optimal monetary rule. The reason is that under monetary targeting, given the structure of the underlying model (see Appendix), the response to the risk premium shock does not require movements in the non-traded goods price. But an optimal monetary rule operates by adjusting the money supply (or interest rates) so as to keep marginal cost and the price of non-traded goods prices constant. Thus, an optimal monetary rule and a money-targeting rule are effectively equivalent. In summary then, the model economy suggests that, in the absence of financing constraints on investment of firms, the preference among monetary rules is in the following order: monetary targeting, then a Taylor rule, then price stability, then a fixed exchange rate. Table 2 tends to confirm this suggestion. The top panel gives the standard deviations of GDP, the real exchange rate, and consumption for all different monetary rules, in the presence of a risk premium shock with persistence parameter 0.25. The scale of the shock is set so that the standard deviation of GDP under the optimal policy rule is unity. The preference ranking suggested holds true in the order of variability of GDP and consumption, and inversely for the order of variability of the real exchange rate. A clear conclusion from the table is that there is a trade-off between the variability of consumption and GDP and the variability of the real exchange rate. A policy of fixed exchange rates maximizes the variability of real magnitudes at the same time as it minimizes the variance of the real exchange rate. The optimal rule (and the money-targeting rule) minimize the variability of real magnitudes while maximizing the variability of the real exchange rate.

Table 2: Monetary Rules

Standard Deviations	Money	Price	Taylor	Optimal	Fixed E. Rate
No Financing Constraints					
Output	1.1	2.8	1.2	1.0	3.8
RER	12.0	5.8	11.0	12.2	3.5
Consumption	2.4	5.2	3.5	2.4	6.2
Financing Constraints					
Output	1.8	4.1	3.2	4.6	4.5
RER	16.4	9.4	14.3	19.6	6.7
Consumption	3.0	6.4	4.1	1.7	8.0

Note: RER is the real exchange rate.

We also note that the pattern of response to the capital market shock in the model is quite consistent, qualitatively, with the experience of Thailand illustrated in Figure 1. The simultaneous occurrence of real exchange rate depreciation, output and consumption collapse, and current account reversal is generated by the model when monetary authorities use a fixed exchange-rate rule, a price-stability rule or a Taylor rule.

Introducing Financial Market Frictions

We now turn to the evaluation of alternative monetary rules in the model with financing constraints on entrepreneurs. Does this alter the calculus against floating exchange rates? At first glance we could think this might be the case. The reason is that unanticipated exchange rate fluctuations cause volatility in the foreign currency liabilities of the entrepreneurs, leading to volatility in both the external finance premium and investment in the emerging market.

Figures 3a-3d illustrate the effects of risk premium shocks in the model with the financing constraint. In fact, as the figures illustrate, most of the conclusions of the previous case remain unchanged. The notable difference is that the impact effects and persistence of the risk premium shocks are much greater with financing constraints on investment. The intuition for this is quite clear. A rise in the risk premium will directly reduce entrepreneurial wealth, as it raises interest payments on outstanding debt. This pushes up the finance premium on investment, leading to a further increase in the effective cost of capital for entrepreneurs, and thus causing a bigger fall in investment than observed in the model with frictionless financing of investment. The fall in investment reduces the real price of capital, and this generates a further fall in entrepreneurial wealth, in a "financial accelerator" effect, as presented by Bernanke, Gertler and Gilchrist (1999). Due to the effect of the rise in the entrepreneurial risk premium, investment and output fall by more in this model, and the real exchange-rate depreciation is greater.

Under floating exchange rates of any kind, there is a further impact on the entrepreneurial risk premium, arising from the effects of exchange-rate depreciation on entrepreneurial wealth. The exchange-rate depreciation generates an increase in the outstanding value of foreign currency denominated debt, reducing entrepreneurial wealth still further and pushing up the investment-financing premium. The finance premium increases under all rules, but it rises by less under fixed exchange rates than any of the other rules. Thus, a policy of fixed exchange rates does have the effect of stabilizing the premium that the economy must pay on investment financing.

But despite this, the fixed exchange-rate regime is still clearly worse than all others in its ability to respond to the capital market shock. This point comes out obviously from Figure 3. Despite the stabilizing of the external finance premium for investors, the inability of the exchange rate to adjust dampens the potential real exchange-rate depreciation (Figure 3c), and thus generates a much greater real interest rate increase in the fixed exchange rate regime than for any of the other rules. This leads to a much bigger fall in investment, consumption, and GDP than for the other monetary rules. Our conclusion in this respect then is that the presence of the external financing constraint does not in fact alter the calculus in favour of fixed exchange rates. The moment calculations in Table 2 confirm this. Fixed exchange rates limit the variability of the real exchange rate, but significantly increase the variability of real GDP and consumption. Furthermore, fixed exchange rates do worse under the external finance constraint than in its absence. While the stability of the nominal exchange rate helps to stabilize the external finance

Figure 3a: Output

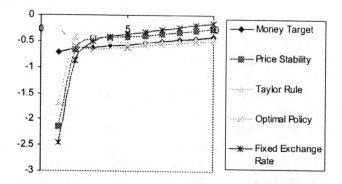

Figure 3b: Consumption

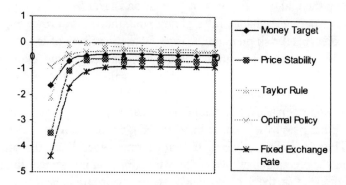

Figure 3c: Real Exchange Rate

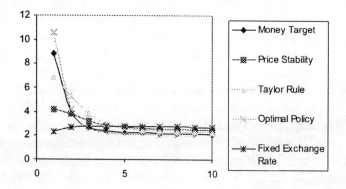

Figure 3d: Trade Balance

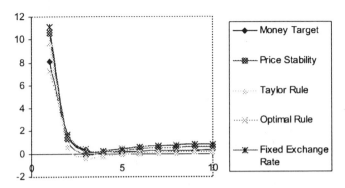

premium, the multiplier effects of shocks to the external finance premium itself are larger under fixed rates.

The ranking of alternative monetary rules carries over unchanged from the model without financing constraints. The monetary target does better, followed by the Taylor rule, followed by the price stability rule, and then the fixed exchange-rate rule. Output and consumption variability increases as we move from best to worst, and real exchange-rate variability decreases. One notable fact from Figure 3 and Table 2 is that in the presence of the external finance constraint, the money-targeting rule is no longer equivalent to the optimal rule which replicates the flexible price economy. Under monetary targeting, the interest rate shock generates a required fall in the nominal price of non-traded goods. This means that an optimal monetary policy should be more expansionary than allowed by the money-targeting rule.

Conclusions

It is important not to place too much emphasis on the results of the theoretical model of this paper. While the model has suggested that it is difficult to make a case for fixed exchange rates, that is, that more exchange rate variability is necessary than is typically allowed within the usual operating rules for monetary policy, there are some realistic limitations on the ability of the model to address all the relevant issues in macroeconomic policy making for emerging markets. The model ignores shocks coming from the domestic financial system. These shocks may place limitations on the ability to conduct monetary targeting as an operating rule. In addition, the very features that we have outlined as being important sources of financial market fragility in emerging markets — high exposure to foreign currency in balance sheets, and thin domestic currency financial markets — actually reduce the ability of central banks to conduct effective monetary policy in the first place. Without a thick market in government, short-term securities, the ability to use open market operations and interest rate adjustment — the hallmarks of monetary policy procedures in developed countries — is quite limited. Finally the type of financial fragility that we have outlined in the model is somewhat limited, as it does not encompass the importance of the banking system, nor does it allow for important direct supply-side effects of exchange rate movements through the availability of trade credit for imported intermediate goods. In the experience of the East Asian economies during the 1997–1999 crisis, these elements were noted to be important explanatory factors for the extent of the economic contraction. We leave it for the future to investigate these issues further.

Appendix

The Small Open Economy Model

Consumers

We will describe the model in terms of the representative consumer. He or she has preferences given by

(A1) $\quad U = E_0 \sum_{t=0}^{\infty} \beta u(C_t, H_t, \frac{M_t}{P_t})$,

where C_t is a composite consumption index, H_t is labour supply, and $\frac{M_t}{P_t}$ represents real balances, with M_t being nominal money balances, and P_t being the consumer price index. Let the functional form of u be given by

$$u = \frac{1}{1-\omega} C^{1-\omega} + \frac{\chi}{1-\varepsilon} \left(\frac{M_t}{P_t} \right)^{1-\varepsilon} - \eta \frac{H_t^{1+\upsilon}}{1+\upsilon}$$

Composite consumption is a function of consumption of non-traded goods and traded goods, where $C_t = (aC_{Nt}^{1-\frac{1}{\rho}} + (1-a)C_{Tt}^{1-\frac{1}{\rho}})^{\frac{\rho}{\rho-1}}$. The implied consumer price index is then $P = (a^\rho P_{Nt}^{1-\rho} + (1-a)^\rho P_{Tt}^{1-\rho})^{\frac{1}{1-\rho}}$. In addition, the consumption of non-tradable goods is differentiated as follows

$$C_{Nt} = \left(\int_0^1 C_{Nt}(i)^{1-\lambda} di \right)^{1/(1-\lambda)} .$$

Exchange Rates in Emerging Markets　　　　　　　　　　109

We assume that consumers do not face any capital market imperfections. Therefore, the consumer can borrow directly in terms of foreign currency at a given interest rate. Agents face an interest cost of borrowing one period nominal debt given by i_t^*.

Consumer revenue flows in any period come from their supply of hours of work to firms for wages W_t, receive a transfer T_t from government, receive profits from firms in the non-traded sector (see below) Π_t, hold domestic money, and repay their debts from last period D_t. They then obtain new loans from foreign capital markets, and use these to consume, and acquire new money balances. Their budget constraint is thus:

$$(A2) \quad P_tC_t = W_tL_t + \Pi_t + S_tD_{t+1} + M_t - M_{t-1} - (1+i_t^*)S_tD_t + T_t$$

The household will choose non-traded and traded goods to minimize expenditure conditional on total composite demand C_t. Demand for non-traded and traded goods is then

$$C_{Nt} = a^\rho \left(\frac{P_{Nt}}{P_t}\right)^{-\rho} C_t \qquad C_{Tt} = (1-a)^\rho \left(\frac{P_{Tt}}{P_t}\right)^{-\rho} C_t$$

The consumer optimum can be characterized by the following conditions.

$$(A3) \qquad \frac{1}{(1+i_{t+1}^*)}C_t^{-\omega} = E_t\beta\frac{S_{t+1}}{S_t}\frac{P_t}{P_{t+1}}C_{t+1}^{-\omega}$$

$$(A4) \qquad \frac{W_t}{P_t} = \frac{\eta C_t^\omega}{1-H_t}$$

$$(A5) \qquad \left(\frac{M_t}{P_t}\right)^{-\omega} = C_t^{-\omega}(1-E_td_{t+1}^h)$$

Equation (A4) represents the Euler equation for optimal consumption. Equation (A5) is the labour supply equation, while equation (A6) gives the implicit money demand function. Money demand depends on domestic nominal interest rates. The domestic nominal discount factor is defined as

$$\text{(A6)} \quad d_{t+1}^{h} = \frac{C_{t+1}^{-\omega}}{C_{t}^{-\omega}} \frac{P_{t}}{P_{t+1}}.$$

The combination of (A3) and (A6) gives the representation of uncovered interest rate parity for this model.

Production Firms

Production is carried out by firms in the non-traded and traded goods sectors. The sectors differ in their production technologies. Non-traded goods are produced using labour and a fixed factor (land). Non-traded firm i has production technology

$$\text{(A7)} \quad Y_{Nit} = A_N F_i^{\varepsilon} L_{Nit}^{1-\varepsilon}.$$

Traded goods production, on the other hand, employs capital and labour, using the production function

$$\text{(A8)} \quad Y_{Tt} = A_T K_t^{\gamma} L_{Nt}^{1-\gamma}$$

Non-traded goods firms hire labour and land from consumers, and sell their output to consumers and capital-producing firms. Traded goods firms hire labour from consumers and capital from entrepreneurs, again selling their output to consumers and capital producers. We imagine that the non-traded goods sector is monopolistically competitive, while the traded goods sector is competitive. Profit-maximizing behaviour then implies the following equations

$$\text{(A9)} \quad W_t = MC_{Nt}(1-\varepsilon)A_N F^{\varepsilon} L_{Nt}^{-\varepsilon}$$

$$\text{(A10)} \quad W_t = P_{Tt}(1-\gamma)A_N K_t^{\gamma} L_{Tt}^{-\gamma}$$

$$\text{(A11)} \quad R_t = P_{Tt}\gamma A_T K_t^{\gamma-1} L_{Tt}^{1-\gamma}$$

Exchange Rates in Emerging Markets

Entrepreneurs

Capital is provided by entrepreneurs. Following the set-up of BGG, we assume that the economy is populated by entrepreneurs who purchase capital in order to invest in uncertain individual-specific projects. Each project then produces "finished" capital which is rented to firms in the traded goods sector. The project returns are private information to the individual entrepreneur. Financing for the project is provided by foreign lenders, but subject to the credit market imperfections discussed in BGG. In particular, because project returns can be monitored by creditors only at a cost, as in Townsend (1979), external finance is more costly to entrepreneurs than internal finance. The external finance premium; the excess of the return on capital for entrepreneurs over the external cost of capital, is negatively related to the internal funds, or net worth, of entrepreneurs.

Assume that the aggregate capital stock evolves according to

(A12) $\quad K_{t+1} = \phi(\dfrac{I_t}{K_t})K_t + (1-\delta)K_t$

where the function ϕ satisfies $\phi' > 0$, and $\phi'' < 0$. Competitive capital producing firms will then ensure that the price of capital sold to entrepreneurs is

(A13) $\quad Q_t = \phi'(\dfrac{I_t}{K_t})$.

Entrepreneurs must borrow in foreign currency. We set this as a constraint on the types of borrowing contracts rather than deriving it endogenously. An entrepreneur who wishes to invest K_t units of capital must pay nominal price $P_t K_{t+1} Q_t$. The entrepreneur begins with nominal net worth given by N_{t+1}. Then he or she must borrow in foreign currency an amount given by

(A14) $\quad D_{t+1}^e = \dfrac{1}{S_t}(P_t K_{t+1} Q_t - N_{t+1})$

The contract structure closely follows BGG. We abstract from the details of the contract, and note merely that the contract will imply that the "internal finance premium"; the excess of the return on capital, R_{Kt+1}, over the real cost of borrowed funds, $R_{t+1}^* = (1+i_{t+1}^*)\dfrac{S_{t+1}}{S_t}\dfrac{P_t}{P_{t+1}}$, will be a negative function of the entrepreneurs net worth, relative to the value of capital. This is given by equation (2) of the text. Following the assumptions of BGG, entrepreneurs are assumed to exit the economy randomly with probability $(1-\zeta)$ every period. Aggregate net worth for all entrepreneurs then evolves as equation (3) of the text.

(A15) $N_{t+1} = \sigma(P_t R_{Kt} Q_{t-1} K_t - (1+i_t^*)S_t D_t^e ...)$

The return on capital for entrepreneurs depends on both the price of capital and the rental rate offered by traded goods firms. Thus

(A16) $R_{Kt+1} = \dfrac{R_{t+1} + (1-\delta)Q_{t+1}}{Q_t}$

Price Setting

Firms in the non-traded sector set prices in advance. Following the method of Calvo (1983), assume that firms face a probability $(1-\kappa)$ in every period of altering their price, independent of how long their price has been fixed. Following standard aggregation results, the non-traded goods price follows the partial adjustment rule

(A17) $P_{Nt}^{1-\lambda} = (1-\kappa)\widetilde{P}_{Nt}^{1-\lambda} + \kappa P_{Nt-1}^{1-\lambda}$

where $\widetilde{P}_{Nt}$ represents the newly set price for a firm that adjusts its price at time t. The evolution of $\widetilde{P}_{Nt}$ is then governed by

(A18) $\widetilde{P}_{Nt} = (1-\beta\kappa)MC_t + \beta\kappa\widetilde{P}_{Nt+1}$.

Exchange Rates in Emerging Markets

References

Agenor, P.R. and P. Montiel (1998), *Development Macroeconomics* (Princeton, NJ: Princeton University Press).

Aghion, P., P. Bachetta and A. Banerjee (2000), "Currency Crises and Monetary Policy in an Economy with Credit Constraints", unpublished paper.

Backus, D., F.E. Kydland and P.J. Kehoe (1992), "International Real Business Cycles", *Journal of Political Economy*.

Bernanke, B., M. Gertler and S. Gilchrist (1999), "The Financial Accelerator in a Quantitative Business Cycle Model", in J. Taylor and M. Woodford (eds.), *Handbook of Macroeconomics*, Vol. 1c (Amsterdam: North Holland).

Calvo, G. (1983), "Staggered Prices in a Utility Maximizing Framework", *Journal of Monetary Economics* 12, 383-398.

_____ (1999a), "On Dollarization", unpublished paper (College Park, MD: University of Maryland).

_____ (1999b), "Fixed versus Flexible Exchange Rates", unpublished paper (College Park, MD: University of Maryland).

Calvo, G. and C. Reinhardt (2000), "Fear of Floating", unpublished paper.

Caramazza, F. and J. Aziz, (1998), "Fixed Versus Flexible: Getting the Exchange Rate Right in the 1990's", *IMF Economic Issues*, No. 13.

Cook, D. (1999), "Monetary Policy in Emerging Markets", Hong Kong University of Science and Technology.

Devereux, M. and D. Cook (2000), "The Macroeconomics of Capital Market Panics", unpublished paper (Vancouver, BC: University of British Columbia).

Devereux, M. and P. Lane (2000), "Exchange Rates and Monetary Policy in Emerging Markets", unpublished paper (Vancouver, BC: University of British Columbia).

Eichengreen, B. and R. Hausmann (1999), "Exchange Rates and Financial Fragility", NBER Working Paper No. 7418 (Cambridge, MA: National Bureau of Economic Research).

Honohan, P. and P.R. Lane (1999), "Pegging to the Dollar and the Euro", *International Finance* 2(3) (November).

King, R.G. and A. Wolman (1999), "What Should the Monetary Authority Do when Prices are Sticky?", in J.B. Taylor (ed.), *Monetary Policy Rules* (Chicago, IL: University of Chicago Press).

Krugman, P. (1999), "Balance Sheets, the Transfer Problem and Financial Crises", *International Tax and Public Finance* 6(4), 459-472.

Mishkin, F. and M.A. Savastano (2000), "Monetary Policy Strategies for Latin American", NBER Working Paper No. 7617 (Cambridge, MA: National Bureau of Economic Research).

Sachs, J. (1998), "The Causes of the Asian Crisis", unpublished paper.

Svensson, L. (1999), "Inflation Targeting as a Monetary Policy Rule", *Journal of Monetary Economics* 43(3), 607-654.

Taylor, J.B. (1993), "Discretion Versus Policy Rules in Practice", Carnegie Rochester Conference Series on Public Policy.

Townsend, R.M. (1979), "Optimal Contracts and Competitive Markets with Costly State Verification", *Journal of Economic Theory* 2, 265-293.

Yun, T. (1996), "Nominal Price Rigidity, Money Supply Endogeneity, and Business Cycles", *Journal of Monetary Economics* 37, 345-370.

Money, Markets and Mobility

Part IV:

The Macro Mix

Reflections on the Mundell-Fleming Model on its Fortieth Anniversary

Russell S. Boyer

Introduction

The Royal Swedish Academy of Sciences awarded the 1999 Prize in Economic Sciences to Robert A. Mundell in part for his formulation of the Mundell-Fleming model. The Academy identifies "Capital Mobility and Stabilization Policy under Fixed and Flexible Exchange Rates", published in the *Canadian Journal of Economics and Political Science* in 1963 as the key contribution to the Mundell-Fleming model. In the course of the Queen's Conference underpinning this volume, Mundell pointed out that the approach employed in his 1963 paper is similar to that in an earlier paper in *The Quarterly Journal of Economics* (1960). Therefore, he argues, this 1960 paper should be viewed as the pioneering work in the development of the Mundell-Fleming model. If we use that dating, precisely forty years have elapsed between the time of publication and this conference to honour Mundell's work.

As part of celebrating Mundell's contributions, and in particular his creative analytical approach to the "macro-mix" issue under alternative exchange-rate regimes, the ensuing analysis begins with a general framework that encompasses the early Mundell work as well as that by Marcus Fleming (1962). Among the numerous ways in which the Mundell-Fleming model evolves, I shall focus on the two key modifications introduced by Mundell in

119

his 1963 paper. The first of these is a redefinition of what constitutes a given stance of monetary policy. Mundell and Fleming had emphasized in their earlier work the distinction between a central bank's domestic assets (or domestic credit) and its foreign assets (or international reserves) with the sum of the two being equal to the value of the money supply. By defining a given stance as being a given amount of domestic credit, Mundell was able to frame a simple way of presenting the fixed and flexible rate results for both fiscal and monetary policy in both the short and long runs. As a device for expounding the effects of macroeconomic policies, the Mundell model diagram is still unsurpassed at the undergraduate textbook level.

The second assumption in Mundell (1963) is perfect capital mobility. In tandem, these assumptions allow Mundell to avoid the pitfalls into which one stumbles when conducting a more general analysis.[1] Therefore, Mundell (1963) can be seen as a bridge between earlier models that have a flow specification of the capital account and the later models which adopted the portfolio balance approach and which quickly won the day. Despite the paper's similarity to earlier models which are written explicitly in the flow specification, many economists have interpreted this 1963 paper as being the first presentation of a portfolio balance model.[2] In contrast Fleming, instead of getting credit for jointly developing the general case (of which Mundell (1963) is a particular, although highly relevant and inciteful application), is now dismissed as epitomizing the high-water mark of an antiquated approach.

By publishing such a neat and accessible framework, Mundell was then able to dominate research for many years thereafter, with even distantly-related models identifying themselves as "modified" Mundell-Fleming structures.[3] Thus, Mundell's papers provide a graphic example of the fact that the way in which an argument is phrased and framed can be a key

---

[1]McCallum (1996) sees the Mundell-Fleming model as flawed because of its specification of the capital account. Nonetheless he finds Mundell (1963) to be immune from this criticism.

[2]Dornbusch (1975) cites the results of Mundell (1968) (which embodies the 1963 model) as though they fall naturally into the portfolio balance mold.

[3]See, for example, Marston (1985) in Jones and Kenen (1985). Most readers would probably agree that this model is sufficiently internally motivated that its links to the Mundell-Fleming model are barely discernible.

determinant of the amount of attention that it will receive. As Mundell says about his work "Hard writing makes easy reading." Without doubt the 1963 paper is a classic example of this dictum.

The Model

The starting point of the model is a small, open economy which has unencumbered trade with the rest of the world. This economy takes as given the foreign-currency price of its imports and the rate of return on assets issued in the rest of the world. But the economy produces its own unique good which is an imperfect substitute for imports, and it has a domestic bond whose rate of return can differ from that on foreign bonds, at least in the short run, and perhaps for longer if there is less than perfect substitution in portfolios between the two different kinds of bonds. Conditions of production are such that there are unemployed factors which can be hired at given money wages. With constant returns to scale in production, these conditions guarantee fixity of domestic-currency prices in the economy.

This is the setting which Fleming (1962) and Mundell (1960, 1961a, 1961b, 1963) employ and so it would be surprising if their analyses came to markedly different conclusions. Mundell notes about his own contributions in this area that they are all based on essentially the same model. Much the same statement could be made about how it compares with Fleming's paper. What differs between the earlier papers and the ones published in 1962 and 1963 is that the argument is now phrased in terms of comparative statics rather than dynamics. Dynamics had been at the heart of Mundell (1960), and there is general agreement that its argument is "formidable".[4] In contrast Fleming (1962) and Mundell (1963) can be understood very simply in terms of matrix algebra.

Both authors note that the condition for equilibrium in the economy is that three markets must clear: for goods, for money, and for foreign exchange. The diagrammatic framework introduced in Mundell (1961a) is reproduced below as Figure 1 in order to start off our discussion. Interestingly

---

[4]This is the term which Dornbusch (2000) uses to characterize the model in Mundell (1960).

Reflections on the Mundell-Fleming Model   *121*

Figure 1

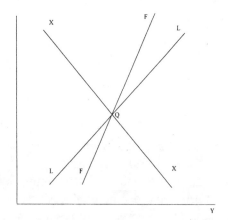

it is the low capital mobility case that is portrayed throughout that paper. This certainly is a contrast with the perfect capital mobility approach which is the only case considered in Mundell (1963).

The goods market equilibrium locus, denoted by XX, is negatively sloped in output, Y, and interest rate, r, space for the conventional reasons. An increase in income creates an excess supply of output which requires a fall in interest rates to restore goods to equilibrium. XX is drawn for a given value of the exchange rate, which is defined as the domestic-currency price of a unit of foreign exchange. If the exchange rate increases (a depreciation of the domestic currency in terms of foreign currency) this creates an excess demand for goods which, for any interest rate, requires an increase in Y to re-equilibriate the goods market. Thus, XX is shifted to the right.

The money-market equilibrium curve, LL, is upward sloping in r-Y space: for a given money supply, an increase in interest rates requires an increase in income to maintain equilibrium. An increase in the supply of money will shift LL to the right. Finally, the foreign exchange market is in equilibrium when the balance of payments is equal to zero. The locus of points for which this is true is identified by the positively sloped locus denoted by FF. The balance of payments is made up of two parts: the current account and the capital account. The current account is assumed to be negatively related to output: as output increases, so does the demand for imports, while exports, dependent on magnitudes in the rest of the world, are unchanged. The capital account is assumed to be a positive function of the level of interest rates, so the locus of points for which the balance of payments is equal to zero must be positively sloped.

The external balance curve FF shifts to the right as a result of an increase in the exchange rate (a depreciation), because the resulting current account surplus requires, for external balance, either an increase in Y or a fall in r. It can be shown that a rise in the value of the exchange rate causes the rightward shift in FF to be *greater* than the rightward shift in XX. The reason is that a depreciation causes an increase in exports and a reduction in imports, so that the trade account improves. In the case of FF, output needs to rise sufficiently so that imports increase enough to offset this improvement in the trade account, thereby restoring it to its former value. This occurs via the mechanism of the marginal propensity to import. In contrast, to restore internal balance (XX), output needs to rise only to the extent that through both the marginal propensity to import and the marginal propensity to save the exchange-rate-induced improvement in the trade account is offset. Since imports and saving work in tandem, the increase in output needed for this to happen is less than it is when imports alone do the job.

Before proceeding it should be noted that we have used the Hicksian notion of a given monetary policy. That is, we have defined a given monetary policy as one in which the quantity of money is held constant. An alternative definition that is commonly used is that a given monetary policy sets the interest rate at a particular level. Mundell alternated between these two definitions in his writings, before settling on the still-different and ingenious definition that he used in his work in (1963).

When a given monetary policy is defined as a given stock of money, both LL and FF are positively sloped, and the question arises as to which is steeper. The relative slopes are not given by theory. Instead, they depend upon the degree of capital mobility, a parameter whose value must be measured empirically. In the low capital mobility case, an increase in output, causing a worsening of the current account, must be matched by a very large increase in interest rates in order to generate an equivalent improvement in the capital account, since capital responds very little to the interest-rate change. In contrast, in the high capital mobility case the interest rate needs to be raised by only a small amount as output increases. As capital mobility becomes perfect the FF curve becomes horizontal, and, therefore, not as steep as the LL curve. At a sufficiently low level of capital mobility, the FF curve will be steeper than the LL curve.

Reflections on the Mundell-Fleming Model

For equilibrium in all these markets it is necessary that all three loci intersect at a single point. This is accomplished by movement in either the stock of money or the value of the exchange rate or both. The way that this occurs, as shown in Mundell (1961b), is that the "short-run" equilibrium occurs at XX and LL. If there is a balance of payments deficit at that point (as portrayed by this point being below and to the right of the FF locus), then the money supply is falling under fixed exchange rates, or the exchange rate must move to a higher value under flexible exchange rates.

The usual distinction is between the "short-run" equilibrium and the situation that prevails in the steady state. This difference is also identified as that between the sterilization equilibrium and the non-sterilization equilibrium. The argument is that if the central bank conducts an active policy, namely one of offsetting the monetary effects of the balance of payments position, then the short-run equilibrium can be sustained indefinitely for a surplus country, or until reserves run out for a deficit country. Thus, the sterilization equilibrium can persist for a considerable length of time. If the central bank lets the automatic adjustment take its course, then a surplus country will find that its international reserves are increasing over time and the money supply is expanding in step. Conversely a deficit country is losing reserves and its money supply is contracting. In both cases, the economy will move in a monotonic fashion from its short-run position to a long-run one where the balance of payments is equal to zero. This is pictured as the LL locus moving slowly over time from its short-run position so as to eventually slot through the intersection between XX and FF (which remain stationary during this process). In this situation the three markets are once again clearing and the economy can stay in that position indefinitely.

Figure 1 is drawn with values of the money supply and the exchange rate that cause the three curves to slot through a single point, Q, and therefore is a situation of equilibrium that can persist indefinitely. We will use Q to denote the initial (preshock) equilibrium in all the figures that follow. Also, loci that shift as a result of a policy initiative are indicated by primes (') attached to the letters that identify the curves.

We now have the tools to carry out an analysis of macroeconomic policy initiatives in a small, open economy.

The Money Stock and Monetary Policy

The model as set out above enables us to analyze the consequences of monetary and fiscal policy when a constant monetary policy is defined as maintaining a given stock of money in the short run. This is traditionally the way a given monetary policy is defined in closed-economy Hicksian analysis, and applying it to an open-economy setting is certainly an appropriate first step.

From a position of equilibrium, consider the consequences of an increase in the money stock. We know that this policy initiative shifts the LL locus to the right, reflecting the fact that the higher quantity of money is willingly held at either a lower rate of interest or a higher level of output. As shown in Figure 2 (which is drawn with a low level of capital mobility so that the FF is steeper than LL, and where Q denotes the equilibrium that existed before the policy initiative), the new short-run equilibrium under fixed exchange rates is at point S. This is the intersection point between the XX locus and the line L'L', which is the new (post-shock) position of the LL locus.

At this equilibrium, interest rates are indeed lower and output is higher, and the proportions of their movements will depend on the orientation of the XX locus. At this point there is a balance of payments deficit no matter the relative slopes of FF and LL. The reason is that higher output worsens the

Figure 2

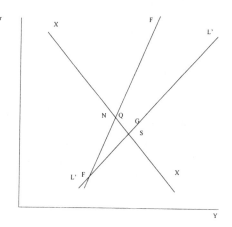

Reflections on the Mundell-Fleming Model   *125*

current account, and lower interest rates worsen the capital account. This shows that considerations of capital mobility do not determine the effects which an expansionary monetary policy has on the balance of payments: unambiguously it goes into deficit.

In the case of fixed exchange rates this short-run equilibrium will not persist so long as the central bank does not engage in any further independent actions. In this non-sterilization world, the loss of international reserves arising from the balance of payments deficit causes the money supply to shrink back toward the level that it obtained before the initiative. In such a case the economy will be automatically returned to its initial equilibrium. This eventual outcome has often been described as indicating that monetary policy is "completely ineffective" under fixed exchange rates. At this juncture, it is worth noting a conclusion from Swoboda (1972), namely that this result does not depend on the degree of capital mobility. As portrayed here, monetary policy ineffectiveness occurs even if the degree of capital mobility is zero, so long as the central bank does not sterilize international reserve flows.

Implicit in this discussion is an important distinction which makes this analysis logically consistent, specifically the distinction between domestic credit and international reserves. Mundell assumes that the increase in the money supply is carried out by buying domestic bonds from the private sector. But when stabilizing the exchange rate, intervention is undertaken in the foreign exchange market. That is, in response to a payments imbalance transactions are carried out in foreign exchange and money. Thus the equilibrium at point Q is reattained even though the proportion of the money supply which is backed by international reserves may be changed considerably.

This distinction provides logical consistency because it argues that there are two independent tools at the central bank's disposal: intervention in the domestic bond (and money) market; and intervention in the foreign exchange (and money) market. Note that a policy-induced increase (decrease) in the quantity of money really means an open market purchase (sale), that is, an increase (decrease) in domestic credit/assets.

In contrast to the adjustment that occurs when balance-of-payments processes have their automatic monetary effects, the central bank may seek to perpetuate (sterilize) the short-run equilibrium by conducting further policy initiatives so as to maintain the higher level of the money supply. That is, it may seek to keep the economy at point S. It would do this by conducting further open market purchases which increase the central bank's holdings of domestic securities (and augment the money supply) and these actions just offset the diminution of the quantity of money due to the loss of international reserves. This is a possibility so long as the government has a sufficient quantity of international reserves. But so long as the economy is at point S, reserves are flowing out, which implies that the situation is unsustainable. On this, Fleming and Mundell clearly agree.

Finally, if the central bank is following a floating exchange-rate regime it is, by definition, not intervening in the foreign exchange market. Instead, the balance of payments deficit causes a depreciation of domestic currency (and the exchange rate rises). We have noted that this has effects on both the XX and FF loci, because both are dependent on exports and imports which are affected by the value of the exchange rate. If we assume that capital market conditions are independent of the actual movement of the exchange rate, then the depreciation of domestic currency moves the FF locus to the right by a greater amount than it does the XX locus, as we noted above. This can be shown in Figure 2 as a movement in their intersection in a southeasterly direction, establishing a full equilibrium represented by a triple intersection of these curves (not shown) at a point such as G.

In contrast with the ineffectiveness results that we found for monetary policy in a non-sterilization regime, the flexible exchange-rate regime has lower interest rates and higher output. Indeed, monetary policy is even more effective than it is in the sterilization situation with fixed exchange rates. Although interest rates are higher for flexible, their effects are more than offset by the favourable movement of the value of the exchange rate. A further contrast between these equilibria is that a flexible exchange-rate regime moves us to a point in which the balance of payments is zero. In contrast, the sterilization equilibrium continues to lose foreign exchange reserves for the economy. It is worth repeating that if we compare long-run equilibria, then monetary policy under fixed exchange rates is ineffective, and this is true no matter what the degree of capital mobility.

The Money Stock and Fiscal Policy

When a constant monetary policy is defined in the short run as a given money stock, it turns out that a fiscal policy shock has ambiguous effects on the balance of payments. As a consequence, the differing outcomes under fixed and flexible exchange-rate regimes are of indeterminate sign, as the following analysis shows.

An increase in government expenditures (defined as a bond-financed increase in government spending, leaving the quantity of domestic credit unchanged) causes the XX locus to shift to the right. The reason is that the exogenous increase in demand causes output to increase at a given level of interest rates. The new equilibrium in the case of sterilization is at point S in Figure 3. This is the short-run equilibrium which holds during a period of time before the consequences of the payments imbalance affect the money supply. Clearly both domestic output and interest rates rise as a result of this policy.

In the case of low capital mobility shown in Figure 3, the effect of higher output in worsening the trade account outweighs the effect of higher interest rates for improving the capital account. As a result, the balance of payments goes into deficit. This means that the money supply will be drifting downward over time, and the long-run equilibrium will be at a point such as N where the level of income, although higher than originally, is not so high as in the short run. And the level of interest rates continues to rise during the adjustment process so that they are higher than in the short run and *a fortiori* higher than originally.

Figure 3

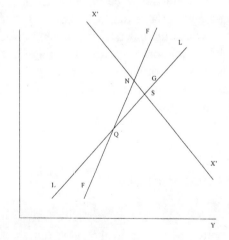

The same diagram shows that, in this low capital mobility case, fiscal policy is more effective under flexible exchange rates than under fixed rates. The reason is that now the incipient deficit in the balance of payments causes the exchange rate to rise, i.e. the domestic currency to depreciate. This rise shifts both the XX and the FF loci to the right, with their intersection moving in a southeasterly direction. The new equilibrium is at point G in Figure 3. At that point output is higher than its comparable, fixed exchange-rate value at either S (short run) or N (long run). In contrast, the interest rate attains its equilibrium at a position somewhere in between these two points. It is higher than the value it has at the short-run fixed exchange-rate situation, but lower than at the long-run, fixed exchange-rate equilibrium.

Figure 4 replays the analysis when capital mobility is high, when LL is steeper than FF. In this case expansionary fiscal policy causes a surplus in the balance of payments. The reason is that the short-run equilibrium, being the same as before in terms of its effects on interest rates and output, now generates a balance of payments surplus. The higher interest rates now generate a capital account surplus which is greater than the current account deficit due to the higher level of output. With this different sign for the balance of payments, the relation between the short-run and the long-run equilibria is reversed. Also reversed is the relation between the fixed exchange rate equilibria and the equilibrium which holds for flexible exchange rates. The reason is that now an increase in the money supply will

Figure 4

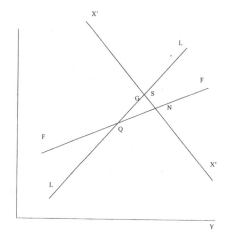

Reflections on the Mundell-Fleming Model

occur as a result of a balance-of-payments surplus under fixed exchange rates. In contrast, the incipient surplus under flexible rates causes the domestic currency to strengthen, driving the XX and FF loci back to the left to a final equilibrium which is north and west of the long-run, fixed exchange-rate equilibrium.

Noting the positions of the points in Figure 4, we see that output is highest in the case of the fixed exchange-rate, non-sterilization (long-run) equilibrium, next highest in the short-run (sterilization) equilibrium, and lowest (but still greater than originally) in the flexible exchange-rate case. Interest rates are higher as a result of this fiscal policy with the ascending order being: fixed exchange rate without sterilization, then flexible exchange rate, and finally fixed exchange rate with sterilization.

Perhaps the simplest statement of these results is that fiscal policy generates higher interest rates and output, with the relative magnitudes under different exchange-rate regimes depending importantly on the degree of capital mobility. The key consideration is the relative slope of the LL locus and the FF locus.

Macroeconomic Policy and the Interest Rate

This ambiguity about the effects of fiscal policy under different exchange-rate regimes can be eliminated by using an alternative definition of a given stance of monetary policy. Specifically, if such a policy is defined in terms of interest rates, then the ambiguity is resolved. The reason is that in defining a given monetary policy as an unchanging rate of interest, the effective LL locus becomes a horizontal line. This guarantees that the FF line is the steeper locus and implies that an expansionary fiscal policy worsens the balance of payments. This is one of the reasons that Mundell (1960, 1961a) uses this definition.

Figure 5 captures the effects of a fiscal expansion when a given monetary policy is defined in this manner. The short-run equilibrium at S is in the area south and east of the FF locus, consistent with the deficit that arises in the external accounts. This forces a depreciation of the domestic currency which, shifting X'X' and FF so as to move their intersection in a southeasterly direction, generates the flexible exchange-rate equilibrium shown as point G.

130   *Russell S. Boyer*

Figure 5

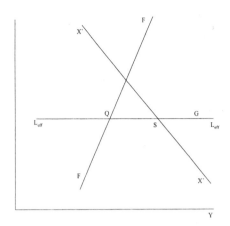

In contrast, there is no attempt to deal with the effects on the quantity of money of the balance-of-payments deficit in the case of fixed exchange rates. Point S is the short-run equilibrium which will persist so long as the authorities sterilize the balance of payments. Since the balance of payments is not driven to zero, this is much like comparing a full equilibrium situation with a disequilibrium one. But to allow the money supply to fall, as would be necessary to eliminate the deficit, interest rates would have to rise. This, of course, is logically inconsistent with the way in which we have defined a constant monetary policy.

Turning to monetary policy, this definition of a given stance of policy has an obvious interpretation: an expansionary policy is one that drives the rate of interest down to a lower level at which it is then held constant. Figure 6 shows the effects of such a policy, where the only noteworthy result is that output is higher under fixed exchange rates (with sterilization) shown by point S. And output is higher still under a flexible exchange regime as is shown by position G. Since an expansionary monetary policy, no matter how defined, causes a balance-of-payments deficit, there is no ambiguity to be resolved.

Again we should note that once we consider the consequences of a payments imbalance on the money supply, then the constant interest rate case is not a full equilibrium. The reason is that a long-run, steady-state situation requires that the balance of payments be equal to zero. But that in turn

Reflections on the Mundell-Fleming Model   *131*

Figure 6

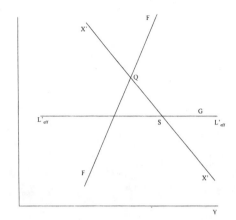

requires that the money supply must be permitted to adjust in order to bring that about. There is no possibility of such an equilibrium if interest rates and exchange rates are both held constant.

Open Market Operations and Perfect Capital Mobility

The analysis thus far indicates that with less than full capital mobility and with monetary policy defined in terms of a given stock of money, fiscal policy has an ambiguous effect on the balance of payments. We then demonstrated that this ambiguity can be resolved if a given stance of monetary policy is defined in terms of maintaining a given level of interest rates. But this leads to the unsatisfactory situation where the equilibrium under analysis is not a long-run one (except by coincidence).

Mundell (1963) developed an ingenious way of dealing with both these difficulties. He defines a given stance of monetary policy as one which maintains the level of domestic credit at a particular value. Consistent with this, he points out that an open market purchase is an expansionary monetary policy action in that it increases the amount of domestic credit.[5] Furthermore, foreign exchange market operations, used to manage the exchange rate, can further alter the size of the money supply in the new equilibrium. But this does not alter the stance of monetary policy, because no change in the amount of domestic credit is taking place. And for capital mobility, the assumption is that it is perfect, thus guaranteeing that an expansionary fiscal policy causes an improvement of the balance of payments. With these changes we are able to proceed very quickly.

For the impact of expansionary fiscal policy the analysis is shown in Figure 7. The noteworthy difference in this figure is that FF is now horizontal. This reflects the fact that only a miniscule increase in interest rates is needed to improve the capital account sufficiently to offset any deficit in the trade account as higher output draws in more imports.

The short-run (sterilization) equilibrium is not included in this diagram on the grounds that with perfect capital mobility such a position is tenable

---

[5]Because this is such an important turning point in the analysis of macreconomic policy, it is instructive to let Mundell speak for himself in terms of the alteration of the definition of monetary policy:

> It may puzzle the reader why I went to some length to alter the definitions of monetary policy and fiscal policy and thus to bring about a seemingly artificial difference between the conclusions based purely upon different definitions. The reason is that monetary policy cannot in any meaningful sense be defined as an alteration in the interest rate when capital is perfectly mobile, because the authorities cannot change the market rate of interest. Nor can monetary policy be defined, under conditions of perfect capital mobility, as an increase in the money supply, since the central bank has no power over the money supply either (except in transitory positions of disequilibrium) when the exchange rate is fixed. The central bank has, on the other hand, the ability to conduct an open market operation (which only temporarily changes the money supply) and that is the basis of my choice of this definition of monetary policy for the present analysis. (1968, p. 258)

In the notation generally employed, the specification of the money market moves from M=L(Y,r) to D+R=L(Y,r), where D and R are domestic and foreign assets, respectively, of the central bank. Earlier in the above footnote (not reproduced) Mundell defines fiscal policy as an increase in government expenditures with no change in domestic credit. (Note that the money supply may increase depending on the operations in the foreign exchange market.)

Reflections on the Mundell-Fleming Model   *133*

Figure 7

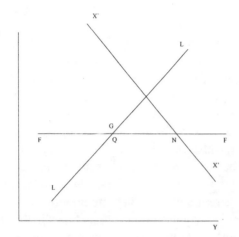

for an infinitesimal length of time. Instead for fixed exchange rates we focus on the non-sterilization equilibrium at point N. For flexible rates the long-run equilibrium position is denoted by G.

In assuming that capital mobility is perfect, Mundell was able not only to eliminate the ambiguity about the effects on the exchange rate, but he was also able to seamlessly incorporate a result that Fleming (1962) had published the year before (with little fanfare), namely that if asset markets do not depend upon the value of the exchange rate, then fiscal policy is completely ineffective under a flexible exchange-rate regime. To see this, note that under perfect capital mobility the incipient increase in interest rates following from expansionary fiscal policy immediately triggers a fall in the exchange rate (an appreciation of domestic currency) such that the trade account worsens by exactly the amount of the expenditure increase. In other words, output is invariant because the increase in the current account deficit matches the increase in the government deficit. Therefore, fiscal policy is ineffective under flexible exchange rates, represented by point G in Figure 7 which is coincident with the initial equilibrium denoted by Q. In other words, the XX curve remains unchanged and, hence, still intersects the LL and FF curves at G (or, equivalently, at Q).

This result can be demonstrated quite easily using only the asset market condition which is included in footnote 5 (D+R=L(Y,r)). The definition of an expansionary fiscal policy is an increase in government expenditure that does not change the value of D. Flexible exchange rates imply that no intervention is undertaken in the foreign exchange market so that R remains unchanged. And perfect capital mobility leaves r invariant. Therefore, Y has to remain unchanged, thus demonstrating the ineffectiveness of fiscal policy under flexible exchange rates and perfect capital mobility.

In a fixed-rate, perfect-capital-mobility environment, expansionary fiscal policy shifts the XX curve upward and to the right (Figure 7). The resulting tendency for interest rates to increase leads to an increase in the money supply (via a capital inflow and an increase in foreign assets of the central bank). In Figure 7, the long-run equilibrium is at N, since the LL curve will shift rightward to intersect XX and FF at this point.

In contrast, monetary policy in a perfect capital mobility environment is wholly ineffective under fixed rates and all-powerful under floating rates. See Figure 8. Under fixed exchange rates, an open market purchase of securities (increase in domestic credit of the central bank) which threatens to increase the money supply leads to an incipient decrease in interest rates which immediately triggers a capital account deficit and a decrease in central bank foreign assets that exactly offsets the increase in domestic assets. The original LL curve in Figure 8 intersected the XX and FF curves at Q. The attempt to increase the money supply via open market operations keeps the LL curve unchanged, with the long term equilibrium at N, coincident with the

Figure 8

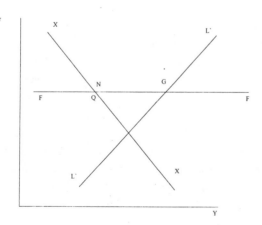

Reflections on the Mundell-Fleming Model

initial equilibrium Q. As noted earlier, in long-run equilibrium, monetary policy is ineffective under flexible exchange rates, irrespective of the degree of capital mobility.

Under flexible exchange rates, an increase in domestic assets (an open market purchase of securities by the central bank), leads to an expansion of the money supply (L'L') and an incipient decrease in interest rates which triggers an immediate currency depreciation. The depreciation increases the current account surplus sufficient to move XX in Figure 8 in a north-east direction so it intersects L'L' and FF at G, well to the right of the original equilibrium Q.

This figure presents us with familiar conclusions. We noted previously that the ineffectiveness result for monetary policy under fixed exchange rates is independent of the degree of capital mobility. This ineffectiveness result is shown in the figure by point N being at the same position as the initial equilibrium, identified by Q. Therefore cranking up the value of this parameter does not alter any of our previous conclusions. In contrast, monetary policy is effective under flexible exchange rates, and high capital mobility forces a greater degree of depreciation, therefore guaranteeing a bigger impact under that exchange-rate regime. This is shown by point G being well to the right of the original equilibrium at Q.

Conclusion

While this discussion has covered various shocks and both exchange-rate regimes, we should not let this taxonomic review distract us from the novelty of what Mundell did in the (1963) paper. By defining discretionary monetary policy in terms of open market operations, he introduced a comparative static mechanism that seamlessly lends itself to investigating two policy initiatives under two exchange-rate regimes in both the short and the long run. In doing this, he was able to draw together and compare conclusions about stabilization policy which had never been done before. It was this unifying vision which caused this paper to supercede both Fleming (1962) and his own previous work.

And by conceptualizing capital mobility as complete or "perfect", Mundell was able to starkly juxtapose the effectiveness/ineffectiveness results for monetary and fiscal policy under fixed and flexible rates — fiscal

136   *Russell S. Boyer*

policy is ineffective under flexible rates and all-powerful under fixed exchange rates whereas monetary policy is impotent under fixed exchange rates while all-powerful under floating rates.

The Royal Swedish Academy of Sciences press release announcing Robert Mundell's Nobel prize noted that "Mundell chose his [research] problems with uncommon — almost prophetic — accuracy in terms of predicting the future developments of international monetary arrangements and capital markets." Nowhere is Mundell's foresight more evident than in his assumption of perfect capital mobility. When introduced in 1963, perfect capital mobility was more in the nature of a creative and insightful analytical device that led to stark and powerful policy implications. On this, the fortieth anniversary of Mundell's seminal paper, perfect capital mobility is more and more an emerging reality, in the process highlighting the prescience of Mundell's analysis.

The impact of Robert Mundell's macro-mix insights on analysis and policy alike have been enormous, sufficient on their own to merit his Nobel Prize in Economic Sciences.

References

Dornbusch, R. (1975), "A Portfolio Balance Model of the Open Economy", *Journal of Monetary Economics* 1(1), 3-20.

_____ (2000), "Robert A. Mundell's Nobel Memorial Prize", *Scandinavian Journal of Economics* 102(2), 199-210.

Fleming, J.M. (1962), "Domestic Financial Policies under Fixed and under Floating Exchange Rates", *International Monetary Fund Staff Papers*, 9 (November), 369-379.

Jones, R.W. and P.B. Kenen, eds. (1985), *Handbook of International Economics, Volume 2* (Amsterdam: North-Holland).

Marston, R.C. (1985), "Stabilization Policies in Open Economies", in Jones and Kenen (eds.), *Handbook of International Economics*, 59-91.

McCallum, B.T. (1996), *International Monetary Economics* (Oxford: Oxford University Press).

Mundell, R.A. (1960), "The Monetary Dynamics of International Adjustment under Fixed and Flexible Exchange Rates", *The Quarterly Journal of Economics* 74, 227-257. Reprinted in an adapted form in Mundell (1968), Chapter 11.

_____ (1961a), "The International Disequilibrium System", *Kyklos* 14, 154-172. Reprinted in an adapted form in Mundell (1968), Chapter 15.

_____ (1961b), "Flexible Exchange Rates and Employment Policy", *Canadian Journal of Economics and Political Science* 27, 509-517. Reprinted in an adapted form in Mundell (1968), Chapter 17.

_____ (1963), "Capital Mobility and Stabilization Policy under Fixed and Flexible Exchange Rates", *Canadian Journal of Economics and Political Science* 29, 475-485. Reprinted in an adapted form in Mundell (1968), Chapter 18.

_____ (1968), *International Economics* (New York: The Macmillan Company).

Swoboda, A. (1972), "Equilibrium, Quasi-equilibrium, and Macroeconomic Policy under Fixed Exchange Rates", *Quarterly Journal of Economics* 86, 162-171.

Problems of Monetary and Exchange-Rate Management in Canada

Pierre Fortin

Under this title, Mundell wrote his first major paper on Canadian macroeconomic policy in the September 1964 issue of the *National Bank Review* (Mundell, 1964b). He provided a broad interpretation of economic developments in Canada between 1946 and 1964, based on the ideas of his famous articles concerning the relative effectiveness of monetary and fiscal policy under fixed and flexible exchange rates (Mundell, 1960, 1963, 1964a).

The *National Bank Review* Article

The NBR article is a model of clear, simple and effective writing in policy analysis. In it Mundell displayed his very detailed knowledge of events, brought deep theoretical insights to bear on the issues, and was careful to derive practical policy prescriptions. Nearly forty years later, it does not look one bit outdated.

I am grateful to Serge Coulombe for helpful suggestions.

139

Mundell stressed the point that "when the exchange rate is flexible, *two* large classes of expenditures are affected [by monetary policy]: the same class of durable goods as under fixed exchange rates; and the additional class of all foreign goods" (1964b, p. 84). This simple observation preceded by 25 years the rise in popularity of the *monetary conditions index* (MCI). This index is a linear combination of the real short-term interest rate and the real effective exchange rate now in common usage among central bankers to provide information about the stance of monetary policy in open economies.

Mundell also gave a clear verdict on the 1961 controversy between Bank of Canada Governor James Coyne and Finance Minister Donald Fleming (see Gordon, 1961 for background). His theoretical ideas about stabilization policy naturally led him to view monetary and fiscal policy as, respectively, very powerful and very weak stabilization tools under the flexible exchange-rate regime in force from 1950 to 1962. This immediately had him conclude that "tight money had done considerable damage to employment since 1959, but it was a mistaken belief that an increased budget deficit would be a useful corrective ...The key question was the monetary policy followed" (ibid., p. 85). In light of the new theory of stabilization policy put forward by Mundell, both the governor and the minister had been in error.

Mundell worried about the propagation to Canada of the U.S. business cycle despite the insulating potentialities of a flexible exchange-rate system. In his view, the reason theory did not match reality was the improper use of monetary policy independence. "It is obvious [he said], that a different monetary policy would have to be followed. Instead of allowing the exchange rate to appreciate at the onset of a recession abroad [as they had done], the authorities must force it to depreciate" (ibid., p. 84).

Finally, Mundell warned that the favourable prospects for the Canadian balance of payments from 1964 on could lead to a massive inflow of autonomous and speculative capital that would eventually force a revaluation of the currency above the fixed parity established in 1962. Here was a clear advanced intuition, based on the Canadian experience, that the Bretton Woods system would have a hard time surviving the spread of capital mobility across international markets. Nowadays, the hypothesis of the "vanishing middle", that there is little room for intermediate exchange-rate systems between full flexibility and common currencies, is held by most students of international money and finance (see Obstfeld and Rogoff, 1995, for a recent survey).

Mundell concluded that, compared to the Bretton Woods fixed-parity system, "the best solution for the Canadian economy at the present time is a resumption of the flexible exchange rate system" (1964b, p. 86). Later events proved him right. In 1970, currency speculation forced an appreciation of the Canadian dollar, and the country returned to the flexible exchange-rate system. It has been there ever since.

The Mundell of recent years has been an advocate of a more advanced alternative: a common North American currency. Along with Tom Courchene and Rick Harris, he has argued forcefully that the adjustment benefits of monetary independence for Canada are nothing to crow about, and that the costs of exchange-rate instability and misalignment have increased sharply with rising north-south economic integration (Mundell, 1991; Courchene and Harris, 1999). I have recently stated my agreement with them that a common North American currency is economically desirable from a Canadian perspective, but I have at the same time recognized that it is not politically feasible for now (Fortin, 2000; see also Buiter, 1999).

Going the route of official dollarization would be felt by Canadians as a national setback. Going for a formal monetary union would generate little interest in the United States, and it would entail a U.S.-dominated North American central bank with zero political legitimacy in Canada. Because the national currency is a major symbol of national identity, few Canadians are now ready to listen to arguments for a common North American currency. Prime Minister Jean Chrétien and Finance Minister Paul Martin have used strong words to reject this idea. Things may change in the future, as they did in the case of the North American Free Trade Agreement, but a sure bet is that tomorrow morning, and the morning after, Canada will still be living with its current flexible exchange-rate system with inflation-targeting.

So I will, in the spirit of Mundell's NBR article, focus on some current problems of monetary and exchange-rate management. I will first clarify the framework for discussion, and then consider three specific questions raised by the functioning of the current monetary regime.

Monetary Policy and the Transmission Mechanism

The framework I have in mind is the usual three-step "transmission mechanism" of monetary policy, already present in Mundell's 1964 NBR article (see also Thiessen, 1995). First, changes in the central bank instrument, taken here to be the short-term interest rate (r), affect the international price of the Canadian dollar (e) through the no-arbitrage interest rate parity condition. An increase in the interest rate attracts foreign capital and induces an exchange-rate appreciation (and increases in other asset returns as well). Second, changes in the interest rate and the exchange rate influence aggregate spending and output (y) relative to potential (y*) through the IS equation. An increase in the interest rate reduces real consumption and investment, and an exchange-rate appreciation reduces the real trade balance; both lower output through standard multiplier effects. Third, changes in the output gap end up modifying the rate of inflation (i). The farther output is below its full potential, that is, the larger the *output gap* (y* − y), the stronger the downward pressure on inflation.

The following arrow diagram gives a simple representation:

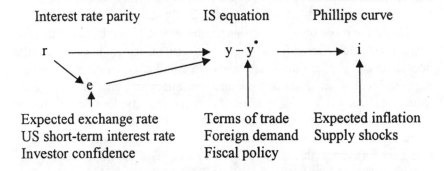

The (non-exhaustive) list of variables below the diagram are influences on the exchange rate, output and inflation other than monetary policy. For example, if the short-term U.S. interest rate rises, capital flows into U.S. dollar assets, and the Canadian dollar depreciates. If the terms of trade deteriorate, as when commodity prices dropped during the Asian crisis of 1997–98, export-generated real income declines and output falls. Simultaneously, markets expect the Canadian dollar to decline, leading to a capital outflow and an actual depreciation. "Supply shocks" include the temporary effects on inflation of indirect tax rate, real commodity price, real import price and exchange-rate changes. Potential output y* is defined as the maximum level of output that can be sustained without inducing a general price acceleration. Depending on the shape of the long-run Phillips curve, it may or may not be a function of the steady-state, target rate of inflation (i*).

Within this framework, the purpose of monetary policy is to achieve its inflation target (currently 2% in Canada) on average and at least cost in terms of deviations of actual from potential output. In accomplishing this task, the central bank must take account of various kinds of uncertainty surrounding the transmission mechanism. Multiplicative uncertainty concerns the exact specification of the three structural relations involved, including the lags in the transmission mechanism. Additive uncertainty concerns the future time paths of variables other than monetary policy, including the formation of market expectations, that influence the exchange rate, output and inflation.

I consider three broad questions raised by the functioning of the current monetary regime. First, has the inflation target been set too low? Second, has actual output tended to be too much below potential on average? Third, have monetary conditions become harder to manage? My answers to these questions will be: yes, yes, and yes.

Has the Inflation Target Been Set Too Low?

Setting an inflation target within a specified range is, in my view, a reasonable way of conducting monetary policy in a country operating under a flexible exchange-rate regime. It helps stabilize inflation expectations, and gives a clear signal to public and private sector agents as to what monetary policy is up to and how it is going to react under various circumstances. This reduces uncertainty. Since 1995 in Canada, the official inflation target has been 2%, which is the mid-point of the official target range of 1–3%. Actual inflation has averaged 1.5%, or 0.5 point below the official target.

According to classical theories of inflation, the long-run Phillips curve is vertical. There is a unique level of potential output (and correspondingly a unique level of unemployment) that is sustainable at *any* chosen level of steady-state inflation (see, for example, Friedman, 1968). However, according to some recent theories, the long-run Phillips curve could be non-vertical within a limited range at low rates of wage and price inflation. Within this range, potential output and the lowest sustainable unemployment rate would not be constant, but would depend on the chosen level of steady-state inflation.

Examples of such theories are that firms and workers would strongly resist absolute wage cuts (Tobin, 1972), or that information on inflation could be underexploited by near-rational wage- and price-setters when the inflation rate is low (Eckstein and Brinner, 1972). If either theory is true,

Problems of Monetary and Exchange-Rate Management in Canada   143

there would exist a long-run exploitable trade-off between inflation and unemployment at low inflation rates. In the past four years, such a trade-off would have been less fully exploited in Canada, where wage growth and core inflation have both averaged 1.5% per year, than in the United States where wage growth has averaged 3.5% per year and core inflation 2.5%.[1]

Akerlof, Dickens and Perry (1996, 2000) in the United States, and Djoudad and Sargent (1997) and Fortin and Dumont (2000) in Canada have uncovered favourable evidence for these newer theories. They have calculated that even such small differences in average wage and price inflation as exist between Canada and the United States could make a difference in excess of one percentage point for the lowest sustainable unemployment rate.

This suggests Canada could gain substantially and permanently from trading off a little inflation for lower unemployment. The cost of raising average inflation, say from 1.5% to 2.5% or 3%, would likely be negligible. The contemporary literature provides no evidence that there would be any significant output cost from this mild shift in the inflation target (Barro, 1997; Sala-i-Martin, 1997). Conversely, the benefit from reducing the unemployment rate permanently by one point, say from 6.5 to 5.5%, would be comparatively large. According to Okun's Law, the resulting capitalized long-term benefit for Canadians would amount to about one year's gross domestic product (GDP) (currently $1 trillion).[2] These numbers should not be viewed as farfetched given that in recent years the United States has been able to wind up at unemployment rates below 4.5% while experiencing average wage and price inflation rates between one and two points higher than Canada.

This kind of trade-off would seem very attractive. It would suggest that the Canadian authorities at least keep the inflation rate in the upper half of the inflation-target range of 1–3% instead of forcing it into the lower half as they have done over the last eight years, or else that they lift the target range itself by 0.5 or one point to a 1.5–3.5% band or to a 2–4% band.

---

[1]"Core" inflation is defined here as the 12-month increase in the consumer price index (CPI) excluding the volatile food and energy components.

[2]This law would indicate that a one-point reduction in unemployment is accompanied by a 2% increase in annual GDP. Capitalizing this annual income gain at a growth-discount rate of 2% gives a present value of 100% of current annual GDP, equal to $1 trillion.

The favourable U.S. and Canadian evidence on the Tobin and Eckstein theories may be shocking to a large number of economists trained in the belief that the long-run Phillips curve is vertical. They will be tempted to reject the evidence on the existence of an inflation-unemployment trade-off in the low inflation range as "unconvincing", or to treat the phenomenon as reflecting transitory "irrational" behaviour. With respect, I would make three points. First, science should be based on empirical evidence, not on faith. Second, the existing evidence on the new theories, while not definitive, cannot be dismissed lightly, even for the long run. Third, given the current uncertainty about the "truth", the optimal strategy is to attach non-zero probabilities to the Tobin-Eckstein and classical outcomes, compare their net cost-benefit balances, and make an honest choice on that basis.

The outcomes of this game played against nature are summarized in the following payoff matrix:

		POLICY OPTIONS	
		Leave Inflation Target Unchanged	*Raise Inflation Target by 1 Point*
ANALYTICAL PARADIGMS	*Classical Theory*	situation unchanged	negligible net loss
	New Theories	situation unchanged	substantial net gain

In cold logic, the optimal decision under uncertainty is clearly to raise the target range under all circumstances except where the probability of the new theories being true is extremely small. Further, the suggested increase in the inflation target does not represent a major change of strategy, and it would likely put Canadian inflation more in line with U.S. inflation — hardly a disaster. The obstacles against this move are psychological. Raising the inflation target would go against the generation-old belief that the long-run Phillips curve does not admit any non-vertical range. It would confront central bank culture — imagine the governor of the Bank of Canada

Problems of Monetary and Exchange-Rate Management in Canada 145

announcing he is going to raise inflation! And it could generate temporary nervousness in financial markets.

Has Actual Output Tended to Be too much Below Potential?

Lags in the transmission mechanism play a key part in the strategy of monetary policy. Broadly speaking, it takes a year or more for changes in the interest rate and the exchange rate (monetary conditions) to affect output, and another year for changes in output to affect inflation. Two implications follow. First, the central bank must make plans today to influence the course of inflation at least two years ahead. Second, the output gap (y^*-y) is not only a key argument of the social welfare function, an ultimate target of policy, but also the major channel through which monetary impulses will change the level of inflation — an intermediate target of policy.

The fact that core inflation has averaged 1.5% over the last eight years despite the official inflation target being 2% or higher, and has been strictly below target more than 90% of the time, raises the question of asymmetrical behaviour around the midpoint of the inflation-target range on the part of the central bank. Extending the question back to the intermediate target, has actual output not been kept too much below potential output most of the time? What would be the causes?

One way to think clearly about this problem is to decompose the actual output gap y^*-y into its three canonical components: the error in implementing planned output, the planned output gap, and the error in estimating potential output. The actual output gap can be written as:

$$y^* - y \quad \equiv \quad (py - y) \quad + \quad (ey^* - py) \quad + \quad (y^* - ey^*) \qquad (1)$$

actual gap ≡ implementation error + planned gap + estimation error,

where ey^* = estimated potential output, and py = planned output.

There is evidence that all three components contributed to keeping the actual gap too large much of the time. Actual output fell short of planned output, planned output was kept below the estimated potential and potential output was underestimated.

Actual Output Below the Planned Level

First, actual output fell systematically short of the planned output. Two Bank of Canada researchers (Freedman and Macklem, 1998) recently reported that a key output equation (Duguay, 1994), previously used by the Bank to measure the response of output to the short-term interest rate and the exchange rate and to construct the Bank's MCI, had overestimated output cumulatively by 12% over the 1992–96 period. They found this implementation error hard to explain, since they thought monetary conditions were easing (the MCI was declining at the time) and saw non-monetary influences on aggregate demand as expansionary during this episode. Freedman and Macklem resorted to the supply side ("intense and disruptive restructuring") to explain the error. However, supply-side shocks are not usually known for large short-run effects on aggregate supply and output. The over-prediction error therefore remains mysterious.

One possible explanation is that the interest-rate elasticity of aggregate demand was underestimated by the Bank, so that the MCI was a misleading indicator of the changing stance of monetary policy. To see what is involved, consider the following simple characterization (lags omitted) of the output (IS) equation:

$$y = a_0 + a_1 r + a_2 e + \varepsilon, \tag{2}$$

where y = output, r = real interest rate, e = (log) real effective exchange rate, a_0 = non-monetary influences on aggregate demand and output (terms of trade, foreign demand, fiscal policy, etc.), a_1 = interest-rate elasticity of output, a_2 = exchange-rate elasticity of output, and ε = zero-mean random shock. Note that a_1 and a_2 are both negative. Equivalently, and as suggested by Mundell, y can be expressed as a simple function of the MCI:

$$y = a_0 + a_1 MCI + \varepsilon, \tag{3}$$

where,

$$MCI \equiv r + (a_2/a_1)e . \tag{4}$$

Problems of Monetary and Exchange-Rate Management in Canada   147

Duguay (1994) estimated his output equation based on the ordinary-least-squares (OLS) method. He found $a_1 = -0.6$ and $a_2 = -0.2$. Assuming these elasticities are correct, suppose the real interest rate is allowed to increase by four points while the real exchange rate depreciates by 21%. Then, a net *rise* of 1.8% will be predicted for output [since $-0.6*4 - 0.2*(-21) = 1.8$]. Correspondingly, the MCI decreases by three points [since $4 + (0.2/0.6)* (-21) = -3$], indicating monetary policy is becoming *easier*. However, if the interest-rate elasticity a_1 is underestimated by the output equation and its true value is -1.4 instead, the actual outcome will be a net output *decline* of 1.4% [since $-1.4*4 - 0.2*(-21) = -1.4$]. The true change in the MCI will be an increase of 1 point [since $4 + (0.2/1.4)*(-21) = 1$], showing monetary policy is in fact becoming *tighter*.

It is possible that the interest-rate elasticity (a_1) was underestimated by the Bank of Canada to such an extent that, at times during the 1990s, monetary policy was seen as easing while it was in fact tightening. Even before Mundell wrote his NBR article, Kareken and Solow (1963) had warned that OLS-estimated output equations would produce biased estimates of the interest-rate elasticity. Their explanation was based on two-way causation between the interest rate and output: a decrease in the interest rate leads to higher aggregate demand and output through the IS equation, but increases in output bring increases in the interest rate through the central bank's stabilizing reaction. This tends to generate a positive correlation between the interest rate r and the random shock ε in the IS equation, which is then known to bias the OLS estimate of the interest-rate elasticity towards zero.

Forty years later, Romer and Romer (1994) actually found evidence of the Kareken-Solow bias in U.S. macrodata. Their estimated interest-rate elasticity was -1.7 based on the OLS method, but -3.6 based on a more sophisticated method that attempted to avoid the estimation bias. While not definitive, this finding suggests the Bank of Canada may have had a serious problem with one crucial ingredient for good monetary policy: knowledge of the slope of the IS curve.

Planned Output Below the Estimated Potential

Second, planned output was likely kept below the estimated level of potential output. Once inflation had been reduced to its target level in 1992, it had to be kept there. After inflation expectations had adjusted, the *deterministic* solution would have called for bringing actual output to match potential, thus leaving neither upward nor downward pressure on the inflation rate. This would have meant planning for a zero output gap.

The practical problem has to be faced, though, that potential output is unobserved and has to be estimated by the central bank. But in this kind of *uncertain* environment, it is not usually optimal to plan actual output to match the estimated potential output as if the latter were certain — the "certainty-equivalent" solution. In general, the optimal solution of this planning problem under uncertainty is to aim for an actual output level that makes the subjective probability of exceeding the true potential output a decreasing function of the perceived cost of doing so.[3] In other words, if you think exceeding the true potential output level is very expensive because you figure the recession cost of eliminating the resulting increase in inflation is large, then you will make sure the probability of making this mistake is very small. For a large enough estimated cost, you will aim for an actual output level *below* your subjective expected value for potential output. You will plan for a positive output gap ($py < ey^*$).

Is there evidence that, during the 1990s, the Bank of Canada was seriously concerned about the prospect of actual output exceeding potential output? Yes. While, understandably, there was no official statement to that effect, the Bank's Research Department published several papers suggesting that the short-run Phillips curve was non-linear, which meant inflation responded significantly more to the output gap when actual output was above potential than when it was below it (e.g., Laxton, Rose and Tetlow, 1993a; Fillion and Léonard, 1997; Macklem, 1997). Laxton, Rose and Tetlow made the policy implications explicit, and further argued that "if a central bank cannot be sure of whether the economy is non-linear or linear, it is better off

---

[3]Assume perceived welfare is equal to y when $y \leq y^*$, and to $y - k(y - y^*)$ when $y > y^*$, where k is the perceived cost of getting rid of inflation per unit of excess of actual output over potential. Then, expected welfare over the subjectively-held distribution of potential output is maximized when the probability that planned output be greater than potential output is equal to 1/k. The larger k, the lower this probability and, hence, the lower planned output will be. For example, if $k = 2$, the central bank should aim for the *median* estimate of potential output (see Tobin, 1983, p. 513).

Problems of Monetary and Exchange-Rate Management in Canada

maintaining the *a priori* position that the economy is non-linear" (1993b, p. 27).[4]

This continued insistence on non-linear inflation dynamics makes it an almost-sure bet that the Bank of Canada aimed for positive output gaps in order to buy insurance against unknowingly crossing over the potential output line. No such view was held at the U.S. Federal Reserve or at the U.S. Council of Economic Advisers (e.g., Blinder, 1998; Stiglitz, 1997). The Fed's active strategy of "testing the waters" of lower unemployment seems to have paid off handsomely, and stands in contrast with the more reluctant strategy adopted by the Bank of Canada.

Potential Output Underestimated

Third, the Bank of Canada recently admitted its methods had previously led to systematic underestimates of potential output (Bank of Canada, 1999, p. 26). It attributed this systematic bias to the greater-than-expected economic restructuring that took place in Canada during the 1990s. Without rejecting this explanation, it would seem that the Bank relied on questionable smoothing techniques and neglected widespread evidence of declining structural unemployment.

The Bank constructed its estimate of potential output by applying trend-fitting techniques (such as the "Hodrick-Prescott filter") to the past history of actual inflation, and by then weighting the results of this operation judgmentally with certain estimated statistical relationships (Butler, 1996). Unfortunately, this methodology seems liable to automatically building sustained slumps into the estimated trend of potential output (Krugman, 1998). One result was that, over the seven-year period 1990–96, the Bank's estimate of the average growth rate of potential GDP per adult for Canada was only 0.4% per year. This did not make sense under any reasonable set of assumptions about trend productivity growth and employment rate change.

Also, the Bank was slow to recognize the major leftward shift, already discernible by mid-decade, of the Canadian Beveridge curve towards less unemployment at given levels of the job offer rate (e.g., Fortin, 1996).

---

[4]Bank researchers seem less inclined to apply this principle to uncertainty about the shape of the *long-run* Phillips curve at low inflation rates, which I have discussed in the previous section. The logic behind this double standard escapes me!

Consistent with this shift, the relative size of the youth labour force was declining, the average level of education was rising rapidly, deregulation and globalization were increasing competitive pressure in labour and product markets, and stiffer regulations were imposed on access to unemployment insurance benefits. All of these factors are known to reduce the lowest sustainable unemployment rate and to increase potential output.

Have Monetary Conditions Become Harder to Manage?

The final question I want to raise is the increasing difficulty for the Bank of Canada to manage its monetary conditions amid volatile financial markets. Recently, Bank of Canada researchers have complained that market expectations were very unsettled over the 1992–96 period, due to recurring market concerns about international financial developments and the domestic political and fiscal situation. At times, the exchange rate fluctuated sharply and the Bank of Canada could hardly keep the MCI on its desired track (Freedman and Macklem, 1998). I extend their argument to one further episode by observing that the same problems were acutely present during the Bank's handling of the Asian crisis of 1997–98. This episode underlines the Bank's limited capacity to take advantage of its monetary independence in helping the Canadian economy absorb declines in world commodity prices.

In Mundellian tradition, the analysis proceeds in three steps. First, I give a simple geometric description of how the interest rate and the exchange rate (monetary conditions) are simultaneously determined by the interaction between the central bank and the market. Second, I use this representation to offer a theoretical and empirical interpretation of the forces that operated on monetary conditions when commodity prices dropped in 1997–98. Third, I discuss two kinds of operational difficulties, with monetary control and effectiveness, which were illustrated by this episode under the current flexible exchange rate *cum* inflation target regime.

Problems of Monetary and Exchange-Rate Management in Canada   151

Determination of Equilibrium Monetary Conditions

The MCI line in Figure 1 traces the locus of interest rates and exchange rates that can achieve a constant level of the MCI (as formalized by equation (4) above). It has a negative slope because, for the MCI to remain the same, the expansionary effect of a reduction in the interest rate on aggregate demand and output must be offset by the restraining effect of an exchange-rate appreciation.[5] Following equation (3), the central bank will normally set the MCI at the desired value $(py - a_0)/a_1$, where py is the intermediate output target it wants to achieve in due time (planned output), a_0 summarizes the anticipated evolution of non-monetary influences, and a_1 is the elasticity of output with respect to the MCI. A downward shift in the MCI line reflects an easing of monetary policy.

Similarly, the IRP line in Figure 1 traces the locus of interest rates and exchange rates along which the no-arbitrage interest-rate parity condition is satisfied in asset markets. It has a positive slope because, to be sustained in international markets, a reduction in the domestic interest rate must be compensated by a greater expected future appreciation of the domestic currency and, hence, an immediate exchange-rate depreciation. The interest rate decline will produce a capital outflow and the currency will depreciate. A leftward shift in the IRP line can arise from an increase in the foreign interest rate, a decrease in the future expected value of the domestic currency, or weaker investor confidence. The IRP line provides the central bank with a market-determined menu from which it selects the particular combination of interest rate and exchange rate that will achieve its desired MCI. The equilibrium combination is located at point A, where the two lines, IRP and MCI, intersect.

---

[5]To avoid complications, I make three simplifications: (i) the interest rate and the exchange rate are left in nominal terms; (ii) real changes are equated with nominal changes; and (iii) the Canadian-dollar exchange rate is defined in terms of the U.S. dollar instead of a trade-weighted basket of foreign currencies. The illustrative short-term interest rate is the three-month rate on prime corporate paper (CANSIM number B14017). The exchange rate is the inverse of the monthly closing spot price of one U.S. dollar (the inverse of CANSIM number B3414).

Figure 1: The Monetary Conditions Index, Interest Rate Parity, and the Determination of Equilibrium Monetary Conditions

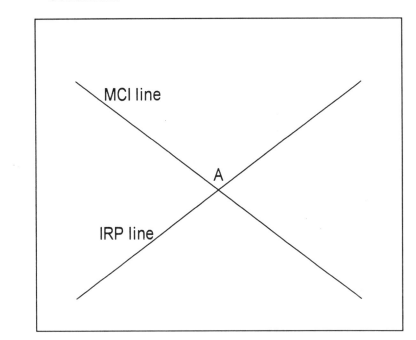

Impact of the Commodity Price Decline

Now, suppose world commodity prices drop, as they did in 1997–98 following the Asian crisis. Then, as shown in Figure 2, the IRP line shifts to the left from IRP0 to IRP1, and the MCI line shifts down from MCI0 to MCI1. The IRP shift occurs because markets realize that such a price shock will lower the equilibrium exchange rate, and also because they have learned from past experience that the central bank will encourage a depreciation of the currency as a macroeconomic stabilizing device. The expectation of a weaker future value of the currency causes an immediate actual depreciation at the going interest rate. The MCI shift confirms market expectations about

Figure 2: Impact of a Commodity Price Decline on Equilibrium Monetary Conditions

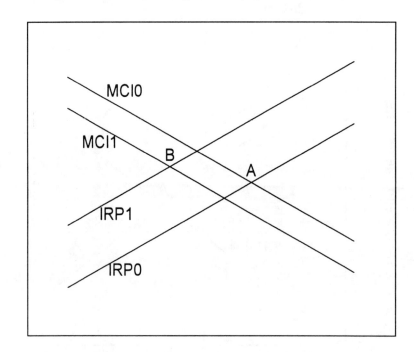

the central bank's reaction. The bank reduces the MCI as an offset to the drop in the terms of trade (a_0 is lower in equation 3) at unchanged output target (py is maintained). The IRP and MCI displacements combine to magnify the exchange-rate depreciation, but work in opposite directions on the interest rate. The particular example pictured in Figure 2 leaves the interest rate higher in the post-shock equilibrium at point B than in the pre-shock equilibrium at point A.

Figure 3 shows the theoretical story told by Figure 2 to be consistent with the actual co-movements of the interest rate and the exchange rate over the period October 1997–February 2000 corresponding to the Asian crisis and its aftermath. To help readability, MCI lines are not pictured on the

Figure 3: Co-Movements of Canadian Short-Term Interest Rate and Canadian-Dollar Exchange Rate, October 1997 to February 2000

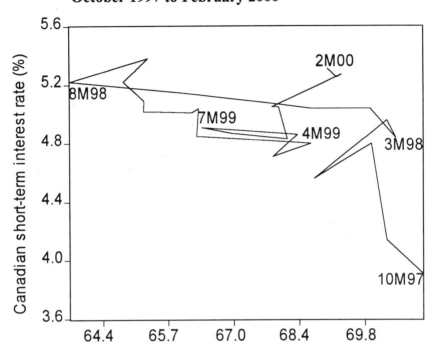

Source: Bank of Canada.

graph, but it turns out that the two endpoints of the path (10M97 and 2M00) are on about the same MCI line as would be estimated by the Bank of Canada. This helps visualize the common negative slope of parallel MCI lines.

Beginning in 1997, the Asian crisis had a depressing effect on Canadian aggregate income and output through two channels: lower world commodity prices and reduced demand for North American goods. The drop in commodity prices increased the U.S. terms of trade by about 5%, but reduced the Canadian terms of trade by about 6%. It also had the usual negative

Problems of Monetary and Exchange-Rate Management in Canada   155

expectations effect on the Canadian dollar. As Figure 3 shows, between October 1997 and April 1998 there was a mild downward pressure on the Canadian dollar. But, by and large, the Bank of Canada was able to steady the MCI through offsetting increases in the interest rate.

From April to mid-August 1998, the Canadian dollar depreciated steadily. There was no increase in the Bank rate, which was probably interpreted by markets as a signal that the Bank wanted to ease monetary conditions to offset the Asian shock. They were prompt to seize upon this opportunity for making successful one-way bets, until the Bank put an end to the game by raising the Bank rate by a full point at the end of August.

Thereafter, markets calmed down, the Canadian dollar recovered, and the Bank of Canada was even able to reduce the Bank rate, first in lockstep with the U.S. discount rate, and then in solo. During the first half of 1999, it became clear that both Canada and the United States had weathered the Asian crisis. The Bank of Canada allowed the reappreciation of the Canadian dollar to tighten monetary conditions again.

Problems with Control and Effectiveness

Not much success can be claimed for this stabilization episode. In addition to the allocative and distributive problems raised by Mundell and others, the experiment underlines two kinds of operational problems for monetary policy under the current regime, one with control and the other with effectiveness.

The control problem arises from the tendency for the game-like interaction between the Bank of Canada and financial markets to exaggerate movements in the exchange-rate component of the MCI. Sometimes, being transparent can hurt. The fact that the Bank has always made clear its intention to allow its MCI to fluctuate in a stabilizing way against terms of trade movements by itself constitutes an explicit invitation to speculate against the Canadian dollar at the slightest news of a commodity price decline. As Figure 3 indicates, over the two years 1998 and 1999 most fluctuations in the MCI arose from wide exchange-rate movements. The interest rate was contained within the narrow range of 4.6% to 5.4%. Decreases in the MCI in 1997–98 involved exchange-rate decreases and interest rate *increases*. The theoretical example in Figure 2 shows that this can happen when the leftward shift of the IRP line dominates the downward shift in the MCI line.

156   *Pierre Fortin*

Overall, just as earlier in 1992–96, the Bank of Canada had to work hard much of the time to calm financial markets and restore confidence, and could not prevent the MCI from displaying considerable volatility and sometimes wandering away from its desired track. Figure 3 looks more like a Brownian movement than like a controlled stabilization experiment. The problems of 1997–98 occurred not too long after the 1992–95 episode of unsettled markets. But this time, the domestic fiscal and political situation was not the concern, and markets understood fully the nature and working of the new monetary regime put in place in 1991. This suggests the problems of managing the new regime have become more the rule than the exception.

The effectiveness problem has to do with the timing and magnitude of the output response to the intended stabilizing decline in the MCI. The *timing* aspect is that, while the Bank of Canada commodity price index fell throughout 1997 and 1998, the Bank did not allow a decline in the MCI to occur before the second half of 1998. Moreover, this decline was already half-reversed by mid-1999. Given the usual outside lags of monetary policy, it would then be at least another year (until late 1999 and beyond) before the full effect on aggregate output would be felt. The excessive importance taken by exchange-rate changes in MCI fluctuations also exacerbated the timing problem, because the lag in the response of output to such changes is probably six months to one year longer (delayed until mid-2000) than in the case of interest rate changes.

The *magnitude* of the output response to the exchange-rate depreciation is also in question for two reasons. First, this magnitude depends on how long firms expect the depreciation to last. With half of the depreciation lasting less than a year, the effects on the trade balance and output were significantly weakened. Second, a depreciation is known to operate initially as a *depressor* of aggregate demand and output, because the income-reducing increase in import prices begins to occur immediately, while real trade volumes take time to react favourably. The dynamic multiplier effect of the depreciation has the shape of a "J-curve".

In fact, to the extent *some* stabilization job was done in 1998, it was due to the fall 1998 reduction in the Canadian interest rate that mimicked the concomitant U.S. reduction. This is exactly what would have occurred under a North American monetary union, or if the Canadian-dollar exchange rate had been pegged in some credible way to the U.S. dollar — such as under a currency board with full backing of the U.S. Federal Reserve.

Problems of Monetary and Exchange-Rate Management in Canada   157

Conclusion

Mundell and others have argued, correctly in my opinion, that a North American monetary union would provide the best monetary arrangement for Canada. However, this solution does not seem to be politically feasible at present. Canada will continue to live with its current flexible exchange rate system with inflation-targeting for some time. It is therefore of some practical importance to examine Canada's recent experience with its flexible exchange rate and to see if some improvement in monetary strategy is possible within this framework.

After reviewing an important paper on Canadian monetary policy written by Mundell in 1964, I have borrowed its title and considered some current problems of monetary and exchange-rate management in Canada. These arise from the uncertainty surrounding the transmission mechanism of monetary policy. I have developed three arguments: over the past eight years, (i) the inflation target pursued by the Bank of Canada has been too low, (ii) actual output has tended to be too much below potential, and (iii) monetary conditions have become harder to manage.

Why has the Bank of Canada kept inflation and output too low on average? Partly, this may have reflected the Bank's conservative views concerning time preference and the cost of inflation relative to unemployment. But partly also, this must be due to deficiencies in everyone's basic knowledge about how the economy works. There is a crying need for better understanding of how important the non-linearities in the long- and short-run Phillips curves are, how steep the slope of the IS curve is, and how estimates of potential output and the lowest sustainable unemployment rate could be made more reliable. These are simple, Econ-101-level questions about which even small improvements in knowledge could yield large social benefits.

If it is confirmed that inflation and output have been too low, then the required intervention will have the simplicity of the "Nike solution": you just do it, that is, you just raise them a bit. But the difficulty of managing monetary conditions will not have such an easy solution. It is, in my view, the most troublesome problem over the long run. Here, our valiant central bank seems to do the best it can within an increasingly fragile exchange rate system. I am afraid there is little Canada can do other than learn to live with this fragility, until a North American monetary union, or some kind of armoured currency board, finally becomes politically as well as economically feasible.

References

Akerlof, G.A., W.T. Dickens and G.L. Perry (1996), "The Macroeconomics of Low Inflation", *Brookings Papers on Economic Activity* 1, 1-59.

_____ (2000), "Near-Rational Wage and Price Setting and the Optimal Rates of Inflation and Unemployment", *Brookings Papers on Economic Activity* 1, 1-60.

Bank of Canada (1999), *Monetary Policy Report* (Ottawa: Bank of Canada).

Barro, R.J. (1997), *Determinants of Economic Growth: A Cross-Country Empirical Study* (Cambridge, MA: MIT Press).

Blinder, A.S. (1998), *Central Banking in Theory and Practice* (Cambridge, MA: MIT Press).

Buiter, W. (1999), "The EMU and the NAMU: What Is the Case for North American Monetary Union?", *Canadian Public Policy/Analyse de Politiques* 25 (September), 285-305.

Butler, L. (1996), *A Semi-Structural Method to Estimate Potential Output: Combining Economic Theory with a Time-Series Filter*, Technical Report No. 77 (Ottawa: Bank of Canada).

Courchene, T.J. and R.G. Harris (1999), *From Fixing to Monetary Union: Options for North American Currency Integration*, Commentary No. 127 (Toronto: C.D. Howe Institute).

Djoudad, R. and T.C. Sargent (1997), "Does the ADP Story Provide a Better Phillips Curve for Canada?", Working Paper (Ottawa: Economic Studies and Policy Analysis Division, Department of Finance).

Duguay, P. (1994), "Empirical Evidence on the Strength of the Monetary Transmission Mechanism in Canada: An Aggregate Approach", *Journal of Monetary Economics* 33 (February), 39-61.

Eckstein, O. and R. Brinner (1972), *The Inflation Process in the United States*, Joint Economic Committee of the Congress of the United States (Washington, DC: Government Printing Office).

Fillion, J.-F. and A. Léonard (1997), "La courbe de Phillips au Canada: un examen de quelques hypothèses", Working Paper No. 97-3 (Ottawa: Bank of Canada).

Fortin, P. (1996), "The Great Canadian Slump" (Presidential Address to the Canadian Economics Association), *Canadian Journal of Economics* 29 (November), 761-787.

_____ (2000), "Le Canada doit-il changer de régime monétaire?", paper presented at the seminar on "The Monetary Future of the Americas", organized by the Raoul Dandurand Chair of the Université du Québec à Montréal, and by the Montreal Council on Foreign Relations, Montreal, April.

Fortin, P. and K. Dumont (2000), "The Shape of the Long-Run Phillips Curve: Evidence from Canadian Macrodata, 1956-98", Working Paper (Montreal: Département des sciences économiques, Université du Québec à Montréal).

Freedman, C. and T. Macklem (1998), "A Comment on 'The Great Canadian Slump'", *Canadian Journal of Economics* 31 (August), 646-665.

Friedman, M. (1968), "The Role of Monetary Policy", *American Economic Review* 58 (March), 1-17.

Gordon, H.S. (1961), *The Economists versus The Bank of Canada* (Toronto: Ryerson Press).

Kareken, J. and R.M. Solow (1963), "Lags in Effect of Monetary Policy", in Commission on Money and Credit, *Stabilization Policies* (Englewood Cliffs, NJ: Prentice-Hall), 14-96.

Krugman, P. (1998), "It's Baaack: Japan's Slump and the Return of the Liquidity Trap", *Brookings Papers on Economic Activity* 2, 137-187.

Laxton, D., D. Rose and R. Tetlow (1993a), "Is the Canadian Phillips Curve Non-Linear?", Working Paper No. 93-7 (Ottawa: Bank of Canada).

_____ (1993b), *Monetary Policy, Uncertainty, and the Presumption of Linearity*, Technical Report No. 63 (Ottawa: Bank of Canada).

Macklem, T. (1997), "Capacity Constraints, Price Adjustment, and Monetary Policy", *Bank of Canada Review* (Spring), 39-56.

Mundell, R.A. (1960), "The Monetary Dynamics of International Adjustment under Fixed and Flexible Exchange Rates", *Quarterly Journal of Economics* 75 (May), 227-257.

_____ (1963), "Capital Mobility and Stabilization Policy under Fixed and Flexible Exchange Rates", *Canadian Journal of Economics and Political Science* 29 (November), 475-485.

_____ (1964a), "A Reply: Capital Mobility and Size", *Canadian Journal of Economics and Political Science* 30 (August), 421-431.

_____ (1964b), "Problems of Monetary and Exchange Rate Management in Canada", *National Bank Review* 2 (September), 77-86.

_____ (1991), "De la surévaluation du dollar canadien", *L'actualité économique* 67 (March), 5-36.

Obstfeld, M. and K. Rogoff (1995), "The Mirage of Fixed Exchange Rates", *Journal of Economic Perspectives* 9 (Fall), 73-96.

Romer, C.D. and D.H. Romer (1994), "What Ends Recessions?", in S. Fischer and J.J. Rotemberg (eds.), *NBER Macroeconomics Annual 1994* (Cambridge, MA: MIT Press), 13-57.

Sala-i-Martin, X. (1997), "I Just Ran Two Million Regressions", *American Economic Review* 87 (May), 178-183.

Stiglitz, J. (1997), "Reflections on the Natural Rate Hypothesis", *Journal of Economic Perspectives* 11 (Winter), 3-10.

Thiessen, G.G. (1995), "Uncertainty and the Transmission of Monetary Policy in Canada", The Hermes-Glendon Lecture, *Bank of Canada Review* (Summer), 41-58.

Tobin, J. (1972), "Inflation and Unemployment", *American Economic Review* 62 (March), 1-18.

_____ (1983), "Monetary Policy: Rules, Targets, and Shocks", *Journal of Money, Credit, and Banking* 15 (November), 506-518.

Money, Markets and Mobility

Part V:

Real Trade Theory

Factor Flows: Immigration in a Specific Factor Framework

James R. Melvin and Robert Waschik

Introduction

Although the work for which Bob Mundell is best known, and for which he received the Nobel Prize in Economics, is in the area of international finance, it is appropriate to recognize that he also made important contributions in the area of real trade theory as well. Among the most significant of these, and one of his very first papers, was entitled "International Trade and Factor Mobility" and was published in the *American Economic Review* in 1957. One of the present authors, Melvin, has used the methodology of this paper extensively in his own work, and it has formed the starting point of many of his own published pieces. Other authors have also used this Mundell paper as a starting point for their own research. Doug Purvis's first paper, published in the *Economic Journal* in 1972, was an extension of the Mundell analysis to consider situations in which production functions in the two trading nations were not identical. In this same lineage, in the commemorative volume for Doug Purvis published as a special issue of the *Canadian Journal* in 1995, two of the authors, Peter Neary and James Melvin, continued the Purvis tradition and made additional extensions of the Mundell model. Peter Neary considered extensions to the case of the specific factor model where capital is mobile, and Melvin compared the consequences

165

of factor flows in constant returns-to-scale and increasing returns-to-scale models.

Two of the appealing features of the Mundell (1957) paper are its clarity and its simplicity. One of the main messages was that within the Heckscher-Ohlin framework, capital flows and trade could be regarded as substitutes in the sense that, under certain circumstances, both would lead to exactly the same final world equilibrium. This important proposition had not been recognized theretofore, and although now well understood by every practitioner of economics, it was Mundell who first brought the idea forward and who presented it in full generality. Of course the Mundell paper is much more than this equivalence proposition, for it also deals extensively with the effects of tariffs in a trading world, and investigates the role that commercial policy would play in determining whether or not countries would choose to trade or achieve equilibrium through factor mobility.

In this paper we will pursue another extension of the Mundell analysis. Specifically, we will consider the effects of labour mobility in a specific factor model. It is, of course, well-known that many of the standard Heckscher-Ohlin results do not carry through to the specific factor model, and in particular the factor-price-equalization result cannot be proved. This suggests, and it is easily shown, that the substitution result of trade for factor flows identified by Mundell will not, in general, hold in the specific factor model. We will formalize this result in terms of well-defined CES production functions and examine the consequence for trading countries of the fact that trade, by itself, will not equalize factor prices. As a help in developing our analysis we will consider, in the next section, the basic reason for the factor-price-equalization result in the Heckscher-Ohlin model, and then indicate why this result is not to be expected for the specific factor model. In the third section we introduce the specific factor model and summarize some of the main results that have been established. In section four we introduce factor flows and analyze their consequences. We then consider the effects of international trade and introduce both trade and factor flows. The concluding section provides a summary of the results and a summary of the policy implications.

The Factor-Price-Equalization Result

As mentioned earlier, one of Mundell's principle results is that, under certain assumptions, commodity trade and factor mobility are substitutes in the sense that both lead to the same world equilibrium, such that all factors in the world will receive the same real incomes. Central to this result is the factor-price-equalization theorem. It is well-known that in the specific factor model trade does not result in the equalization of factor prices among countries and this, of course, is important in determining the relationship between factor flows and international trade. In this section we provide a brief overview of the factor-price-equalization result with a view to showing why it does not hold in the specific factor framework.

The factor-price-equalization result can be seen to depend crucially on two assumptions found in the Heckscher-Ohlin model. The first is the assumption of constant returns to scale and the second is the assumption that in the final equilibrium two goods are produced using the same two factors of production.[1] The simple two-commodity two-factor version of the Heckscher-Ohlin model is given by equations (1) to (4).

$$X = F_x(K_x, L_x) \tag{1}$$

$$Y = F_y(K_y, L_y) \tag{2}$$

$$K = K_x + K_y \tag{3}$$

$$L = L_x + L_y \tag{4}$$

Here, equations (1) and (2) provide the production functions assumed to exhibit constant returns to scale, and equations (3) and (4) provide the factor constraints. Throughout our analysis we will also assume that no factor intensity reversals are present and on the demand side we assume that all individuals in the world share identical homothetic utility functions.

---

[1] The factor-price-equalization theorem does not depend on two factors and two goods, but as Chipman (1966) has shown, can be proved as long as there are equal numbers of factors and commodities.

Factor Flows: Immigration in a Specific Factor Framework   *167*

The assumption of homogeneity of the first degree, or constant returns to scale, imposes important restrictions on the production side of the model. Of particular importance is the fact that the marginal product of each of the factors is uniquely determined by the capital labour ratios, or in other words by the a_{ij}s . In a competitive world these marginal products are equal to the real returns to the factors, and thus when the a_{ij}s have been determined the real returns to factor are also known. Putting things slightly differently, if we have a situation in which the a_{ij}s for an industry are identical in two countries, then the real factor rewards will also be identical in these two countries. Thus establishing that trade equalizes factor prices depends on showing, given that trade equalizes commodity prices between countries, that trade also equalizes the a_{ij}s of the industries in the two countries.

The assumption of constant returns to scale is common to both the Heckscher-Ohlin model and the specific factor model, and therefore cannot explain the differences in the relationship between factor flows and commodity trade in these two models. To provide such an explanation we must look to the production structures of the two models. In the Heckscher-Ohlin analysis given by equations (1) to (4), we have noted that both commodities use the same two factors in the production process. The unit-value isoquant diagram could be used to show that, given commodity prices, and with known technology exhibiting constant returns to scale, the equilibrium wage rental ratio is uniquely determined as long as both X and Y are produced. Because of constant returns to scale the ratio of marginal products, and indeed the marginal products themselves, are uniquely related to the capital labour ratios in the two industries. As a consequence it can be shown that commodity prices and technology uniquely determine the capital labour ratios in the two industries as long as both goods continue to be produced. In this situation endowments play no role in determining real and relative factor prices.

These relationships can be shown in Figure 1, which is the diagram used by Mundell in his 1957 paper. Figure 1 shows overlapping factor box diagrams for two countries that differ in their relative endowments. O_x is the common origin for the production function for X in both countries while O'_y and O_y are the origins for the Y industry in the two countries. The factor boxes O_x and O'_y and $O_x O_y$ give the endowments for countries H and F respectively. Clearly, H is relatively well-endowed with K_1. Because commodity prices are equalized by trade the k_y and k_x ratios (the capital labour ratios in the Y and X industries) are identical in the two countries. The fact that k_y and k_x intersect inside the factor box means that both goods

Figure 1: Box Diagrams for the Heckscher-Ohlin Model

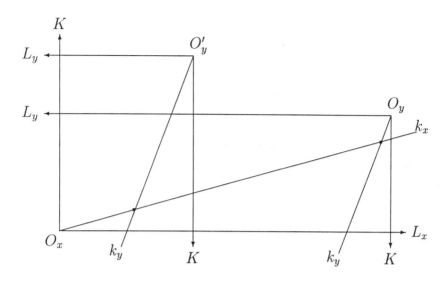

are produced in both countries. As we noted earlier, real and relative factor prices are uniquely determined by the capital labour ratios and these are the same in both countries in spite of the fact that the endowments are quite different. We also note that changes in the endowments in the two countries will leave the k_y and k_x ratios unchanged as long as commodity prices remain unchanged and as long as both goods continue to be produced. Thus, as noted earlier, endowments play no role in the determination of real and relative factor prices as long as both goods continue to be produced.

We now turn to a consideration of the specific factor model as developed by Jones (1971) and given by equations (5) to (9).

$$X = F_x(K_x, L_x) \tag{5}$$

$$Y = F_y(T_y, L_y) \tag{6}$$

$$L = L_x + L_y \tag{7}$$

$$K_0 = K_x \tag{8}$$

$$T_0 = T_y \tag{9}$$

Although similar to the Heckscher-Ohlin model in that two goods are produced using two factors, we note that the factors in the two industries are not the same. In the X industry capital and labour are used, while in the Y industry, land (T_y) and labour are employed. Because capital is used only in the X industry and land only in the Y industry these factors are said to be specific to these two industries.

Because the two industries do not use the same factors of production, a factor-box diagram of a kind used in Figure 1 cannot be drawn for this specific factor model. Instead, we have illustrated the equivalent relationship in Figure 2. Here O_x O_y shows the total quantity of labour available to this economy, and O_x K_0 represents the total amount of capital while O_y T_0 represents the total amount of land. In this model an equilibrium production configuration can be shown by any allocation of labour between the two industries. Consider L_1 for example. Here the X industry uses the amount of

Figure 2: Factor Allocation in the Specific Factor Model

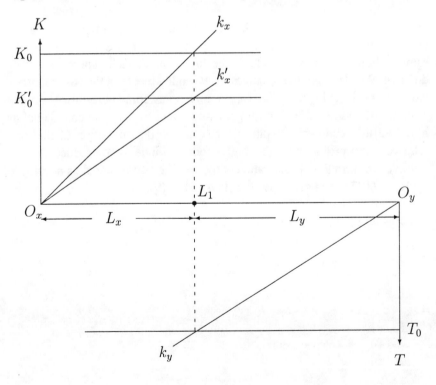

$L = O_x L_1$ and employs K_0 of capital so that the capital-labour ratio is k_x. In the Y industry $L_1 O_y$ of labour is used combined with T_0 of land producing a land-labour ratio of k_y. All possible production equilibria for this model can be traced out simply by choosing different points on the labour axis between O_x and O_y.

Given the assumption of constant returns to scale, and with commodity prices given, the capital-labour ratios in Figure 2 uniquely determine the real and relative factor rewards in the economy.

From Figure 2 it is clear that, unlike the Heckscher-Ohlin model, endowments are crucial to the determination of the capital-labour ratios and thus the real factor rewards. For example, consider two countries which have identical labour supplies and identical endowments of land but differ in the amount of capital. Suppose, for example, that the foreign country has K_0' of capital. Then even if the same amount of labour is allocated to the two sectors in both countries, resulting in the same k_y ratios in the two countries, k_x is clearly not equal to k_x' and thus the real return to capital must differ in the two countries. In this model the equalization of factor prices requires that k_x and k_y be equal in the two countries, and as can be seen from Figure 2 this would be true only by the most remote chance. Thus trade that equalizes commodity prices will in general not equalize factor prices. This in turn implies that in a trading equilibrium there will still be motivation for factors to move after trade, because factor prices still differ in the two countries. But while Figure 2 is useful in showing that factor prices will differ in the two countries it is not instructive in terms of illustrating the relationship between trade and factor flows. To make such comparisons we must now turn to a different set of diagrams.

Diagrams for the Specific Factor Model

In this section we develop the diagrammatic techniques that will be used throughout the paper. It is important to note that the figures drawn are computer-generated from real production functions in the CES class. In each case the production functions and the parameters are given below the diagram. In Figure 3 we show the standard four-quadrant diagram that is often used to represent the specific factor model. Quadrant 2 represents the total product curve for industry Y, quadrant 4 represents the total product

Figure 3: Home Country's Total Product Curves and Production Possibility Frontier

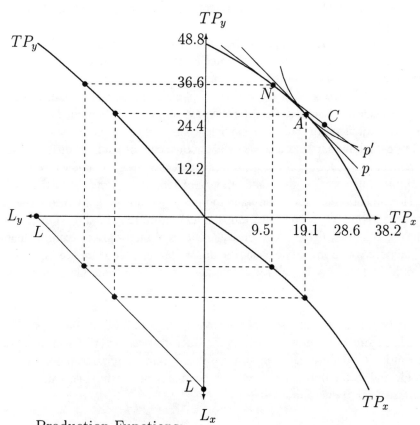

Production Functions:

$$q_i = A_i \left[\alpha_{ti} T^{-\rho_i} + \alpha_{ki} K^{-\rho_i} + \alpha_{li} L_i^{-\rho_i} \right]^{-1/\rho_i}, \quad i = x, y$$

LAND $= 20.0$ LABOUR $= 30.0$ CAPITAL $= 10.0$
$A_y = A_x = 1.000$
$\alpha_{tx} = \alpha_{ky} = 0$ $\alpha_{ty} = \alpha_{kx} = 0.064$ $\alpha_{ly} = \alpha_{lx} = 0.363$
$\rho_y = \rho_x = 1.500$ $\rightarrow$ $\sigma_y = \sigma_x = 0.400$

curve for industry X and the labour constraint is represented in quadrant 3. These two total product curves along with the labour constraint are used to generate the production possibility curve shown in Figure 1. In this diagram point A is assumed to be the initial autarky position with equilibrium prices p. At a different price line p′ we would have production at point N, resulting in a new allocation of labour as shown in quadrant 3.

Figure 4 can be considered to be a variant of this diagram where the marginal products are plotted in quadrant 1 as opposed to the total outputs as in Figure 3. Thus quadrants 2 and 4 show the marginal product curve corresponding to the total product curves of Figure 3 and quadrant 3 shows the same labour constraint as in Figure 3. We know that in equilibrium the marginal products are equal to the real factor rewards. Thus $MP_y = w/p_y$ and $MP_x = w/p_x$. Thus the line MM′ in quadrant 1 is the price line p from Figure 3 but also represents the budget constraint for the representative worker. Thus point A on budget constraint MM′ represents the utility level enjoyed by a representative worker with prices p.

Figure 4 allows for an easy demonstration of how an increase in the labour supply for the economy would affect the real income of workers. An increase in labour results in a move in the labour constraint from LL to L′L′ and consequently a shift, at constant commodity prices, of the budget constraint for workers from MM′ to QQ′. It is clear that such a shift will unambiguously reduce the real return to workers, for the indifference curve tangent to QQ′ represents a lower utility level. Of course this is just the standard result that an increase in the labour supply will unambiguously reduce the real return to workers.

The effect of a change in commodity prices is also clear from Figure 4. Suppose prices change from p to p′ resulting in a shift in the budget constraint for the representative worker from MM′ to NN′. This results in a new allocation of labour between the two industries as shown in quadrant 3. Given the particular production functions and utility functions chosen, it is clear that this change in price has resulted in a reduction in the utility level for workers for the point C, the tangency between the highest community indifference curve and budget line NN′ is clearly on a lower indifference curve than I_0. Thus in this case a reduction in the price level has made the representative worker worse off. As noted, this result depends on the particular choice of production functions and utility functions, and it is clear that with a different choice of utility functions workers could have been made better off by this change in prices. Thus we have demonstrated what has come to be called the neoclassical ambiguity: for any change in the

Figure 4: Representative Labour's Budget Constraints and an Increase in Labour Endowment

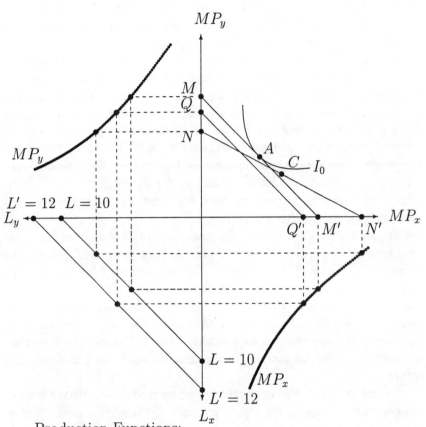

Production Functions:

$$q_i = A_i \left[\alpha_{ti} T^{-\rho_i} + \alpha_{ki} K^{-\rho_i} + \alpha_{li} L_i^{-\rho_i} \right]^{-1/\rho_i}, \quad i = x, y$$

LAND = 40.0   CAPITAL = 40.0 $A_y = A_x = 1.000$
$\alpha_{tx} = \alpha_{ky} = 0$ $\alpha_{ty} = \alpha_{kx} = 0.882$ $\alpha_{ly} = \alpha_{lx} = 0.106$
$\rho_y = \rho_x = 1.500$ $\rightarrow$ $\sigma_y = \sigma_x = 0.400$

commodity price ratio it is unclear whether workers will be made better off or worse off.

Other standard results of the specific factor model can also be shown with these diagrams. For example, an increase in the specific factor T in the Y industry would shift out the total product curve in Figure 3 and the marginal product curve in Figure 4, and with the same commodity prices would result in an upward shift of the budget constraint for the representative worker. Thus we have the result that an increase in the specific factor will unambiguously make workers better off, but will lower the real return to both specific factors. Note that because of the assumption of constant returns to scale, an increase in the marginal product of labour will necessarily imply a reduction in the marginal product of the specific factor in that industry.

The two price lines MM' and NN' shown in Figure 4 are, of course, just two of the infinite number of price lines that could be considered in this model. It is of interest to inquire how these price lines relate to one another, and one possibility is shown in Figure 5. Here three representative price lines are shown and it is clear from the diagram that of these three, the representative worker is better off at point C on indifference curve I_0 on price line mm'. Thus given a choice between the three price lines RR', NN' and MM', the representative worker would choose the price line MM'.

This leads to the question of whether there is a best-price lines as far as workers are concerned, and the fact that there can be is shown in Figure 6. Here we have shown the whole family of price lines, and together these form an envelope. It is clear, given appropriate assumptions about convexities, that there is a unique best-price line in this situation. In the case shown it is MM', and it occurs where the highest community indifference curve is tangent to this envelope. The significance of this result is that it indicates that for the representative worker the price line MM' provides the highest level of utility that the workers can enjoy. Any price line other than this will result in a lower utility level. Thus if C represents the free trade equilibrium, it is clear that any change in prices due to tariffs, for example, would make workers worse off. Alternatively, C could represent a situation in which tariffs exist. If this is the case then any movement away from this tariff-ridden situation will again make workers worse off. Thus whether tariffs are beneficial for workers entirely depends on the nature of production functions and on the utility assumptions assumed.

Another point of interest is that the particular type of envelope shown in Figure 6 depends on the parameters of the production functions used to construct this figure. In this diagram an elasticity of substitution in

Figure 5: Marginal Product Curves and Representative Labour's Budget Constraints

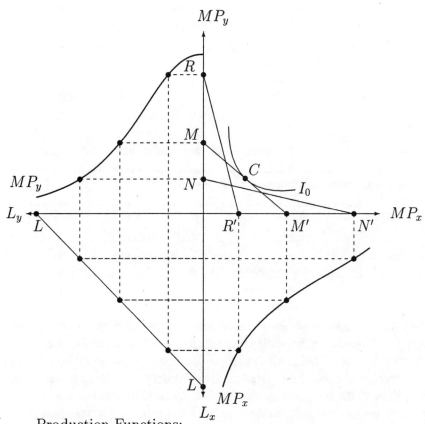

Production Functions:

$$q_i = A_i \left[\alpha_{ti} T^{-\rho_i} + \alpha_{ki} K^{-\rho_i} + \alpha_{li} L_i^{-\rho_i} \right]^{-1/\rho_i}, \quad i = x, y$$

LAND $= 10.0$ LABOUR $= 10.0$ CAPITAL $= 10.0$
$A_y = A_x = 1.000$
$\alpha_{tx} = \alpha_{ky} = 0$ $\alpha_{ty} = \alpha_{kx} = 0.182$ $\alpha_{ly} = \alpha_{lx} = 0.047$
$\rho_y = \rho_x = 2.333$ $\rightarrow$ $\sigma_y = \sigma_x = 0.300$

Figure 6: Frontier of Marginal Product Curves with CES Production Technology

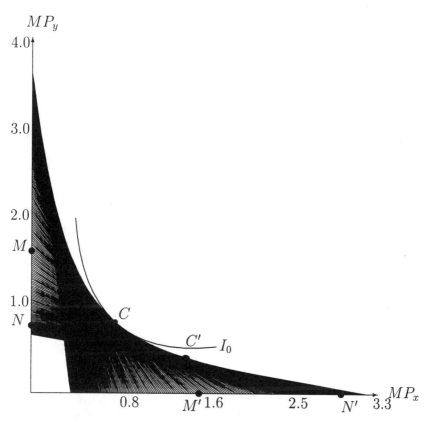

Production Functions:

$q_i = A_i \left[\alpha_{ti} T^{-\rho_i} + \alpha_{ki} K^{-\rho_i} + \alpha_{li} L_i^{-\rho_i} \right]^{-1/\rho_i}$, $i = x, y$

LAND $= 10.0$ LABOUR $= 10.0$ CAPITAL $= 10.0$

$A_y = A_x = 1.000$

$\alpha_{tx} = \alpha_{ky} = 0$ $\quad \alpha_{ty} = \alpha_{kx} = 0.182$ $\quad \alpha_{ly} = \alpha_{lx} = 0.047$

$\rho_y = \rho_x = 2.333$ $\quad \rightarrow \quad \sigma_y = \sigma_x = 0.300$

Factor Flows: Immigration in a Specific Factor Framework

production of 0.4 has been assumed for both industry X and industry Y. In Figure 7 we represent the case for a Cobb-Douglas production function with elasticity of substitution equal to unity, and here we see that the envelope formed by the infinity of possible price lines has quite different characteristics than the one in Figure 6. In particular, points on this envelope represent the minimum utility level that a representative worker would enjoy. Thus suppose that price line MM' exists, giving rise to a tangency with the highest community indifference curve at point A. Suppose this is the free trade equilibrium. From Figure 7 it is clear that any other price line will make workers better off. It is also clear that the utility level of workers will rise as the price ratio gets either very high or very low, and indeed workers would prefer extreme prices, that is either a very high price of X or a very low relative price of X, and they are largely indifferent as to which of these two situations would occur.

The situations of Figures 6 and 7 indicate the crucial importance of the assumptions about the production functions. They have illustrated that no assumptions about how workers will be expected to gain or lose from such policy changes as tariffs or free trade can be made unless the specific forms of the production functions are known. It should also be noted that much more complex situations than the one shown in Figures 6 and 7 are possible. Some of these other cases have been examined by Melvin and Waschik (2000).

Factor Flows

It has been established that the relationship between commodity trade and factor flows differs significantly between the Heckscher-Ohlin model and the specific factor model. Mundell's result that factor flows and trade are substitutes in the Heckscher-Ohlin model does not carry through to the specific factor framework, and this suggests that an examination of how the effects of factor flows and trade differ would be appropriate. In this section we consider how inflows (or outflows) of labour will affect outputs, commodity prices, and factor rewards, and in the next part we will compare the results derived here with the results for the traditional trade model.

Figure 7: Frontier of Marginal Product Curves with Cobb-Douglas Production Technology

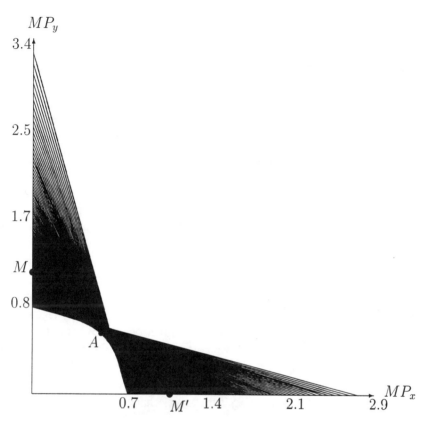

Production Functions:

$q_i = A_i \left[T^{\alpha_{ti}} K^{\alpha_{ki}} L_i^{\alpha_{li}} \right], \quad i = x, y$

LAND $= 10.0$ LABOUR $= 10.0$ CAPITAL $= 10.0$
$A_y = A_x = 1.960$
$\alpha_{tx} = \alpha_{ky} = 0 \quad \alpha_{ty} = \alpha_{kx} = 0.600 \quad \alpha_{ly} = \alpha_{lx} = 0.400$
$\rho_y = \rho_x = 0.000 \quad \rightarrow \quad \sigma_y = \sigma_x = 1.000$

We have already seen, from Figure 4, that an inflow of labour will unambiguously make labour worse off and the specific factors better off at unchanged commodity prices. Additional evidence of this is provided in Figure 8. Suppose with marginal product curves MP^1_y and MP^1_x and an initial labour supply L_hL_h we have an initial autarky equilibrium at A^h. This produces the budget constraint QQ' for the representative worker. Now suppose the labour supply doubles to L_fL_f with a new equilibrium at A^f. The new budget constraint is NN', and we can see that doubling the labour supply has resulted in a more than proportional fall in the real income of workers. It is clear that in this model large inflows of workers can substantially reduce the income and welfare of workers already resident in the economy.

The fact that the large change in income of workers associated with immigration is not a necessary result can be seen by considering, as alternatives to marginal products MP^1_y and MP^1_x the marginal products MP^2_y and MP^2_x. In this case the same increase in the labour supply for the economy results in a shift in the budget constraint from RR' to MM', resulting in a very modest reduction in income and welfare for the representative workers. It is thus clear that the effect that immigration will have on the existing workers in an economy will very much depend on the production functions for the economy. As can be seen from the legend for Figure 8, the differences in the production functions depend simply on the choice of α. With $\alpha_y = \alpha_x = 0.363$ we have that labour's share is large in the production of both commodities, and in this case substantial changes in the labour's supply have only modest effects on the real return of workers. With $\alpha_y = \alpha_x = 0.106$ we observe very substantial changes in the real return of workers associated with immigration.

There are several interesting implications from these results. First, it is clear that large inflows of labour can have very substantial effects on residents of the economy, and that the size of these effects will depend crucially on the production functions for the goods being produced. Now suppose that the two factor constraints in quadrant 3 represent two different countries. For the case with $\alpha_y = \alpha_x = 0.106$ this would result in very substantial differences in real wages between the two economies. In the example shown, since commodity prices are equal to the slopes of the budget constraints, since these are the same, even if trade were possible no trade would take place. Nevertheless, there would still be a very substantial wage differential and factors would flow if labour mobility is permitted. In this case labour would move to equilibrate the real returns to labour, resulting in

Figure 8: Effects of Changes in the Labour Supply on Worker's Budget Constraints

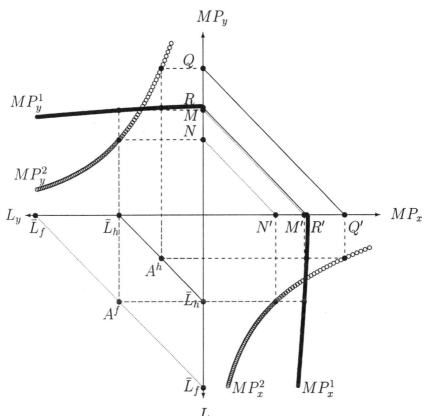

Production Functions:

$$q_i = A_i \left[\alpha_{ti}T^{-\rho_i} + \alpha_{ki}K^{-\rho_i} + \alpha_{li}L_i^{-\rho_i} \right]^{-1/\rho_i}, \quad i = x, y$$

Home: LAND = 40.0   LABOUR = 10.0   CAPITAL = 40.0
Foreign: LAND = 40.0   LABOUR = 20.0   CAPITAL = 40.0
$A_y = 1.000 \quad A_x = 1.000 \quad \alpha_{tx} = \alpha_{ky} = 0$
$\alpha_{ty}^{\bullet} = \alpha_{kx}^{\bullet} = 0.064 \quad \alpha_{ty}^{\circ} = \alpha_{kx}^{\circ} = 0.882$
$\alpha_{ly}^{\bullet} = \alpha_{lx}^{\bullet} = 0.363 \quad \alpha_{ly}^{\circ} = \alpha_{lx}^{\circ} = 0.106$
$\rho_y = \rho_x = 1.500 \quad \rightarrow \quad \sigma_y = \sigma_x = 0.400$

Factor Flows: Immigration in a Specific Factor Framework

a substantial increase in the wage rate in the country with a large population and a substantial reduction in the real return to labour in the country with a smaller population. For the case for $\alpha_y = \alpha_x = 0.363$, even with large differences in the population there would be very small differences in the real return to factors in the two countries. If immigration costs were taken into account, it is possible that there would be no labour movements. On the other hand, if labour does move to equalize real income between the two countries then a very large migration would be required to generate a small change in factor prices in the two countries.

As a third case we could consider the situation where labour's share is large in one country and small in the other. This could be due to differential rates of technological change taking place in the two countries. If the country well endowed with labour has production functions where labour's share is small, then both the labour that migrates and the labour that remains at home will benefit substantially from immigration. Labour in the smaller host country will be largely unaffected by the immigration. On the other hand, if the small country has production functions where labour share is small then immigration from the larger country will significantly reduce workers' real income while in the country that is losing labour wages will be largely unaffected. These results could well have important implications in situations where technological change is uneven. It seems quite possible that in many situations, technological improvement results in labour's share in production falling, and this would make such economies vulnerable to large factor inflows in situations where the wage rates in these countries are high.

Implications of International Trade

We now turn to a consideration of how equilibrium would be achieved in a model in which commodity trade is allowed but in which there are no factor flows. In Figure 9 two countries are represented with country F having twice as much labour as country L so that the labour constraint lies twice as far from the origin in quadrant three. We make the same assumptions about production functions but have changed the endowments of land, labour and capital from what we made in the construction of Figure 8. As before, we assumed that all consumers in the world face the same Cobb-Douglas utility functions. The autarky allocations of labour between the two industries in the

Figure 9: Autarky Equilibrium and Equilibrium with Trade in Goods

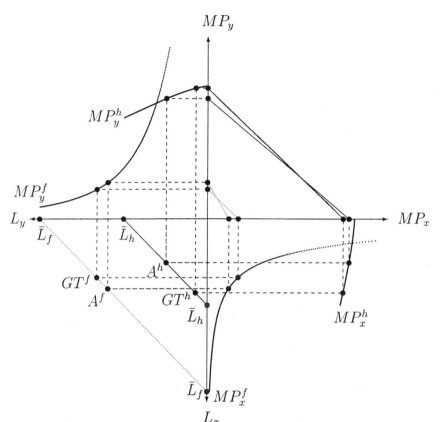

Production Functions:

$$q_i = A_i \left[\alpha_{ti} T^{-\rho_i} + \alpha_{ki} K^{-\rho_i} + \alpha_{li} L_i^{-\rho_i} \right]^{-1/\rho_i}, \quad i = x, y$$

Home: LAND = 10.0 LABOUR = 10.0 CAPITAL = 20.0
Foreign: LAND = 20.0 LABOUR = 20.0 CAPITAL = 10.0
$A_y = 1.000 \quad A_x = 1.000$

$\alpha_{tx}^h = \alpha_{ky}^h = 0$ $\qquad\qquad \alpha_{tx}^f = \alpha_{ky}^f = 0$

$\alpha_{ty}^h = \alpha_{kx}^h = 0.064$ $\qquad \alpha_{ty}^f = \alpha_{kx}^f = 0.410$

$\alpha_{ly}^h = \alpha_{lx}^h = 0.363$ $\qquad \alpha_{ly}^f = \alpha_{lx}^f = 0.049$

$\rho_y = \rho_x = 1.500 \quad \rightarrow \quad \sigma_y = \sigma_x = 0.400$

Factor Flows: Immigration in a Specific Factor Framework

two countries is shown in Figure 9 by points A^f and A^h. The equilibrium price lines for the two countries, or in other words the slope of the budget constraints faced by the representative workers, for these two countries are shown in quadrant 1. Note that the price line for the foreign country is steeper than the price line for the home country.

We now assume that trade is allowed and calculate the new equilibrium for both countries. This results in a labour allocation of GT^f and GT^h for countries F and H respectively. The new equilibrium price lines for the two countries shown in quadrant 1 are parallel since trade is assumed to equalize relative commodity prices between the two countries.

We now turn to a consideration of how commodity trade has affected the welfare of the two countries. We note that for both countries the commodity price lines for trade and for autarky intersect, and indeed this will always be the case for trade in a specific factor model. In general this means that the effect of trade on the representative worker is indeterminate. It is clear from Figure 9 that, depending on the assumption about utility, workers may be better off or worse off depending entirely on where the indifference curve is tangent to the budget constraint. This is what has become known as the neoclassical ambiguity. With trade, while the welfare of owners of the specific factor used in the industry whose price has risen will necessarily rise and the utility of the other specific factor necessarily falls, the effect on labour is indeterminate. In the particular situation of Figure 9, if the indifference curves were drawn in it would be seen that trade results in an increase in the utility of workers in country F and a reduction in the utility of the representative workers in country H. Thus trade can affect workers in the two countries quite differently. And of course a variety of other outcomes are possible. Thus workers could be better off in both countries, worse off in both countries or better off in one country and worse off in the other.

But however the trade affects workers in the two countries it nevertheless remains clear that workers in H are much better off than workers in F both before and after trade takes place. While trade has resulted in some change in the real wage in both countries, there certainly has been no general tendency for trade to equalize the real return to workers. In fact, trade is just as likely to result in a divergence in real income of workers as it is to result in a tendency towards equalization. The important point is that there is no reason to expect that international trade, in the specific factor model, will do anything towards equalization of real factor rewards for labour between the two trading countries. There will be as much incentive for factors to move between countries after trade as there was before, and indeed there could be more depending on how the real wages have been affected by trade. Real wage differentials fundamentally depend on the relationship between factor supplies and such differences could be very large. In Figure 9 countries differ in labour endowment by a factor of about two, but this is a small difference relative to the differences in populations found in real world situations. Thus the real returns to factors in a world of free trade that might be observed in the real world could be substantial and after trade there will still remain significant incentives for labour to move from countries with abundant labour to countries where labour is scarce. As noted earlier, the movement of factors between countries will equalize real factor rewards but the cost to workers in countries receiving this immigration could be extremely high.

International Trade and Labour Mobility

We have seen that in the specific factor model, neither trade nor factor mobility taken by themselves result in a full equilibrium for the world economy. Trade does not equalize factor prices across countries, and if factor endowments are very different then equilibrium factor prices may also be very different in a trading equilibrium. Allowing full mobility of labour will equalize the return to workers in the two countries, but will not equalize commodity prices. Such a situation is shown in Figure 10. Thus a full equilibrium for the world will require the movement of both commodities and at least one of the factors. In our case we consider that labour is the mobile factor. In this section we consider an equilibrium in which both labour and commodities are free to move between countries and we compare the results achieved in this equilibrium with the situations described in the previous two sections. In Table 1 we provide a full description of the model beginning with the summary statistics describing the endowments and the parameters of both the production functions and the utility functions. We then describe the autarky equilibrium, the equilibrium with labour mobility, the equilibrium with trade, and the equilibrium with both labour mobility and trade. In Tables 2 to 5 we report the utility levels enjoyed by the two countries, in Table 2 for the total populations of the two countries, and in Tables 3, 4 and 5 for the three types of factor owners. This allows for an easy comparison of how the different equilibria affect the economies as a whole and the individual

Factor Flows: Immigration in a Specific Factor Framework   *185*

Figure 10: Autarky Equilibrium and Equilibrium with Trade in Labour

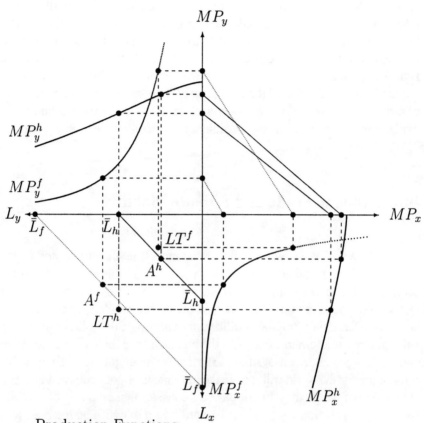

Production Functions:

$$q_i = A_i \left[\alpha_{ti} T^{-\rho_i} + \alpha_{ki} K^{-\rho_i} + \alpha_{li} L_i^{-\rho_i} \right]^{-1/\rho_i}, \quad i = x, y$$

Home: LAND = 10.0 LABOUR = 10.0 CAPITAL = 20.0
Foreign: LAND = 20.0 LABOUR = 20.0 CAPITAL = 10.0

$A_y = 1.000 \quad A_x = 1.000 \quad \alpha_{tx} = \alpha_{ky} = 0$

$\alpha_{ty}^h = 0.064 \quad \alpha_{kx}^h = 0.064 \quad \alpha_{ty}^f = 0.410 \quad \alpha_{kx}^f = 0.410$

$\alpha_{ly}^h = 0.363 \quad \alpha_{lx}^h = 0.363 \quad \alpha_{ly}^f = 0.049 \quad \alpha_{lx}^f = 0.049$

$\rho_y = 1.500 \quad \rightarrow \quad \sigma_y = 0.400$
$\rho_x = 1.500 \quad \rightarrow \quad \sigma_x = 0.400$

Table 1: Equilibria with Autarky, Trade and Immigration

Summary Statistics		Home	Foreign
Endowments	Land	5.0000	25.0000
Endowments	Labour	6.0000	60.0000
Endowments	Capital	20.0000	10.0000

Production

$$y = A_y\left[\alpha_{ty}T^{-\rho y} + \alpha_{ly}L_y^{-\rho y}\right]^{-1/\rho y}$$
$$x = A_x\left[\alpha_{kx}K^{-\rho x} + \alpha_{lx}L_x^{-\rho x}\right]^{-1/\rho x}$$

		Home	Foreign
Subst. elast.	$\sigma_x = 1/(1+\rho_x)$	0.4000	0.4000
Subst. elast.	$\sigma_y = 1/(1+\rho_y)$	0.4000	0.4000
Alpha	α_{tx}	0.0000	0.0000
Alpha	α_{ty}	0.2197	0.2197
Alpha	α_{lx}	0.1393	0.1393
Alpha	α_{ly}	0.1393	0.1393
Alpha	α_{kx}	0.2197	0.2197
Alpha	α_{ky}	0.0000	0.0000

Autarky

		Home	Foreign
Relative Price Ratio		0.5725	2.2957
Consumer Price Index		0.3807	1.3908
Nominal input prices	Land	0.2405	1.4101
Nominal input prices	Labour	0.8601	0.3281
Nominal input prices	Capital	0.0173	4.0061
Supply	X	12.1013	24.5143
Supply	Y	6.9282	56.2772
Demand	X	12.1013	24.5143
Demand	Y	6.9282	56.2772
Utility	Land	0.3282	0.5513
Utility	Labour	1.1737	0.1283
Utility	Capital	0.0237	1.5663
Utility	TOTAL	9.1564	37.1429

Factor Flows: Immigration in a Specific Factor Framework

Table 1–Continued

Trade		Home	Foreign
Relative Price Ratio		1.3852	1.3852
Consumer Price Index		1.2518	1.2518
Nominal input prices	Land	0.0044	1.8508
Nominal input prices	Labour	3.7740	0.3456
Nominal input prices	Capital	0.2605	2.7990
Supply	X	18.4310	23.8244
Supply	Y	1.0263	57.5062
Demand	X	9.5859	32.6694
Demand	Y	13.2785	45.2540
Net exports	X	8.8450	-8.8450
Net exports	Y	-12.2522	12.2522
Net exports	Lab	0.0000	0.0000
Utility	Land	0.0018	0.7491
Utility	Labour	1.5275	0.1399
Utility	Capital	0.1054	1.1329
Utility	TOTAL	11.2821	38.4502
Migration			
Relative Price Ratio		0.3125	2.1658
Consumer Price Index		1.3137	1.2086
Nominal input prices	Land	3.6346	0.9126
Nominal input prices	Labour	0.5965	0.5989
Nominal input prices	Capital	0.6502	2.8295
Supply	X	37.2371	22.7273
Supply	Y	11.6367	49.2236
Demand	X	37.2371	22.7273
Demand	Y	11.6367	49.2236
Net exports	X	0.0000	0.0000
Net exports	Y	0.0000	0.0000
Net exports	Lab	-19.8354	19.8354
Utility	Land	1.6240	0.4061
Utility	Labour	0.2665	0.2665
Utility	Capital	0.2905	1.2591
Utility	TOTAL	20.8162	33.4473

Table 1–Continued

Both		Home	Foreign
Relative Price Ratio		1.0000	1.0000
Consumer Price Index		1.0239	1.0239
Nominal input prices	Land	1.3553	1.3553
Nominal input prices	Labour	0.6770	0.6770
Nominal input prices	Capital	1.3553	1.3553
Supply	X	41.0179	20.5090
Supply	Y	10.2545	51.2724
Demand	X	25.6362	35.8907
Demand	Y	25.6362	35.8907
Net exports	X	15.3817	-15.3817
Net exports	Y	-15.3817	15.3817
Net exports	Lab	-21.5000	21.5000
Utility	Land	0.6618	0.6618
Utility	Labour	0.3306	0.3306
Utility	Capital	0.6618	0.6618
Utility	TOTAL	25.6362	35.8907

Table 2: Total Utility

	H	F
Autarky	9.2	37.1
Trade	11.3	38.5
Migration	15.5	38.7
Both	18.5	43.0

Note: H = home country   F = foreign country

Factor Flows: Immigration in a Specific Factor Framework

Table 3: Workers' Utility

	H	F
Autarky	1.174	0.128
Trade	1.528	0.140
Migration	0.267	0.267
Both	0.331	0.331

Table 4: Landowners' Utility

	H	F
Autarky	0.328	0.551
Trade	0.002	0.749
Migration	1.624	0.406
Both	0.662	0.662

Table 5: Capital Owners' Utility

	H	F
Autarky	0.024	1.566
Trade	0.104	1.133
Migration	0.291	1.259
Both	0.662	0.662

factor owners in each. Note that because of our simple utility function where $U = \sqrt{XY}$ the utility measure is a good approximation for the real incomes of factors and of the GNP of the economies. In this section we will use the terms real income and utilities interchangeably.

One of the important features of the information provided in Table 2 is the comparison between the real income associated with autarky, trade and factor mobility for the two economies. For the foreign country, with a relatively large labour supply, the effects of any liberalization are quite modest. Utility increases from 37.1 to 38.5 in moving from autarky to trade and from 37.1 to 43 in moving from autarky to the full equilibrium with both trade and factor mobility. Thus the full equilibrium results in a real-income increase of approximately 16%. For the home country, on the other hand, the welfare improvements associated with trade or factor mobility are significantly larger. Allowing commodity trade increases utility by 23% and allowing a full equilibrium with factor mobility and trade more than doubles real income for the economy as a whole. It is also of interest to note that for the home country labour mobility is much preferred to trade if a choice had to be made between these two. Immigration provides a 68% increase in real income while trade results in a 23% increase. For the foreign country the difference between trade and factor mobility is very small, although it is still the case that migration is preferred to international trade, and recall that in this case labour is leaving the foreign country. Turning to Tables 3, 4 and 5 one of the striking features is the significant difference in how the individual factor owners are affected by the three scenarios. Workers in both countries prefer commodity trade to autarky — the utility of the workers in the home country is improved by over 30% but in the foreign country by less than 10%. Even more striking is the fact that trade has made the divergence between the welfare of workers in the two countries even larger. In autarky workers in the home country have incomes nine times as high as those in the foreign country. After trade incomes in the home country are almost 11 times those in the foreign country. Trade has made the disparity between real wages in the two countries even larger than it was in autarky.

With labour mobility wages in the two countries will be the same and we note that in the home country wages fall so that the new wage rate is only 23% of what it was in the autarky situation. In the foreign country, on the other hand, wages are more than twice their autarky level. For both countries a full equilibrium with trade and factor mobility is preferred to migration, and for both the increase is 24%.

Factor Flows: Immigration in a Specific Factor Framework   *191*

The other factors are also affected differently by trade and factor mobility. The effect on land owners is relatively modest for the foreign country with international trade being the preferred situation and labour mobility being the least desirable case. Just the opposite is true for the home country, and the differences here are very striking. With trade the real return to land falls to less than 1% of its autarky level, while with immigration the return to land owners increases almost five-fold from its autarky position. In H, land owners have a real return 800 times as high with migration as with international trade.

The returns to capital are also differentially affected by trade and factor mobility. Again we note that the capital owners in the foreign country are affected much less than their counterparts in the home country. In H, trade raises the return to capital by a multiple of 4.3 while both trade and factor mobility result in an increase to 28 times the autarky level. We also note that in the home country autarky is far and away the worse situation for capital owners while, in the foreign country autarky is the preferred situation.

Policy Implications

Bob Mundell, in 1957, provided a very elegant demonstration that in the Heckscher-Ohlin model trade and factor mobility are substitutes in situations where factor prices will be equalized through international trade. We began our analysis by outlining the conditions necessary for this substitution result, and showed that these conditions did not hold for the specific factor model. We developed a diagrammatic approach that allowed us to consider the effects of trade and factor mobility in terms of well-defined CES production functions and examined the differences between capital flows and international trade in terms of the specific factor model.

It is well-known that international trade does not result in the equalization of factor prices in the specific-factor model, but nevertheless the extent to which factor prices can differ in a trading world has not, to our knowledge, been explored. We have shown that for normal production functions, modest differences in factor endowments between two trading countries can result in substantial differences in real factor rewards. In our example, with one country having ten times as large a labour force as another we found that wages, even after international trade, could be less than one-tenth of the levels existing in the country where labour is relatively scarce. These are large differences, and certainly the differences in labour endowments assumed here are not out of line with what we observe in the real world. In discussions of the reason that some less-developed countries have such low wages, it is often suggested that the fault lies in the efficiencies of the production technology in these countries. Our example shows that, even if technology is exactly the same between the two countries, wages may differ in orders of magnitude simply because of the relatively large population in one of the countries. It was also shown that while trade will improve the welfare for trading countries, and may even raise the real income of workers, it may do little to alleviate the difference in real factor rewards that exist.

Real wage differentials can, of course, be eliminated by the free mobility of labour. Indeed, it was shown that such labour mobility would generally result in an increase in the welfare level and real incomes of both countries. But while such labour mobility will undoubtedly be beneficial to the workers in the country well-endowed with labour, labour in the recipient country could suffer a substantial loss in real income. In the example given, migration reduced the wages in the home country to only 23% of what existed in autarky.

While labour will be disadvantaged by inflows from another country, specific factors will benefit, and again these benefits can be very substantial. This raises the possibility of political conflict, for the interests of labour and specific factor are clearly at odds when it comes to the issue of trade versus factor flows.

References

Chipman, J.S. (1966), "A Survey of the Theory of International Trade: Part 3, The Modern Theory", *Econometrica* 35, 18-76.

Jones, R.W. (1971), "A Three-Factor Model in Theory, Trade and History", in J.N. Bhagwati *et al.* (eds.), *Trade, Balance of Payments and Growth: Essays in Honor of Charles C. Kindleberger* (Amsterdam: North-Holland).

Melvin, J.R. (1995), "Trade and Investment with Constant and Increasing Returns to Scale", *Canadian Journal of Economics* 28 (Special Issue), 24-25.

Melvin, J.R. and R. Waschik (2000), "An Examination of the Neoclassical Ambiguity in the Specific Factor Model", Working Paper (Waterloo, ON: University of Waterloo and Wilfrid Laurier University).

Factor Flows: Immigration in a Specific Factor Framework

Mundell, R.A. (1957), "International Trade and Factor Mobility", *American Economic Review* 47, 321-335.

Neary, J.P. (1995), "Factor Mobility and International Trade", *Canadian Journal of Economics* 28 (Special Issue), 4-23.

Purvis, D.D. (1972), "Technology, Trade and Factor Mobility", *Economic Journal* 82, 991-999.

Money, Markets and Mobility

Part VI:

International Economy

Perspectives on the Evolution of the Global Trading System

Sylvia Ostry

Introduction

In the ongoing discussion about Seattle it is important to make a distinction between the possibility versus the probability of the failure to launch a new round. The latter required a catalyst to trigger the outcome of failure. But the transformation of the trading system combined with the structural weakness of the World Trade Organization (WTO) would have ensured that even "success" could not guarantee the future of a rules-based multilateral system in the absence of fundamental reform of the WTO.

What I plan to do in this paper is first to summarize the main transformative changes in the global trading system which include the impact of the Uruguay Round as well as changes in the policy *ambience* and the policy *process*. I will then highlight the most urgent reforms needed to keep the system going and briefly note the longer term changes required in the international governance architecture.

Transformative Changes in the Trading System

Even the term "trading system" is an anachronism today since the WTO is less and less centred on trade rather than on domestic regulatory and legal systems. But the shift in focus resulting from the Uruguay Round is only one of the changes that has transformed the system. I have grouped these into three categories: the *ambience,* the *political economy* and the *process of policy making.*

The Ambience

The end of the Cold War has had, and will continue to have, a profound effect on the role of the United States in international economic policy not only because of a secular decline of congressional deference but also because the postwar spillover from "high" to "low" policy which acted as a constraint on trade disputes has now greatly diminished or even reversed. That being said, the major impact of the Cold War finale is really more relevant to the next session and the leadership issue. What I want to touch on here are more pervasive albeit less obvious developments.

There was very little public interest in the Uruguay Round negotiations. As the new director-general of the WTO, Mike Moore, has described it: "The Uruguay Round was launched in the silence of public apathy" (WTO, 1999a). The same could be said about the previous seven rounds since the creation of the General Agreement on Tariffs and Trade (GATT) in 1948. The negotiations were handled by governments although the GATT model involved lobbying by so-called distributional coalitions, chiefly business and trade unions, as an important element in the process and outcome. In the Uruguay Round, the role of multinational corporations and farmers was unique because of the unique character of the so-called new issues (services, intellectual property and investment) and the centrality of agriculture as a deal-maker or breaker in the ultimate settlement. While the United States was the leader in launching and guiding all GATT negotiations, it is fair to argue that all the negotiations ultimately depended on cooperation between the two biggest players, the Americans and the European Community.

In Seattle there must have been many governments who sorely missed the "silence of public apathy". The publicity surrounding the Seattle meeting was not due only to the role of street theatre on CNN. I would argue that the

198   *Sylvia Ostry*

absence of apathy also reflects a broader and more pervasive secular change in the industrialized countries — an alienation from the elites. The American sociologist V.O. Key Jr. wrote about the "permissive consensus" of the earlier postwar decades (Key, 1963). While the broad public had little detailed knowledge of international policy, opinion polls demonstrated consistent support for the government's foreign policy which would, of course, include trade policy. As Key noted: "when a permissive consensus exists, a government may be relatively free to work out a solution of the issue or it may be free to act or not to act" (ibid., p. 35). The deference to government, and more broadly to the establishment as it was then termed, underlay the permissive consensus and has dramatically declined since the 1960s in all Organisation for Economic Co-operation and Development (OECD) countries as many recent analyses of opinion polls have demonstrated (*The Economist*, 1999). Perhaps the Uruguay Round was the last gasp of the permissive consensus — and barely that.

There are many reasons for the decline in deference to government and to the elites — a word of opprobrium in North America and even in Europe today. One major cause has been the much wider access to information and the role of the media. In the context of trade policy, the latest stage in the information technology revolution — the accelerating use of the Internet since the mid-1990s as exemplified by the role of the non-governmental organizations (NGOs) in Seattle — will be described shortly. But another development, more difficult to discern, is also at work: the ongoing debate in academia about the impact of trade on growth and equality and the growing emphasis on issues of values and morals is generating a change in the climate of ideas which is likely, over time, to have an effect on policy. As Keynes famously observed: "The ideas of economists and political philosophers, both when they are right and when they are wrong, are more powerful than is commonly understood. Practical men, who believe themselves quite exempt from any intellectual influences, are usually the slaves of some defunct economist. Madmen in authority, who hear voices in the air, are distilling their frenzy from some academic scribbler from a few years back."

One of the most important academic scribblers of this century was Joseph Schumpeter whose work on the capitalist engine of innovation, or creative destruction as he termed it, is enjoying a major revival in the new growth theory. But when read today his views about the future of capitalism, as expressed in his 1942 book *Capitalism, Socialism and Democracy*, seem absurd. His lengthy and brilliantly argued answer to the question: *Can Capitalism Survive?* boils down to one word, "no". He argued that the fatal

Perspectives on the Evolution of the Global Trading System   *199*

flaw at the heart of the capitalist system is that its fundamental ethos, rationality, cannot be defended against the attacks of its progeny, the intellectual. The intellectuals, defined as people "who wield the power of the spoken and the written word" (Schumpeter, 1942, p. 147), live on criticism and their "whole position depends on criticism that stings" (ibid., p. 15). Capitalism is based on freedom so the intellectuals cannot be controlled. But the "unheroic and rationalist" defence of the capitalist is no match for the criticism that "nothing is sacrosanct" (ibid.) and renders indefensible the system's institutions.

So the weakness of the system which provides the target for the intellectuals (who, he notes, have many more outlets as books become cheaper, newspaper chains spread and radios proliferate) is the absence of an heroic and binding ethos, or set of moral values. As he so trenchantly put it: "The stock exchange is a poor substitute for the Holy Grail" (ibid., p. 137). But there it is, how wrong could he get? In the United States, at least, the Stock Exchange *is* the Holy Grail!

From the vantage point of the new millennium, when capitalism has been embraced by all but a few countries in the world, Schumpeter's dire prediction seems almost bizarre. Nor is it just capitalism that reigns supreme. Its core ethos — economics — can well boast of having invaded most of the other social sciences, a phenomenon (proudly) termed "economic imperialism" (Lazear, 1999). Even, *pace* Schumpeter, religion has not been safe from the discipline's imperial reach. For example, one can develop a really neat model of church attendance as investment under uncertainty, the uncertainty being whether or not you go to heaven.

Yet despite his erroneous forecast, was Schumpeter all wrong? Perhaps it would be unwise to dismiss the penetrating insight of his core argument about moral values. Echoes of the diatribes of his "intellectuals" can be heard daily, and certainly could be read hourly on the Internet in the weeks leading up to Seattle.

Okay, I agree that the term "intellectuals", even in inverted commas is inappropriate. Does the term "global village idiots" sound better? Or, "real nut cases"? Yet that does not trump Schumpeter's argument about the weakness of the "rationalist" defence. Unless all Americans are global village idiots, the opinion polls taken after Seattle reveal that very large majorities want the environment and labour standards included in trade agreements.[1]

These views — supported by citizens in many other OECD countries — present a formidable challenge to the WTO membership since they are adamantly opposed by virtually all non-OECD countries, who represent two-thirds of the membership. This particular north-south divide is but one aspect of the second transformative change: the *political economy* of trade policy making.

The Political Economy

Before the Uruguay Round, the GATT model of reciprocity, irrationally mercantilist though it was for Manchester liberals, worked very well. Border barriers erected in the disastrous thirties were reduced in negotiation rounds and trade grew faster than output. The model was premised on the idea that protectionist lobbies could be offset by export interests. In these rounds developing countries negotiated mainly to secure unreciprocated market access to OECD countries. Most lacked the expertise and analytical resources for trade policy making but that did not really matter much because of the nature of negotiations.

The Uruguay Round was dramatically different. The negotiation to launch the negotiation, as it were, took almost as long as the Tokyo Round. After repeated efforts by the Americans beginning in the early 1980s, the Uruguay Round was launched in Punta del Este in September 1986 and formally concluded in Marrakesh, Morocco in April 1994, several years later than the target completion date originally announced. The extraordinary difficulty in both initiating and completing the round stemmed essentially from two fundamental factors: the nearly insuperable problem of finishing the unfinished business of past negotiations, most of all agriculture; and the equally contentious issue of introducing new agenda items, notably trade in services and intellectual property and, though in a more limited way, investment. The Europeans blocked the launch to avoid coming to grips with the Common Agricultural Policy and a number of developing countries led

---

[1]*The Economist*, April 15, 2000, p. 26 and Harris Poll, <wto-activist@iatp.org>, April 18, 2000. See also *Business Week*, April 24, 2000, p. 202.

Perspectives on the Evolution of the Global Trading System   *201*

by Brazil and India were bitterly opposed to including these so-called "new issues". In the end, the final trade-off involved a north-south deal across the old and new issues. In exchange for improved access for agricultural and labour-intensive products, especially textiles and clothing, the developing countries yielded on the new issues and accepted the restructuring of the GATT and the transformation of the world trading system.

Although the "new issues" are not identical — obviously negotiations on telecommunications or financial services differ from intellectual property rights — they do have one common or generic characteristic. Thus, they involve not the border barriers of the original GATT but domestic regulatory and legal systems embedded in the institutional infrastructure of the economy. The Uruguay Round launched the deepening integration of the global economy. The degree of intrusiveness into domestic sovereignty bears little resemblance to the shallow integration of the GATT with its focus on border barriers. Thus, for example, the barriers to access for service providers stem from laws, administrative actions or regulations which impede cross-border trade and investment. Hence liberalization or improved access of necessity involves changes in domestic economic regulatory regimes and involves an inherent pressure for convergence. Moreover, the telecommunications agreement included a reference paper that set out a common framework for the regulation of competition in basic telecom-munications. The inclusion of intellectual property rights in the world trading system was arguably an even more radical transformation of the traditional concept of a trading system and the shift to positive regulation was even more fundamental. In the case of intellectual property, the negotiations covered not only comprehensive standards for domestic laws but, perhaps more importantly, detailed provisions for enforcement procedures to apply individual (corporate) property rights. The WTO had shifted from the GATT model of *negative* regulation — what governments must not do — to *positive* regulation or what governments must do. This new agenda will require significant upgrading of the institutional infrastructure of many (most?) developing countries: governance, education, legal systems, regulatory systems, etc.

Moreover, it is important to underline another aspect of the irrelevance of reciprocity for the developing countries in accepting the General Agreement on Trade in Services (GATS). By the end of the 1980s a major change in economic policy was underway. The revolution of what might be termed "Ronald Thatcherism" began in the OECD countries but was adopted by many developing countries, including countries in Latin America and in

Central and Eastern Europe by the onset of the 1990s. Economic reform — deregulation, privatization, liberalization — were seen as essential elements for launching and sustaining higher growth. Even without the regulatory reform thrust from the Uruguay Round, the postwar economic regulatory state was no longer a dominant paradigm and reform of key service sectors such as telecommunications and finance were regarded as essential building blocks in the soft infrastructure underpinning growth.

But the law of unintended consequences was at work. Because of the focus of attention on *economic* regulation, the negotiations on *social* regulation concerning product standards, health and safety measures and environment received little publicity and little attention from the senior policy ranks. In the OECD countries social regulation started in the late 1960s and has been accelerating since then. The OECD has called the phenomenon "regulatory inflation". One could, with a bit of a stretch perhaps, say that the postwar economic regulatory state of the advanced countries is withering away, while the social regulatory state is alive, well, and growing: a curious mix of *laissez-faire* and *laissez-regler*. Thus social regulation, covering the environment, labour, food safety, product labeling, etc., has grown by 300–400% in the industrialized countries since 1970 (OECD, 1997). This is decidedly not the case in the developing countries, nor are they likely to embrace the social regulatory state unilaterally: *au contraire!* Moreover, while the positive regulatory approach in social regulation — Technical Barriers to Trade (TBTs) and Sanitary and Phytosanitary Measures (SPS) — is more *procedural* than *substantive*, the infra-structure implications are equally demanding involving sophisticated administrative procedures law as well as highly trained scientific human resources.

Thus for many developing countries, especially the poorest, the "grand bargain" of the Uruguay Round seemed by 1999, a bum deal. They got less access than they had hoped for and the burden of the new agenda was far greater than they had understood. In Geneva during the preparatory meetings for Seattle they argued for better access in agriculture and textiles as well as an extension of time before implementation of the more difficult aspects of the "new issues" along with enhanced technical assistance, a kind of redress for the Uruguay deal. So a north-south divide was expected in Seattle. Unexpectedly, however, the meeting ended with a walkout by a coalition of virtually all the developing countries from Latin America, Asia and Africa (hardly a homogenous group) not over agriculture or textile tariffs, but because of the U.S. president's insistence on the inclusion of labour standards which would be enforced by trade sanctions. But while this proved to be the catalyst, it is important to note that the bitterest complaints of many of these countries was the "undemocratic" nature of the negotiation process.

Finally, another major difference between the GATT and the WTO is the greatly strengthened Dispute Settlement Mechanism. This new juridified system — described by some as a form of international constitutional law — will be discussed in other papers so the only point I want to make here concerns the impact on both the political economy and the process of policy making. Since the establishment of the WTO the most high-profile and contentious disputes have concerned social regulatory issues (food safety and environment) which are very sensitive in terms of public opinion. Inevitably the dispute panels and especially the Appellate Body have been forced to interpret the relevant WTO rules. And inevitably, as is the case with all courts and all legal rules, but even more so because some WTO rules are deliberately imprecise or "creatively ambiguous", the interpretation has essentially involved these internationally appointed judges making law, that is, defining the boundary for domestic policy space and reinforcing the perception, and reality, of the intrusive nature of the new system (see Bronckers, 1999; and Sampson, 2000). It is this "sovereignty" thing that has enraged and emboldened a new group of policy actors, the NGOs, and will have a significant impact on the policy process.

The Process

> You taught me language; and my profit on't
> is I know how to curse.
>   Shakespeare: *The Tempest*

While economists and business and trade officials ponder how e-commerce will affect the market for goods and services, few seem to have given much thought as to how the Internet has and will affect the market for policy ideas and therefore the policy-making process.

We will long debate the effect of the political opera mounted by the NGOs in Seattle but it would be unwise to concentrate only on that. A major impact of the Internet has and will be to make the market for ideas contestable, a radical transformation which will affect the domestic and international policy-making process. Inexpensive, borderless, real-time networking provides the NGOs with economies of scale and also of scope by linking often widely disparate groups with one common theme. Equally important, it offers the opportunity to disseminate strategic knowledge formerly concentrated in governments and business. As is the case for all innovations there are also important positive feedback loops. The NGO network established at the Rio Summit in 1992 was used by American, Canadian and Mexican anti-North American Free Trade Agreement (NAFTA) advocacy groups and this experience was vital to mobilizing the fight against the Multilateral Agreement on Investment (MAI). The lessons from the attack on the MAI were put to use in preparing for Seattle and the Seattle experience was helpful in planning for Washington and then for a new series of demonstrations on different occasions and different locations.

An analysis of a large number of Web sites concerning Seattle and post-Seattle developments suggests that there are three broad functional categories of NGO coalitions or networks: what might be termed "mobilization networks" whose chief objective is to rally support for a specific set of activities; "technical networks" designed to facilitate and provide specific information; and networks dedicated to servicing developing countries which I call a "virtual secretariat".

Two examples of mobilization networks preparing for Seattle were the International Civil Society Opposing a Millennium Round (ICS) and People's Global Action (PGA). The ICS claimed to represent more than 1,400 local, regional and international NGOs from over 87 countries. The list is attached to their statement and includes environmentalist, religious and human rights organizations, labour coalitions, women's groups, student groups and small farmer groups who are opposed to the agri-business oligopoly, from all OECD countries and a large number of developing countries.[2] The PGA is also a very broad coalition which was dedicated to organizing a conference in Seattle on November 30, 1999, at the outset of the WTO meetings. On the Internet the conference was termed N30. The PGA describes itself as "an instrument for coordination, not an organization" and was formed in Geneva in February 1998.[3] The PGA organized a "carnival against capitalism" in the city of London on June 18, 1999. The J18 carnival, as reported in *The Daily Telegraph* (1999), deteriorated into violence, resulting in more than six hours of rioting and vandalism in the financial district.

---

[2]See <http://www.twnside.org.sg/souths/twn/title/wtomr-cx.htm>.

[3]See <http://www.agp.org/agp/en/PGAenfos/about.html>.

The mobilization networks are coalitions of a widely diverse set of NGOs often with conflicting interests. They pride themselves on their pure form of "participatory democracy" with no centre and no hierarchy. However in Seattle (and Washington) both the libretto of the carefully choreographed street operas and the sound bites on television carried a simple, common theme — anti-globalization or, rather, anti-corporate globalization and pro-democracy. The charge was that the WTO (or the International Monetary Fund or the World Bank) is dominated by the interests of transnational corporations; that rules and procedures are "undemocratic"; that it is harming the environment; and increasing inequality both within and among countries. The sound-bite versions were the slogans: "fix it or nix it"; "no new round but turnaround"; "shrink it or sink it".

So one must distinguish between the loose mobilization networks of diverse NGOs around the world and the "headquarters executives" responsible for creating and marketing the message. These headquarter organizations such as Ralph Nader's *Public Citizen* and *Global Trade Watch*; the U.S.-based *Preamble Center*; *Friends of the Earth* in the United Kingdom (which organized the ICS manifesto) were aided in logistics planning by a number of groups including the *Direct Action Network* or DAN and the *Ruckus Society*, and in press relations and media management by *Turning Point*, an NGO formed only in 1999 to produce a series of advertisements in the *New York Times* on the effects of globalization on the environment. Some analysts have argued that NGOs like these are part of a new industry: the protest business (see Jordan and Maloney, 1997).

The protest business could be a new market created by the Internet, after all technological innovation can generate wholly new products and services. It is difficult at this point in time to predict the viability of the new business but it seems to have combined three key ingredients or what I have termed the three Ms: a saleable *message,* a skillful *media* strategy and *money* (from mass-mailings and a number of philanthropic institutions, mainly American).[4] The objective is to influence the policy process through public opinion. It is very important to underline that these new actors do not resemble the distributional coalitions sparring over the division of the pie. Indeed, in the traditional version of the political economy of trade, their

---

[4]The *Chronicle of Philanthropy* (acewald@mindspring.ca) noted that after Seattle and Washington a conference of the National Network of Grant-makers drew some 350 participants to Boston to discuss why philanthropies should care about globalization and promote NGO's concerned with the issue.

support is quite irrational because of the free-rider problem associated with collective action for public goods. This definition of rationality needs a re-examination.

Following from that it is important to distinguish the prominent role of a traditional distributional lobby, the American unions in Seattle (less so in Washington) from the mobilization networks. The so-called Turtle-Teamster alliance between the unions and the greens was probably a marriage of convenience to influence American trade policy but it seems unlikely that a lasting alliance could be forged given the profound divisions between these two groups. The U.S. advantage in a period of ongoing change stems from its Exit model (as compared with the European Voice paradigm) because change is governed by an anonymous mechanism that rewards the most efficient. Winners prosper and losers appear to disappear. What was heard in the streets of Seattle was the Voice externalized, but workers of the world are more likely to compete than unite.

In marked contrast to the mobilization networks are the technical networks such as, for example, *Centre for International Environmental Law* in Geneva and Washington; the *International Institute for Sustainable Development* in Winnipeg; the *Institute for Agriculture and Trade Policy* in Minneapolis; the *International Centre for Trade* and *Sustainable Development* in Geneva; WEED *(World Economy, Ecology and Development)* in Bonn; and the *Institute for Global Communications* in Palo Alto. California which directs and supports the Association for Progressive Communication (APC) linking 15,000 NGO computers in 95 countries. It was the APC that played a major role in providing communications services for NGOs at Rio. The primary purpose of these, and a number of similar networks, is to facilitate the greater participation of NGOs in the policy process by providing a flow of strategic and technical information, very heavily weighted to environmental and legal issues. Some were present in Seattle but probably not many on the streets.

These technical groups are interested in influencing policy mainly by operating through institutional channels both governmental and intergovernmental. Events like Seattle provide an opportunity to access national delegations and network with other NGOs. One example of their operational effectiveness has been the ongoing debate over genetically modified organisms (GMO). The meeting in Montreal on the Cartagena Biosafety Protocol at the end of January 2000 was widely expected to be another Seattle but, in fact, ended in an agreement (albeit as a result of brilliantly ambiguous drafting!) (See WTO, 2000, pp. 7-9; *The Economist*, 2000a,b).

Perspectives on the Evolution of the Global Trading System   *207*

The large number of NGOs engaged in the meeting proclaimed victory, especially in inserting the precautionary principle, a very contentious subject at the WTO. *En route* to the WTO there will be a number of other steps being carefully planned, including meetings of the Codex Alimentarius, the institution that establishes international food standards recognized by the WTO.

Finally, a remarkable and recent development has been the proliferation of NGOs dedicated to providing information and undertaking advocacy on behalf of developing countries — a virtual secretariat. Examples are *Third World Network* in Malaysia with offices in India, Uruguay, Ghana, London and Geneva, and established links with other NGOs in both north and south and a wide range of publications; TWN collaborates with the *South Centre* in Geneva which is funded by LDC members with the mission of networking with other institutions "to promote south solidarity" on policy; SEATINI (Southern and East African Trade and Information and Negotiations Initiative) with several offices in African countries and funding from UNDP and UNCTAD and a mission to build the knowledge base and capabilities of African countries; *Focus on the Global South* in Thailand with a mission to link grassroots NGOs working on development issues to broader policy concerns including WTO and the Asia-Pacific Economic Cooperation Conference; and CUTS (Consumer Unity and Trust Society) in India with a research and advocacy mission in trade and sustainable development. In addition, there are also a number of northern NGOs with a focus on southern issues in the WTO such as *Rongead* (European NGO Network on Agriculture, Trade Environment and Development) based in France and funded by the European Commission, the French government and a private foundation; *Intrac* (International NGO Research Centre) based in Oxford to train NGOs in developing countries and act as a consultancy; as well as a number of traditional development NGOs (such as *Oxfam*, *Christian Aid* and other religious organizations) which are now focusing on trade and environmental issues.

This south "virtual secretariat" provided a continual flow of information on negotiations in Geneva; helped formulate policy positions on all major issues; and many of their leaders were present in Seattle. Once again, they are not a homogenous group and may differ on specific subjects but, as Seattle demonstrated, the strategic assets of information and political know-how can provide a base for a significant increase in bargaining power in the WTO.

Finally, the new prominence of the NGOs in trade policy making should be evaluated in a broader context. Thus far the American business community — in marked contrast to their activist transnational role in the Uruguay Round — has maintained a low profile with respect to WTO negotiations. Apart from the service industries, the business community in both Europe and the United States has demonstrated little in the way of what might be termed generic or systemic interest and even in the case of services the interest is sector-specific rather than cross-cutting, although that may well change over time, and perhaps e-commerce will be the catalyst. However, the current lack of activism is remarkable and one can only speculate as to the reasons. Perhaps the Uruguay Round was truly a singular event because it involved a radical transformation of the GATT system and the stakes were very high. Moreover, the global span of many corporations today facilitates direct negotiation with host governments so, ask many of them, why bother with lengthy and tedious intergovernmental negotiations? Privatization of trade policy may be an attractive option. Another factor is the restructuring of American corporations over the past decade which has required a sharper focus on a limited number of specific governmental lobbying objectives with shorter term impact on the bottom line. Thus Chinese accession to the WTO has been a top priority. (That also seemed to be the case for the U.S. government whose objectives for a new round were minimal and defensive, while the EU position was far more assertive, including new issues such as investment and competition policy.) In the absence of a multilateral option which would require a narrowing of the transatlantic divide not only over agriculture but also more fundamental issues, as the 1980s so clearly demonstrated, a revival of unilateralism, bilateralism and regionalism should not be ruled out.

To sum up, if one were asked to predict the future of the world trading system the best single word would be "uncertain". But maybe that is too terse a reply. A layman's definition of Heisenberg's uncertainty principle is: we can know where we are but not where we are going, or we can know where we're going but not where we are. So, how about Heisenberg squared as a more specific response? Yet that too is not adequate. Many lessons can to be learned from the Seattle experience. But most important is the urgent need to reform the WTO, a necessary but not sufficient condition to ensure the survival of a global rules-based trading system since there will also have to be some change in the existing architecture for international cooperation.

Perspectives on the Evolution of the Global Trading System

Governance of WTO

Policy Forum

It is not clear that the negotiators really understood the full implications of the fundamental shift in policy template marked by the Uruguay Round. However, there *was* recognition that the GATT would not provide an adequate foundation for the much more ambitious and comprehensive trading system embedded in the negotiating agenda. Thus, the Punta Declaration established the Functioning of the GATT System or the FOGS negotiating group. FOGS was promoted by a coalition of middle powers, both developed and developing, since institutional issues were not a priority for either the United States or the European Union. The middle powers recognized that the alternative to a rules-based system would be a power-based system and, lacking power, they had the most to lose.

Nonetheless, the goals of FOGS were relatively modest: to improve the adaptability of GATT to respond to accelerating change in the global economy through improved surveillance of country trade policy and regular ministerial conferences designed to raise the public and political profile of trade policy; to improve the "coherence" of international policies by establishing better linkages between the GATT and the Bretton Woods institutions; and, most importantly, to strengthen the enforcement of the trading system's rules of the road by improving dispute-settlement arrangements. The creation of a new institution was not included among these objectives, and the proposal by Canada for a new institution, the WTO, was not put forward until April 1990. It was soon endorsed by the European Union, which had opposed stronger dispute settlement in the Tokyo Round and which had taken a position of benign neglect with respect to FOGS. The European Union became an active supporter of a new institution that could house a single, strong dispute settlement mechanism, out of growing concern about U.S. unilateralism.

Unfortunately, an attempt to establish a successor to the Consultative Group of Eighteen (CG18), the GATT's policy forum for debate and discussion, failed and the WTO is a minimalist legalist institution — a Mercedes Benz without gas. Since Seattle the issue of the governance structure of the WTO has again hit the radar screen but only in terms of the negotiation modality. That issue, while important, is rather like putting the cart before the horse. If there is no understanding let alone agreement on the broad and complex policy issues the best negotiating structure in the world will not help much.

A brief review of the history of the CG18[5] is useful in the light of the current debate on the structure or governance of the WTO. It was established in July 1975 not by trade ministries but as a result of a recommendation of the Committee of Twenty Finance Ministers after the breakdown of Bretton Woods. (The Committee of Twenty also established the IMF's Interim Committee). Originally termed the GATT Management Group, the name was changed because its purpose was to provide a forum for senior officials to discuss policy issues and not to, in any way, challenge the authority of the GATT Council. The composition of the membership was based on a combination of economic weight and regional representation but there was provision for other countries to attend as alternates and observers or by invitation. Each meeting was followed by a comprehensive report to the GATT Council. In 1979 the Council agreed to make CG18 permanent but it was suspended in 1990 by the director-general (for reasons that have never been made public) and has never met since.

Because it was a forum for senior officials from national capitals it provided an opportunity to improve coordination of policies at the home base. And because of the creation of the Interim Committee, the Committee of Twenty felt the need for a similar body in the GATT to facilitate international coordination between the two institutions. Papers were prepared by the secretariat on important global economic issues such as, in its early years, balance of payments and related financial matters and the nature and scope of cooperation with the IMF. After the Tokyo Round the CG18 was the only forum in the GATT where agriculture was discussed and, in the long lead-up to the Uruguay Round, trade in services. Indeed the CG18 was the only forum for a full, wide-ranging, often contentious debate on the basic issues of the round. There was an opportunity to analyze and explain issues without a commitment to specific negotiating positions. Negotiating committees *inhibit* discussion because rules are at stake. The *absence* of rules is essential to the diffusion of knowledge which rests on a degree of informality, flexibility and adaptability. Thus a policy forum can promote discussion of norms, principles and concepts which may or may not underlie longer term strategies for new rules.

---

[5]*The Consultative Group of Eighteen*, MTN.GNGIN14/W15, June 1987, secretariat document prepared for Negotiating Group on FOGS.

The establishment of a policy forum (or executive committee if that term is preferable) is essential to fostering more comprehensive structural reform and should be accorded the highest priority. Since Seattle the mindset in Geneva is pretty much that the WTO ain't broke so why fix it. There has been some discussion about "transparency" and the opacity of that word has now been significantly increased by distinguishing between *internal transparency* (WTO-speak for adapting the traditional negotiating process to include more developing countries) and *external transparency* (improving access to documents, etc. and dealing with demands of the NGOs for more participation). The I-transparency issue is gridlocked essentially because of disagreement over how to design the main negotiating committee or, in other words, what weights should be assigned to economic power, numbers and geography. The so-called trade-off between efficiency and inclusion will involve delicate negotiations and is unlikely to be settled on its own but only as part of a package for a new round. Even more conflicted is the E-transparency issue and the role of NGOs. But, of course, these and many other issues could be the subject of discussion and debate in the policy forum which could meet regularly at the official level and, as required, at the ministerial level.

How would the policy forum be established? One possibility is to use the Trade Policy Review Mechanism as a formula. For the TPRM, after lengthy and difficult negotiations, an agreement was forged that different countries would be subject to different review schedules on the basis of geography and share of world trade. Thus the TPRM formula could be used for establishing a committee of reasonable size and rotating membership which would ensure that all countries and regions would be represented within a given time frame. If a formula cannot be agreed upon it may be necessary to make the establishment of the policy forum part of a new north-south package which would include the so-called "confidence-building" measures of zero tariffs for the products of the poorest countries; extension of implementation periods of some measures such as TRIMs, TRIPS and customs valuation; and, most important, enhanced technical assistance and training.

While the establishment of the policy forum would be a great step forward, it is unlikely to function effectively without an increase in the WTO's research capability. If member governments are unwilling — as they have been up to now — to provide funding other avenues should be explored such as private donors, after all Ted Turner donated one billion dollars to the UN! As was the case for CG18, it will be necessary to provide analytical papers on key issues to launch serious discussions and to improve the diffusion of knowledge in national capitals where improved coordination of policy among a number of different governmental departments and agencies is essential. If such a forum was deemed necessary in 1975 when border barriers were the main focus of trade policy, it is obviously crucial today if the system is to survive. There is no "trade" minister any longer because the domain of trade policies spans a growing range of both international and domestic policies and is linked to other policy domains such as the environment or competition policy, and so on. And the dominant global paradigm of neoliberalism is being challenged by an emerging new model, unclear and inconsistent as yet, which asserts the need to meld efficiency with ecology, equality and community. Quite a challenge!

In order to keep up to date and reasonably small in size, the WTO could not possibly generate all its policy analysis in-house. Like most research bodies today, the WTO secretariat would have to establish a research network linked to other institutions such as the OECD, the Bretton Woods institutions, private think-tanks, universities and the like. Knowledge networks are key elements in promoting cooperation and coordination and fostering the achievement of consensus. This networking should also include NGOs such as environmental groups, business groups, international labour associations and intergovernmental organizations such as the International Labour Organization and the United Nations Environment Program. The establishment of a research or knowledge network, "soft power", is also important to enhance the ability of the WTO director-general to play a more effective role leading and guiding the policy debate. In the terminology of the international regime literature the policy forum could become a broad meta-regime founded on mutually agreed basic principles and fostered by a combination of strategic assets: a knowledge infrastructure in the form of a research capability; a meeting infrastructure for knowledge diffusion, debate, peer group pressure; strategic planning and monitoring of policy performance. But no "hard power" to make or enforce rules.

Thus it is essential to underline that the new forum must not be a decision-making body and must report regularly to the General Council. Of course, as was the case for CG18, it should be able to make recommendations to the Council and proffer suggestions for further analysis or action. In reading the document prepared for the FOGS group by the GATT secretariat, one is struck by the perceptiveness and prescience of the Committee of Twenty. But perhaps an even more prescient historical footnote is the Report on Organizational and Functional Questions adopted by the Contracting Parties in 1955 which recommended that an "Executive

Perspectives on the Evolution of the Global Trading System   *213*

Committee, restrictive in size and representative in character" be established! Let us hope an executive committee will be established before 2005, after all, 50 years is more than enough.

Transparency

The GATT decision-making system worked well because there were far fewer countries and the issues were less complex. The traditional Green Room process, inherited from the GATT, has not been established by explicit rules but by a self-selection process and includes a small and varying number of participants involving the larger OECD countries and a group of middle powers; a number of the more powerful developing countries; and perhaps a few of the transition economies. The demand for change came not only from the largely excluded poorer countries, but also from Pascal Lamy, the trade director-general of the European Commission, whose term the "medieval process of decision-making" was widely quoted. A number of suggestions for structural reform have been made by trade experts (see, e.g., Schott and Watal, 2000; and Lal Das, 2000, pp. 14-16) and some minor, mainly procedural changes have been put forward in Geneva, but none agreed upon. This is hardly surprising since any significant restructuring of the negotiating committee arrangements would involve "winners" and "losers". In the absence of an agreed target date for the launch of a new round, there is no incentive for the countries now inside the "Green Room" to agree to any change. And as noted above this is not a serious matter for concern since the priority should be the establishment of a policy forum where, *inter alia*, the negotiating structure, or improved I-transparency, could be discussed and alternative proposals from a range of countries and outside experts considered.

However, the question of E-transparency (external transparency), or the role of NGOs, is much more complex and contentious and raises a number of issues concerning the WTO's institutional design. There are, broadly speaking, three main requests in the NGO's demand for democratization: more access to WTO documents; the right to observer status and to present *amicus curiae* briefs before dispute settlement panels and the Appellate Body; and more participation in WTO activities such as committee meetings, "a seat at the table", though this usually stops short of a request to be included in negotiations. Of these three, the first is generally agreed by most member countries though there will be niggling and haggling over release of some documents. Indeed the WTO has already greatly improved the access to documentation via its Web site and this is likely to expand either voluntarily or by leaks! The other two aspects of E-transparency are, however, very contentious and will not be easily or quickly resolved.

The U.S. has been the strongest proponent of "opening up" the WTO dispute procedure including the right of private parties to submit *amicus* briefs to panels and the Appellate Body. This proposal is supported not only by environmental, labour and human rights groups but also by private lawyers who specialize in international trade and by the international businesses who are their clients. Indeed, since *amicus* briefs often carry little weight in judicial decisions, it is likely that the next step for all these non-governmental actors would be a demand for the right to bring cases directly: real democracy must be based on *laissez-litiger*!

These demands are strongly rejected by southern governments and their NGOs who regard the present evidentiary-intensive and increasingly legalistic system as already biased against them. (Indeed these legitimate complaints have resulted in the establishment of a legal advisory centre housed in the WTO.) (Van der Borght, 1999). A number of these countries have voiced serious concern over the 1998 ruling of the Appellate Body in the turtle-shrimp case which opened the door to *amicus* briefs. This reaction underlines a broader complaint, not confined to southern countries, that the Appellate Body is engaged in law-making and, in this instance, taking a position in a highly sensitive political debate. As Robert Hudec asserts, a demand for "a right to appear before an international tribunal is a partial repudiation of the role being performed by national governments in those proceedings" (Hudec, 1999, p. 47).

The *amicus*/right of standing aspect of E-transparency is, of course, also related to the broader issue of the reform of the dispute settlement mechanism noted earlier. Suggestions to reduce the legalization of the WTO and even to go back to the GATT mode of diplomacy or perhaps conciliation and arbitration in the case of politically sensitive disputes deserve to be considered because the fundamental question of the boundary line between international rules and domestic policy space should be determined by governments and not by judges (see Sampson, 2000; Barfield, 1999).[6] The

---

[6]See the Meltzer Commission's *Final Report* which recommends that any ruling by the WTO "that extends the scope of explicit commitments under treaties or international agreements must remain subject to explicit legislative enactment by the U.S. Congress", Washington, DC, 2000, p. 1116.

Perspectives on the Evolution of the Global Trading System   *215*

international compact which underlay the GATT involved liberalizing trade through successive negotiations aimed at reducing border barriers; creating rules to govern and sustain the liberalizing momentum; and safeguarding domestic policy space by rules to permit temporary blockage of imports under clearly specified terms as a *buffer* or *interface* to safeguard domestic policy. That compact is, it hardly needs repeating, no longer relevant in the new global trading system. Sooner or later it will have to be renegotiated or the system will not survive. So while some redesign of the dispute mechanism is desirable (perhaps even urgent given the growing concern over sovereignty in the United States)[7] the broader debate should be launched in the policy forum as a matter of highest priority. And that debate should include the role of the NGOs in the WTO — the third issue in E-transparency.

The NGO demand for participation, a seat at the table, is the most difficult and controversial. The WTO is an intergovernmental organization and most member governments want to keep it that way. They argue that NGOs should deal with their own governments if they wish to play a role in the policy process. The response of the NGO advocates of participation is that only they have a truly transnational vision which is lacking in national governments so that, for example, "a citizen who cares very deeply about ending whaling ... will find his or her views better represented in international fora by the Worldwide Fund for Nature than by his or her own government, which has many goals it must simultaneously pursue" (Esty, 1998, p. 133). But it is not clear what the word citizen means in this context. There are no "world" citizens but only citizens of nation-states. Governments are accountable to their citizens, albeit some more so than others. How would we define accountability in the case of non-governmental organizations? And what about transparency? Who and where are their members? What is their source of funding? Are they "accountable" to their membership or to their funders? These are simply examples of some of the questions that would have to be settled before a meaningful proposal on "participatory democracy" in the WTO could be debated. But any such proposal would be

---

[7]The Meltzer Commission recommendation reflects a much wider attack on the issue of the international incursion into U.S. domestic sovereignty and is not confined to leftist NGOs and trade unions. Justice Robert H. Bork, for example, has argued that the trend towards legal globalism "may be capable of changing our Constitution" (*United Press International* April 4, 2000, re: speech to American Enterprise Institute).

216 *Sylvia Ostry*

fiercely opposed by most developing countries in the WTO, especially after their experience in Seattle.

Another complication in this debate is that there is enormous diversity among NGOs. There are operational NGOs whose main function is service delivery in developing countries. Some of these are local but others are "subsidiaries" of northern NGOs or funded by northern governments and foundations. Among the advocacy NGOs, as noted earlier, there are wide differences in focus and function between the mobilization networks in the "protest business" and the technical groups which lobby inside the system. Nor is there any agreed taxonomy among the NGOs themselves or the international institutions, especially the UN agencies with whom they have the closest contacts. And among these agencies and others such as the World Bank or the Multilateral Environmental Agreements (MEAs) there is a wide variation in the specific terms for accreditation and the nature of participation.[8]

Yet there is an interesting new development in the NGO community which might be worthy of exploration by the WTO. As their profile and influence has been heightened many positions of the NGOs have been criticized as simplistic, ignorant and driven by a need for media attention. The Brent Spar oil rig controversy is often cited as an example of a major policy shift catalysed by Greenpeace's erroneous information. But many other examples could be cited, such as the ongoing debate over GMOs as well as their attacks on the WTO and the IMF and World Bank. Of course, other actors distort and manipulate information or are economical with the truth. But if corporations engage in serious distortion and are exposed (which is increasingly feasible in the new information environment) they are accountable to shareholders. The same thing is true of governments (at least democratic governments) and of unions in democratic countries. There is no comparable constraint on NGOs or, at least, no visible or obvious one. In response to the continuing criticism — that NGOs are the only major policy actors who are not accountable — some have undertaken new self-regulatory initiatives.

Because the NGO world is so diverse and covers so many different functions, a universal system of accountability would likely be impossible. But there is now a number of examples of a code of conduct drawn up by NGOs and monitored by them, covering ethical practice, transparency,

---

[8]For a very useful review see ICTSD (1999).

Perspectives on the Evolution of the Global Trading System   *217*

funding accountability, accuracy and other factors. A comprehensive example of self-regulation at the global level is the NGO Steering Committee of the UN Commission on Sustainable Development which includes NGOs, trade union representatives and corporations.[9] This is an experiment which deserves to be closely monitored and indeed is being emulated in other UN fora. It is, in fact, part of a broader trend towards what has been called hybrid governance which involves a combination of "hard law" (implemented by the coercive power of the government or intergovernmental institutions) and "soft law" or codes of conduct which provide principles and norms for guidance and emulation.

However, these developments alone will not solve the problem of the demand by NGOs for a seat at the WTO global table side by side with national governments. Certainly it would assist the WTO in formulating more meaningful accreditation procedures for NGO participation in symposia and other fora such as TPRM meetings on a voluntary basis.[10] But even for that purpose there would need to be some concerted effort at capacity-building in developing countries whose NGOs lack the personnel and expertise to implement the codes. The charge, by some southern countries of neocolonialism is not without merit. Moreover, because the WTO is an intergovernmental organization which administers and enforces global rules negotiated by nation-states it is argued that NGOs should be involved in the policy process through national mechanisms. But, of course, because of cultural political or legal difference, not all member countries are willing to permit this. As a recent survey by Freedom House demonstrates, 58% of the present WTO membership (calculated in terms of population) can be considered democracies and after China accedes the percentage will fall to 43% (Jessup, 2000).

So what is to be done? Certainly the new experiments in codes of conduct should be monitored by the WTO and perhaps it would be useful to convene a symposium to discuss these and other ideas with NGOs, governments, unions and business. Among the most important issues to be discussed should be the national mechanisms required to involve accredited

---

[9]This and other examples are discussed in Edwards (2000).

[10]This is a proposal of the European Commission Trade Directorate submitted to a Workshop on WTO Institutional Reform sponsored by the South Center and Oxfam, Geneva, February 2, 2000. They also recommended the establishment of a WTO Parliamentary Assembly.

NGOs, parliamentarians, academics and business groups in the formulation of policy. Through discussion and peer group pressure (and considerable patience!) it may be possible to improve the "transparency" of policy making in countries which at present may well regard the term transparent governance as an oxymoron.

While establishing an Executive Committee and improving the WTO's analytic and networking capabilities would help entrench the legitimacy and credibility of the institution, these reforms alone would not do much to prevent further marginalization of many developing countries, especially the least developed. Technical assistance and more effective coordination with other international institutions will be required.

The gap between rich and poor countries has been widening over the past three decades largely due to differences in trend rates of growth of per capita income. The knowledge gap is far greater than the income gap and in the absence of change in domestic policies, as well as development policies directed at upgrading the institutional infrastructure, is bound to widen. This growing marginalization has little to do with trade, but that fact has not prevented the anti-globalization movement from blaming the WTO.

Clearly, the WTO, with very limited technical training resources (less than 1% of its budget) cannot deal alone with the marginalization problem. That may have been acceptable when trade policy was only about trade. But the much more demanding WTO agenda and the litigious and evidentiary-intensive dispute process has placed a burden on many non-OECD countries. The richer countries have access to analytical expertise at the OECD, at their home base, and also have far larger Geneva missions. So an upgrading of WTO training resources is urgently required. And this would also facilitate more effective coordination with the World Bank's efforts to improve the governance and institutional infrastructure, including legal systems and regulatory policies.

Reform of the WTO governance structure and enhanced research and training resources would help tackle the "democratic deficit" but the so-called "trade and ..." issues will require confronting the inadequacy of the postwar international architecture. In the absence of a stronger International Labour Organization (ILO) and a new environmental institution, the WTO will continue to be a magnet for policy overload.

If the objective of the American and other OECD unions is to improve working arrangements in developing countries, the mandate rests with the ILO. (If it is not, then it is a matter for domestic policy designed to ameliorate the distributional consequences of adjustment to global forces.)

Perspectives on the Evolution of the Global Trading System   *219*

But the ILO has no power of enforcement. Moreover, many of its developing country members have resisted repeated attempts to improve enforcement capacity — while at the same time opposing labour standards in the WTO. Indeed in 1997 when the director-general of the ILO proposed that the organization could act to oversee a multilateral system of voluntary social labelling the initiative was rejected by the Non-Aligned Movement (O'Brien *et al.*, 2000, p. 104). This dilemma (or hypocrisy) must be resolved and the ILO monitoring and enforcement mechanisms strengthened. But development institutions will also have to play their role since labour standards are clearly linked to growth. What will be needed, in effect, is reform of the ILO and more effective coordination with the WTO, the World Bank and UNCTAD, that is, improved coherence in international policy making which was in fact one of the objectives of the Uruguay Round, although at the time of the launch coherence was conceived in terms of coordination only with the Bretton Woods institutions.

It is worth noting that while this "macro" approach to labour standards would rest on government policy, an innovative "micro" policy is now rapidly evolving independently of government and, indeed, generated by technical NGOs. The Washington-based *Council on Economic Priorities* (CEP), is a consumer organization established in 1969. In 1998, SA8000 was launched — on the fiftieth anniversary of the Universal Declaration of Human Rights. CEP had established a separate accreditation agency (CEPAA) only the year before which developed a "social accountability" code that includes the ILO basic labour rights plus rules on wages and hours. The codes are technically designed for auditors and their development involved large corporations, unions, and NGOs. They have been endorsed by international certification agencies. Monitoring of the developing country subsidiaries of the transnational corporations which have adopted SA8000 will be carried out by a network of NGOs linked to CEPAA. While the information is designed for a consumer audience, the next step will be to involve investors, beginning with large pension funds. The core strategy of this micro policy is market-like: consumer and investor pressure will force an increasing number of firms to join the SA8000 crowd with a little help from global whistleblowers and the media! This policy innovation is very new (and but one example of a burgeoning of "soft law" projects) (see, Clapp, 1998; and Diller, 1999), but certainly it is worthy of further research, especially as it is also a spin-off from the information technology revolution. As CEP has noted, "With instantaneous media connection and the Internet

... today's remote factory scandal can become tomorrow's global headline."[11]

While labour standards have no place in the WTO the same cannot be said of environmental issues. Trade and the environment are linked in both positive and negative ways as the recent report by the WTO has clearly demonstrated (WTO, 1999b). But using trade policy as an instrument of environmental policy is both ineffective in terms of achieving environmental objection and costly interims of growth. However, in the absence of a strong environmental institution (which the United Nations Economic Program or UNEP is not) using the dispute settlement mechanism to define the boundary between domestic and international policies will not work and the WTO will continue to be under attack. Perhaps as a first step, housing all the multilateral environmental agreements in a reinforced UNEP could help the process but, in effect, only a new World Environmental Organization with a clearly defined mission, political influence, and analytic and technical resources could effectively launch the policy dialogue on the relationship between ecology and economy, including, of course, the role of trade. This will not be easy because there really are significant differences between the two models — the economic and the ecological — even if we reject both utopian formulations. The economists' concepts of maximization and trade-offs, of equilibrium, and the primacy of efficiency, yield unambiguous policy statements. A defining characteristic of the ecological sciences is uncertainty, seen most vividly today in the rapid and unprecedented changes in biotechnology. If risk cannot be accurately estimated then unambiguous assessments are precluded. Moreover, the ecological paradigm stresses the goals of equality, and community as well as efficiency so the two paradigms, even in modified versions, will not be easy to reconcile. What the eventual outcome of the debate will be remains to be seen. But an optimist would opine that where there's a political will there's a policy way. The best hope is that, unlike the Asian financial crisis in 1997, which led to much talk about architecture but little action, the ongoing assault on the global trading system may prove to be the catalyst for a serious re-thinking of global policy.

---

[11]"SA8000: Setting the Standard for Corporate Social Accountability", <http://www.cepaa.org>.

Perspectives on the Evolution of the Global Trading System

References

Barfield, C. (1999), "More than You can Chew: The New Dispute Settlement System in the World Trade Organization?", paper prepared for the International Financial Institution Advisory Commission, November 15, unpublished.

Bronckers, M.C.E.J. (1999), "Better Rules for a New Millennium: A Warning against Undemocratic Developments in the WTO", *Journal of International Economic Law* 2(4), 547-566.

Clapp, J. (1998), "The Privatization of Global Environmental Governance: ISO 14000 and the Developing World", *Global Governance* 4, 295-316.

The Daily Telegraph (1999), "Mobs Put City Under Siege", June 19, 1, 4, 5.

Diller, J. (1999), "A Social Conscience in the Global Market Place? Labour Dimensions of Codes of Conduct, Social Labeling and Investor Initiatives", *International Labour Review* 138(2), 122-128.

The Economist (1999), "Politics Brief: Is There a Crisis", July 17, 49-50.

_____ (2000a), "The Biosafety Protocol: A Conventional Argument", January 29, 95.

_____ (2000b), "Caution Needed", February 5, 69.

Edwards, M. (2000), *NGO's and Global Governance: Rights and Responsibilities* (London: Foreign Policy Centre).

Esty, D.C. (1998), "Non-Governmental Organizations at the World Trade Organization: Cooperation, Competition or Exclusion", *Journal of International Economic Law* 1(1), 123-147.

Hudec, R.E. (1999), "The New WTO Dispute Settlement Procedure: An Overview of the First Three Years", *Minnesota Journal of Global Trade* 8(1), 1-53.

ICTSD (1999), *Accreditation Schemes and Other Arrangements for Public Participation in International Fora* (Geneva: ICTSD).

Jessup, D. (2000), *New Economy Information Service*, February 4, <http://www.newecon.org>.

Jordan, G. and W.A. Maloney (1997), *The Protest Business? Mobilizing Campaign Groups* (Manchester and New York: Manchester University Press).

Key, V.O., Jr. (1963), *Public Opinion and American Democracy* (New York: Knopf), 27-53.

Lal Das, B. (2000), "Full Participation and Efficiency in Negotiations", *Third World Economics: Trends and Analysis* (Penang, Malaysia), January 16-31.

Lazear, E.P. (1999), "Economic Imperialism", NBER Working Paper No. 7300 (Cambridge, MA: National Bureau of Economic Research).

O'Brien, R., A.M. Goetz, J. Aart Scholte and M. Williams (2000), *Contesting Global Governance: Multilateral Economic Institutions and Global Social Movements* (Cambridge: Cambridge University Press).

Organisation for Economic Co-operation and Development (OECD) (1997), *Report on Regulatory Reform*, Vol. II: *Thematic Studies* (Paris: OECD), 191-248.

Sampson, G.P. (2000), *Trade, Environment and the WTO: The Post-Seattle Policy Agenda*, Overseas Development Council Policy Essay No. 27 (Washington, DC: Johns Hopkins University Press).

Schott, J.J. and J. Watal (2000), *Decision-Making in the WTO*, International Economic Policy Brief (Washington, DC: Institute for International Economics).

Schumpeter, J.A. (1942), *Capitalism, Socialism and Democracy*, 3d ed. (New York: Harper & Row).

Van der Borght, K. (1999), "The Advisory Centre on WTO Law: Advancing Fairness and Equality", *Journal of International Economic Law* 2(4), 723-728.

World Trade Organization (1999a), *Press Release* (Geneva: WTO), September 28.

_____ (1999b), "Trade and Environment", *World Trade Organization Special Studies* 4 (Geneva: WTO).

_____ (2000), *World Trade Agenda* (Geneva: WTO), February 14.

Money, Markets and Mobility

Part VII:

North American Currency Integration: Policy Panel

Engaging the Debate: Costs and Benefits of a North American Common Currency

John McCallum

Ships that pass in the night, and speak each other in passing; Only a signal shown and a distant voice in the darkness;

Henry Wadsworth Longfellow

The ongoing debate over Canada's exchange rate system has been a frustrating experience because the debate has not been joined. Like ships that pass in the night, those arguing for a common currency or dollarization have made their case with little or no reference to the counter-arguments of the other side.[1] In this paper, I try to engage the debate by analyzing the costs and benefits of alternative exchange rate regimes. While it will become clear that I have a bias in favour of the monetary status quo (a flexible exchange rate combined with inflation targeting), a serious attempt is made to consider arguments for and against this status quo, as well as to distinguish between realistic and unrealistic alternatives to the current system.

The organization of this paper is as follows:

---

[1]Participants in this debate include Courchene and Harris (1999); Crow (1996); Fortin (1999); Grubel (1999); Laidler (1999); McCallum (1999); and Murray (1999).

227

- What are the real alternatives to the status quo?
- What is the case for the status quo?
- What is the case against the status quo?
- Some pointed questions
- Conclusions

What are the Real Alternatives to the Status Quo?

A North American Common Currency Modelled on the Euro Is a Non-Starter: Europe is not North America

As is obvious to Americans and to Mexicans and others pushing for dollarization, but not, it would seem, to all Canadian economists, the truth of the matter is, for all intents and purposes, captured by a simple equation:

North American common currency = U.S. dollar

Europe is not North America. At least since the end of World War II, many Europeans have dreamed of a united Europe in order to avoid future wars on that continent. Monetary union is a logical step along that path to European unity. No one dreams of a united North America. Certainly not Americans, who hardly ever think about their North American partners, let alone dream about uniting with them. When Americans did dream about an expansion of their effective borders under the Monroe Doctrine or, to a much lesser extent, Helms-Burton, it was always with the United States clearly in charge. The European Union model, in which independent states share decision-making and sovereignty, is alien to American thinking and American history. Closely related to this is the fact that the United States is by far the dominant partner in North America, with more than 80% of continental gross domestic product (GDP), as compared with about one-third for Germany in Europe.

This is consistent with a statement by Deputy Treasury Secretary Lawrence H. Summers (dated April 22, 1999). While recognizing that the United States could not prevent a country from dollarizing, he noted that a dollarizing country would necessarily lose its seigniorage revenue (i.e., the country in question must bear the cost of acquiring the U.S. dollars that would be used in circulation). He also stated that it would not "be appropriate for United States authorities to extend the net of bank supervision to provide access to the Federal Reserve discount window, or to adjust bank supervisory responsibilities or the procedures or orientation of U.S. monetary policy in light of another country deciding to adopt the dollar". If the United States will not contemplate changing the orientation of its monetary policy to suit a dollarizing country, it is obviously light years away from according such a country any formal role in the setting of U.S. policy, let alone contemplating a move to a supranational, euro-style currency.

A Simple Pegged Exchange Rate Is also a Non-Starter in a World of Highly Mobile Capital

Nowadays many economists are of the view that countries have to be black or white. Countries must choose between a flexible exchange rate and monetary union or, perhaps, a currency board. The basic notion is that the scale of international capital flows has become so large that a pegged exchange rate will, at some point, be overwhelmed by massive one-way speculative bets.

Certainly the evidence in terms of what countries have actually done over the past decade or so supports this point of view (Table 1). As of September 30, 1999, not one Organisation for Economic Co-operation and Development (OECD) country had what the International Monetary Fund (IMF) defines as a "conventional fixed peg arrangement", meaning a peg to a currency or basket of currencies where the currency is allowed to fluctuate within a narrow band of at most plus or minus 1% around a central rate (IMF, 2000); not one OECD country. Does this not speak volumes to the non-sustainability of such a currency regime?

Three OECD countries, Denmark, Iceland and Greece, have pegged exchange rates within horizontal bands of 2.25%, 6% and 15% respectively. All other OECD countries are either free floaters (including crawling pegs) or members of the euro zone.

The only major country with a pegged exchange rate is China. Others include Malaysia, Iran, Iraq, Bangladesh, and a collection of small African, Asian and Caribbean countries. Moreover, several countries which had pegged exchange rates in 1991 (Czechoslovakia, Hungary, Norway, Sweden and Thailand) are now characterized by either a crawling peg (Hungary), managed float (Czech Republic and Norway), or independent float (Sweden and Thailand).

Engaging the Debate

Table 1: Currency Regimes of OECD Countries

	1991	1999
United States	FL	FL
Japan	FL	FL
Germany	C/WBP	MU
France	C/WBP	MU
Italy	C/WBP	MU
United Kingdom	C/WBP	FL
Canada	FL	FL
Australia	FL	FL
Austria	PEG	MU
Belgium	C/WBP	MU
Czech Rep.	PEG	FL
Denmark	C/WBP	C/WBP
Finland	PEG	MU
Greece	FL	C/WBP
Hungary	PEG	C/WBP
Iceland	PEG	C/WBP
Ireland	C/WBP	MU
Korea	FL	FL
Luxembourg	C/WBP	MU
Mexico	FL	FL
Netherlands	C/WBP	MU
New Zealand	FL	FL
Norway	PEG	FL
Poland	FL	C/WBP
Portugal	C/WBP	MU
Spain	C/WBP	MU
Sweden	PEG	FL
Switzerland	FL	FL
Turkey	FL	C/WBP

Note: FL = independent float   PEG = Conventional fixed peg
C/WBP = Crawling/Wide band peg   MU = Monetary union

In brief, the evidence of what countries have actually chosen to do, in combination with preconceptions relating to the non-sustainability of pegged rates in a world of extreme capital mobility, paints a decidedly negative picture of the viability of a pegged exchange rate in today's world.

The Real Alternatives to the Status Quo Are a Currency Board and Dollarization

If the reader agrees with the argument that neither a euro-style common currency nor a pegged exchange rate is within the realm of possibility, the two real alternatives to the status quo are a currency board and dollarization. If it is further agreed that dollarization is a non-starter politically, then we are left with a currency board as the only serious alternative to the status quo.

A currency board is as close as one can get to monetary union without explicitly using another country's currency. It means that the country in question no longer has an independent monetary policy, as it fixes its exchange rate "irrevocably" to that of a larger country. Shifts in the balance of payments must impact the domestic monetary base on a one-for-one basis, implying no discretion for the domestic monetary authorities over interest rates or the money supply. On the other hand, in contrast with dollarization, Canadians would still use Canadian dollars, and seigniorage revenue would accrue to Canada.

The two major currency boards in the world today are Argentina and Hong Kong.[2] Last year the government of Argentina was clamouring for dollarization on the grounds that the currency board offers the costs but not the benefits of dollarization. To quote from Lawrence Summers once again, "those who favour this step in Argentina believe, among other things, that under their currency board system, they have already borne most of the costs of dollarization, but they are not yet enjoying dollarization's full benefits". While Argentina has managed to maintain its exchange rate in spite of a turbulent decade, this has been at the cost of severe recessions in the mid-1990s and again in 1999. Moreover, market confidence in the continued

---

[2]As of September 30, 1999, other countries with currency board arrangements included Bosnia and Herzegovina, Brunei Darussalam, Bulgaria, Djibouti, Estonia and Lithuania.

existence of the currency board has sometimes wavered, as in September 1998 when the spread between peso- and dollar-denominated loans was nearly 400 basis points.

In the case of Hong Kong, one only has to read the daily financial press to discern that the security of the Hong Kong peg is less than complete, although the fact that Hong Kong is now a part of China certainly makes it a very special case.

In short, while a Canadian currency board would be viable, the cases of Argentina and Hong Kong suggest that currency boards may represent a slippery slope to dollarization and/or that markets may from time to time lose confidence in the government's commitment to maintain the peg. The Bank of Canada would no longer be able to act as the lender of last resort. Whether, despite these negatives, Canada would be best served by a currency board depends on the strength of the cases for and against the status quo — topics to which we now turn.

What Is the Case for the Status Quo?

Policy Discipline and Credibility Already Exist: Canada Is not Argentina

For Latin American countries with long histories of hyperinflation, dollarization has an obvious appeal: get rid of one's own tainted currency and monetary indiscipline and acquire instant monetary discipline by simply using the U.S. dollar. Canada, on the other hand, has already gone through a long and painful process to vanquish inflation and convert government deficits into surpluses. We already have at least as much policy discipline as the Americans. Witness the fact that our interest rates are lower than in the United States at every point on the yield curve (Figure 1). Moreover, Canada's success in achieving fiscal and monetary discipline under a floating exchange rate contradicts the view that floating exchange rates are inimical to such discipline. In Latin America, dollarization holds out the attractive prospect of reducing the gap between domestic and U.S. interest rates. For

Figure 1: Canada–U.S. Yield Curves
(as of March 9, 2000)

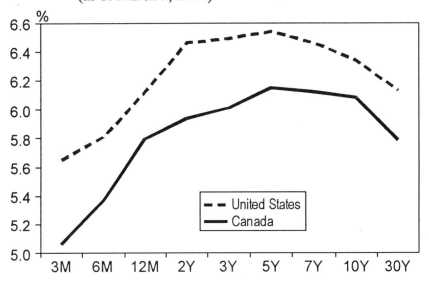

Canada, any move to greater exchange rate fixity offers the prospect of a *rise* in Canadian interest rates to U.S. levels.[3]

Flexibility Is a Good Thing — Providing One Has the Discipline

Given that policy discipline and credibility exist, flexibility is a good thing. My favourite example of such benefits is Canada's experience during the Asian crisis. As commodity prices fell sharply, resource-based economies had to take the hit somehow. Countries like Australia, New Zealand, Chile and Canada experienced significant currency declines, which offered partial mitigation of the shock coming from lower commodity prices (Figure 2). What was the alternative? Had we drawn a line in the sand at an exchange

---

[3]This is not to say that Canadian interest rates will always be lower than U.S. rates. The fact that they are today reflects Canada's lower actual and expected inflation, as well as the relatively expansionary stance of Canadian monetary policy.

Figure 2: Currency Index Against the U.S. Dollar
(Index, June 1997 = 1)

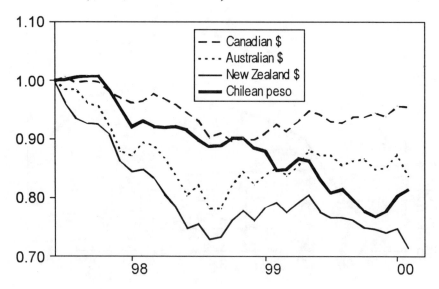

rate of, say, 73 U.S. cents, the Bank of Canada would have been forced to raise interest rates to the point where the economy may well have gone into recession. Better to take the hit through a (hopefully temporary) currency depreciation rather than through higher interest rates, job losses and recession. As things turned out, the Canadian economy enjoyed solid growth in 1999, and the currency has recovered much of its loss.

A change in the monetary order is supposed to last forever. So, in contemplating dollarization, we should have a long time horizon, say 50 years. Any number of totally unpredictable shocks can happen over such a long period of time. Do we really want to put ourselves in the straitjacket arising from the loss of control over our currency when no one can possibly know how the world is going to evolve over coming decades? Maybe we would answer this question in the affirmative if we were currently in a state of monetary and fiscal instability, but that, as we have just seen, is not the case.

Sovereignty Is a Good Thing — Canada Is not Panama

Dollarization, a common currency, and a currency board would all represent not only a major loss in Canadian policy flexibility, but also a major loss in sovereignty. We would, in a more or less permanent way, be conceding full monetary sovereignty to the United States. Even under a common currency, which I have argued would be unacceptable to the United States, Canada would have virtually no monetary sovereignty. At best we would have one vote out of 13 in setting interest rates, which is not much better than no vote at all, and in any case that one representative would be charged with acting in the interests of the entire monetary zone, not in the interests of Canada alone. Under a currency board, the only residue of sovereignty lies in the possibility that we might "let the peg go", and it is this same possibility that could give rise to punishingly high Canadian interest rates from time to time.

How To Get from Here to There?

Let us suppose the reader believes that the above arguments are outweighed by the arguments against the status quo that will be presented shortly. Suppose further, that the conclusion is that a Canadian currency board is the preferred solution. The question that will then arise is how do we get there from where we are today. It will be seen that most of the arguments against the status quo are arguments for currency *strength*, not necessarily currency *fixity*. If, for example, one believes that a weak currency induces laziness and feeble productivity performance in the manufacturing sector, then one's cause will not be served by locking in the Canadian dollar at, say, 69 U.S. cents forever. One will want to lock in at a stronger level. But how do we get to that stronger currency? The Bank of Canada could certainly raise interest rates by enough to reach a target of, say, 75 U.S. cents, at which point the currency board could be established. However, the impact of such a move could be to slow the economy to the point of recession. Alternatively, the federal government could return to large deficits with very large tax cuts and/or expenditure increases. This would generate higher interest rates and perhaps, though not necessarily, a stronger currency — but it would not be good for the Canadian economy.

Some of the fixity schemes (e.g., Courchene and Harris, 1999), modelled on the European experience, involve many years of pegging the exchange rate before moving to dollarization or a currency board, but this, as described

Engaging the Debate   *235*

earlier, runs the risk that at some point during this long period the peg will be derailed by some major shock. In short, even if the balance of the arguments is deemed to favour a currency board or dollarization, proponents must explain to us how we can get to their preferred destination starting from where we are today.

What Is the Case against the Status Quo?

The Currency and Living Standards

As quoted in the *National Post* (June 23, 1999), Thomas Courchene suggests that the large drop in the Canadian dollar from 104 U.S. cents in 1974 to where it is today represented an "enormous collapse" in Canadian living standards relative to those in the United States. While this statement may resonate with the general public, it is a peculiar comment if it is intended to imply causation, that is, the falling dollar has caused the fall in living standards. Indeed, the statement is contradicted by Courchene and Harris (1999), who write that "a falling nominal exchange rate does not necessarily indicate a falling standard of living (and neither does a rising exchange rate indicate the opposite)".

The so-called classical view is that "money is neutral". If the authorities double the money supply or halve the exchange rate, then prices and wages will adjust so as to neutralize any real effect coming from this action. For example, a doubling of the money supply will result in a doubling of all wages and prices and a halving of the currency, leaving real incomes and living standards unchanged. The so-called Keynesian view is that money is not neutral, meaning that changes in the money supply or the currency have real effects on economic activity and living standards.

I would have thought that almost all of today's economists are both "Keynesian" and "classical". In the short to medium run, monetary and exchange rate policy are likely to have real effects, but in the long run money is neutral. The strange thing about the Courchene quote is that he is talking about a period of 25 years. One would have thought that a quarter century was "long run" by just about anyone's standards.

Moreover, if one calculates the actual growth of living standards since 1974, one finds that while growth has been higher in the United States than

236   *John McCallum*

Canada, all of the Canada-U.S. gap stems from the fact that employment has grown faster relative to population in the United States than in Canada (Table 2). This can hardly be attributed to a declining dollar. The other contributors to growth in living standards, productivity and the terms of trade, have been slightly higher in Canada than the United States.

Turning now to the recent Asia-inspired drop in commodity prices, it is clear that Canadian living standards had to take a hit because we are a resource-based economy and the prices of things we produce had fallen relative to the prices of things we consume. The drop in the currency served to sustain economic activity, mitigate the shock to the resource sector, and facilitate the transfer of labour from the resource sector to other sectors. Under a regime of greater exchange rate fixity, living standards would also have had to drop because of the worsening terms of trade, but, as argued earlier, the adjustment process would have been more painful.

Table 2: Contributions to Growth in Living Standards, 1974–1998

	Canada	United States
	%	%
Productivity effect	22.4	20.8
Employment effect	18.0	27.1
Terms of trade effect	0.7	0.3
Interaction term	4.4	5.8
Sum: Total growth in living standards	45.5	54.0

Note: "Living standards" are defined as per capita nominal GDP deflated by the price deflator for final domestic demand. This can be expressed as the product of three components: real GDP per person employed ("productivity effect"), the percentage of the total population that is employed ("employment effect"), and the ratio of the final domestic demand deflator to the GDP deflator ("terms of trade effect"). The numbers shown in the table are the 1974–1998 percentage changes in each of these components, as well as the percentage change in living standards.

Engaging the Debate

As Fortin (1999) and others have stressed, Canadian living standards did suffer a major setback in the 1990s. However, the role of the terms of trade in generating this setback was certainly not dominant, accounting for 20% of the drop in the growth rate of Canadian living standards growth between the 1980s and the 1990s and 19% of the gap between Canadian and U.S. living standards growth in the 1990s.

This is not to say that the choice of currency regime has no real effect. As just argued, a flexible rate is likely to allow smoother adjustment to shocks, while it has also been argued that a flexible rate may have negative effects on economic efficiency. In particular, exchange rate flexibility may inhibit international trade or induce indiscipline or complacency on the part of both the fiscal and monetary authorities and managers in the manufacturing sector. These two issues will be considered next.

Currency Volatility as an Impediment to Trade

As a matter of pure theory, there is little doubt that currency risk is an impediment to trade. Witness the fact that many companies hedge their currency risk and that hedging is not free. It is also true that the North American economy is becoming ever more integrated and that Canadian economic relations with the United States are stronger than the relations of European member states with the other countries of the European Union.

The fact of the matter, however, is that notwithstanding currency volatility, we have experienced what can only be described as an explosion of Canada-U.S. trade over the past decade, much more than had been predicted by studies pre-dating the signing of the Canada-U.S. Free Trade Agreement (Figure 3). This, together with multi-country evidence from Jeffrey Frankel and others suggesting a very small impact of currency volatility on trade, casts considerable doubt on the practical importance of this point. At a minimum, the burden of proof lies with those whose proposals hinge on the assumption that currency risk is highly damaging to Canada-U.S. trade.

Figure 3: Canada–U.S. Trade
(in CDN$ billions)

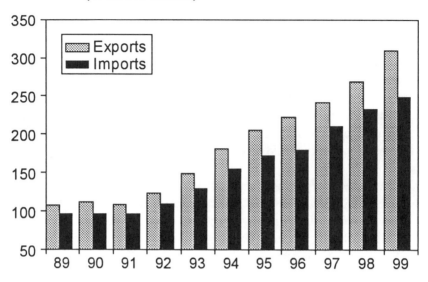

Private Sector Discipline — The "Lazy Manufacturers Hypothesis"

Another argument is that the recent weakness of the Canadian dollar has shielded our manufacturers from international competition and allowed them to become complacent in terms of reducing costs and improving productivity. While supported by anecdotal evidence and some macroeconomic correlations, at second glance this theory runs into a number of problems.

- Over the past decade Canada's productivity performance has exceeded that of the United States in most industries. More than all of our aggregate under-performance has resulted from spectacular under-performance in two industries: industrial machinery and equipment and electronic and other electric equipment. Does this mean that our manufacturers have been afflicted by extreme "laziness" in these two industries but not in the others? That seems unlikely.

- The theory carries an awkward implication. If manufacturers can be induced to become more productive by "punishing" them with a higher currency, then presumably we could get similar productivity gains from a host of alternative punishments such as mass unionization or higher taxation. If the pain of a higher currency will enhance productivity, why not pain from other sources?

- One can see how an overvalued currency that is associated with buoyant demand and full employment might fuel innovation and productivity growth (e.g., the United States in the mid-1980s or today), but this does not mean that a punishingly high exchange rate, one resulting in widespread unemployment, pressures to reduce capacity and downward pressure on wages would produce the same result.

- Even if the theory is true, it is not evident that the problem would be solved by dollarization or a currency board. If we lock in at today's relatively low exchange rate, we do little to solve the "laziness" problem. What the theory implies is a bias towards a stronger currency, not necessarily a fixed currency.

The Wave of the Future?

Some economists, notably Nobel Laureate Robert Mundell and Richard Cooper, argue that in the grand sweep of history, the world will evolve towards only a very small number of currencies, possibly three (the U.S. dollar, the euro and the yen), or maybe only one. While it is difficult to imagine the Chinese using the yen, I concede that Mundell might eventually be right. I also concede that in a world that would otherwise have only three currencies, it is unlikely that the Canadian dollar would constitute the fourth. However, to the extent the reader agrees that the benefits of the status quo exceed the costs, the implication is that Canada should not seek to speed up this grand historical process that is allegedly leading the world to only one, two, or three currencies.

Some Pointed Questions

As stated earlier, a major reason for writing this report was an attempt to engage the debate. To that end, I summarize some of the arguments in the form of a number of questions.

To Those Advocating a Pegged Exchange Rate

- Given that Canada would be the *only* OECD country with a pure pegged exchange rate and given widespread opinion that pegged currencies offer one-way bets to currency speculators, how can you put forward this option at this time of extreme capital mobility?

To Those Advocating a Currency Board, Admittedly the most Realistic Alternative to the Status Quo, or Dollarization

- Given that Canadian interest rates are now lower than U.S. rates, why do you want to pursue an option that would cause Canadian interest rates to rise?

- Had your option been in place from, say, mid-1997 onwards, do you deny that, in the face of the global drop in commodity prices, Canada would have suffered from significantly higher interest rates and, if not a recession, at least a pronounced drop in the number of jobs?

- If not, do you deny that such crises might recur in the future? If not, should we not retain the flexibility provided by a floating exchange rate?

- If you think that exchange rate flexibility is a major impediment to trade, how do you explain the explosion of Canada-U.S. trade (imports and exports) over the past decade?

- If you think that a flexible exchange rate results in fiscal and/or monetary indiscipline, how do you explain the fact that, over the past

Engaging the Debate   *241* decade, Canada has taken giant strides to greater policy discipline under a flexible exchange rate regime?

- Do you subscribe to the "lazy manufacturers hypothesis" (i.e., private sector indiscipline under a flexible exchange rate regime)? If so, how do you explain selective laziness across industries, and do you agree that mass unionization or higher taxes would be an alternative to a strong currency?

- Even if the "lazy manufacturers hypothesis" is true, the implication is that we need a stronger currency, not necessarily a fixed currency. How do we get there from here?

Conclusions

Barring major flaws in the analysis of this report and/or some pointed answers to my pointed questions, it would seem that Canada should and will continue with the monetary status quo. This conclusion, however, should not be taken to imply that everything is just fine. Indeed, in McCallum (2000), I stressed the challenges Canada faces after a decade in which Canadian living standards dropped sharply relative to U.S. living standards. It was there argued that both Canadian governments and business should address the competitiveness issue with a sense of urgency. However, the list of needed policy changes does not include a change in our system of flexible exchange rates with inflation targets.

References

Courchene, T.J. and R.G. Harris (1999), *From Fixing to Monetary Union: Options for North American Currency Integration*, Commentary No. 127 (Toronto: C.D. Howe Institute).

Crow, J. (1996), "The Floating Canadian Dollar in Our Future", in T.J. Courchene (ed.), *Policy Frameworks for a Knowledge Economy*, Bell Canada

Papers on Economic and Public Policy (Kingston: John Deutsch Institute, Queen's University).

Fortin, P. (1999), *The Canadian Standard of Living: Is There a Way Up?* Benefactors Lecture (Toronto: C.D. Howe Institute).

Grubel, H. (1999), "The Case for the Amero: The Economics and Politics of a North American Monetary Union", *Critical Issues Bulletin* (Vancouver: Fraser Institute).

International Monetary Fund (IMF) (2000), *International Financial Statistics* (February), 2-3.

Laidler, D. (1999), *What Do the Fixers Want to Fix? The Debate about Canada's Exchange Rate Regime*, Commentary No. 131 (Toronto: C.D. Howe Institute).

McCallum, J. (1999), "Seven Issues in the Choice of Exchange Rate Regime for Canada", *Current Analysis,* Royal Bank of Canada, February.

_____ (2000), "Will Canada Matter in 2020?" Lecture series *2020: Building the Future* (Waterloo, ON: University of Waterloo).

Murray, J. (1999), "Why Canada Needs a Flexible Exchange Rate", Working Paper No. 99-12 (Ottawa: Bank of Canada).

Toward North American Monetary Union

Herbert Grubel

The case for and against a North American Monetary Union is complex and multidimensional, as is evident from my own work (1999 and forthcoming) and that of others (e.g., Murray, 1999). In the limited space available to me here I will focus my analysis on some new insights relating to the merits of such a union, insights which I have gathered through discussions with a wide range of people over the last year.

By way of an introduction to the ensuing analysis, a short sketch of the proposed North American Monetary Union may be in order. I envisage that on January 1, 20XX all Canadian, U.S. and Mexican currency notes, coins and accounts are converted into a new currency, the Amero, at an exchange rate that will leave each country's competitive position unchanged. (As a relevant aside, this is essentially identical to the process of currency conversion currently ongoing in Europe.) Monetary policy in the union will be set by the North American Central Bank on whose board all three member countries will be represented according to their economic importance. The Bank will be politically independent and responsible only for price stability.

The adoption of the new currency leaves the real income and wealth of people in all three countries unchanged. The benefits will arise from the elimination of costs associated with exchange rate dealings and uncertainty and induced changes in the behaviour of politicians and economic agents. The costs from the union take the form of reduced flexibility of economic policy in dealing with economic imbalances.

245

Most economists trained since Mundell's seminal article in 1961 react to the ideas of monetary union by engaging in lengthy discussions of the costs of reduced policy options in dealing with disturbances. In doing so, they draw on the literature on optimum currency areas, which was generated in the wake of Mundell's famous optimum currency area article (1961), but with no further input from Mundell himself.[1] The papers by John McCallum (this volume) and John Murray (1999) reflect the conventional wisdom in this area. The list of characteristics required for a country's membership in a monetary union to bring benefits would include: no asymmetric shocks, similar industrial mix, high inter-country labour mobility, etc.

On more than one occasion, Mundell has noted that a list of such characteristics can be drawn up for *any* sub-region of a country and that the underlying logic inevitably would lead to the conclusion that each should have its own currency. As he further noted in his series of articles in the *Wall Street Journal* in 1998, his 1961 article used this *reductio ad absurdum* to make a fundamental point missing from Friedman's (1953) analysis contained in "The Case for Flexible Exchange Rates". Friedman's article at the time had a big impact because he equated the exchange rate to the price of foreign exchange. He then produced a powerful polemic in support of flexible prices and their role in the efficient allocation of resources. Mundell insisted that the exchange rate was not just like any other price. It was the price of money and money was not just like any other commodity, a position taken by Friedman in much of his own work.

The conventional wisdom on the subject now is that regions like Kingston should leave the Canadian monetary union only if the macro-economic benefits outweigh the microeconomic cost. Such a calculation quickly shows that it would make no sense to endow Kingston with its own money and flexible exchange rate. On the one hand it would have the benefit of easier adjustment to economic disturbances. But, on the other, the Kingston dollar would not be a successful medium of exchange, unit of account or store of value. Because of its small size, the economy would be inherently less stable, investors would demand a risk premium on funds placed in Kingston and foreign exchange trading costs would reduce the competitiveness of business. The region's real economy would not be as

---

[1]An excellent discussion and analysis of the relationship between Mundell's ideas on currencies and what passes as conventional thinking on optimum currency areas appears in McKinnon (this volume).

246   *Herbert Grubel*

prosperous if it had its own currency as it would be as part of the Canadian monetary area.

Unilateral Fixing

Let me now return to the issues facing countries which contemplate the fixing of their exchange rate to that of another country. This fixing can be achieved by a unilateral commitment to monetary and fiscal balance and unsterilized exchange market interventions, if needed. The problem with unilaterally fixed exchange rates is that the system leaves in place national central banks and currencies. These institutions are vulnerable to speculation even if they pursue very sound monetary policies and the government balances its budgets. The recent examples of the Netherlands and Austria notwithstanding, wherever and whenever unilaterally fixed exchange rates were tried, they eventually have broken down and caused great economic costs. The breakdowns tend to have been the result of some unforeseen problem like unsafe banking, economic cronyism, civil unrest, foreign policy adventures or even the election of governments opposed to markets on ideological grounds. A country can even be the victim of its own good policies if and when the country to which it links its currency suffers from monetary and fiscal imbalances or some exogenous shock, as a result of which the rate fixing country may be the victim of speculative capital inflows. The currency appreciation following such events is as damaging to economic prosperity as the depreciations, which have been the historic norm.

The recent crises in Mexico, Asia and South America are examples of fixed exchange rates being abandoned as a result of speculation in the wake of some unforeseen economic or political events. I am afraid of what might happen to the Canadian currency fixed to the U.S. dollar if the New Democratic Party formed the government in Ottawa or if Aboriginal peoples in Canada began to press their claims for compensation for historic injustices. One way speculation would be rife, regardless of the Bank of Canada's commitment to, and record of, price stability and the federal government's record of balanced budgets.

Toward North American Monetary Union

Currency Boards, Dollarization, Etc.

The inevitable problems associated with unilaterally fixed rates resulted in the design of alternative methods for fixing exchange rates. The European Monetary Agreement led to the euro, Argentina and Hong Kong have adopted currency boards, several countries are in the process of dollarization and much attention is given to proposals for monetary union in North America and the cone of South America.

Currency boards are less likely to suffer from speculative attacks than fixed currencies, but the continued existence of a central bank and national currency will always remain a potential target for such attacks if the right circumstances come along. Hong Kong and Argentina suffered from much distress as a result of the Asian crisis and the devaluation of the Brazilian real during the 1990s, respectively. Both countries had to resort to policies which compromised the integrity of their currency boards. The boards survived on this occasion, but the danger of speculators not believing in their permanence remains a constant threat.

Dollarization eliminates the risk of speculative attack but brings its own costs in terms of opposition from economic and cultural nationalists, as well as from people concerned about the loss of seigniorage and having no input whatsoever into the formulation of U.S. monetary policy.

The Case for Monetary Union

Accommodating Macro Shocks

Let me now challenge the conventional wisdom with an analysis that concludes that a monetary union produces macroeconomic benefits rather than the costs considered in the traditional literature on optimum currency areas. My insight is based on the proposition that labour market flexibility and other institutions determining the ability of an economy to adjust to shocks are determined by the exchange rate system in place. Studies like those by Bayoumi and Eichengreen (1994) reflect the historic results of national policies, which were based on the existence of flexible exchange rates. These studies ignore the fact that history might have been different under fixed exchange rates and the domestic policy constraints they impose.

I find it useful to develop this proposition by considering the recent, and much different, records of the California and Canadian economies in dealing with large exogenous shocks. During the 1990s California's shock stemmed from the end of the Cold War and the dramatic shrinking of the defence industry. Canada's shock arose out of the decline in commodity prices. How different were the reactions of labour and capital in the two countries in the face of these disturbances?

In California, labour immediately faced the reality that a depreciating exchange rate would not absorb the economic shock. Workers did not want to leave their homes, which they could have sold only at low prices in a depressed market. Therefore, they were ready to retrain and, if necessary, accept lower wages and take on longer commutes. Capital at low cost from the rest of the United States promptly moved into California to take advantage of the highly skilled and flexible labour force and the existing, superb infrastructure. California quickly returned to prosperity after the shock of losing its defence industries.

In Canada, in contrast, low commodity prices depressed the exchange rate. The shock absorber, praised by so many, did its job. Canadian dollar prices of commodities remained high and sales abroad at lower U.S. dollar prices increased export shares. Importantly, pressures on labour to adjust were blunted. New industries were not attracted by virtue of the fact that Canada was not characterized by workers flexible in their retraining and wage demands. Canada kept its traditional commodity producing industries and labour did not have to change its ways. But Canada also failed to return to economic growth and low unemployment at a rate equal to that experienced by California. There may be a very long wait for commodity prices to return to their traditional levels.

The important question raised by this tale of two countries is the extent to which the flexibility of labour and other institutions are *endogenous* to the exchange rate regime. I maintain that the greater labour market flexibility in California is, to a considerable degree, caused by the knowledge that exchange rate changes do not come to the aid of labour.

This perspective on the role of exchange rate regimes in the determination of labour market conditions is not new. The Delors Commission Report (1990) suggested that one of the benefits of the European Monetary Union was that it would result in greater labour market flexibility. There is recent support for this prediction from the fact that the introduction of the euro has not resulted in economic problems in any of the member countries linked permanently through fixed exchange rates. To the contrary, the lead story in the April 29, 2000 issue of *The Economist* was "Europe limbers up — EU companies and economies are getting fitter". The article describes how labour markets have become more flexible, mergers and downsizing of firms are making business more productive and capital markets are integrated and rationalized. Most of these developments have their roots in the monetary union and the changes in the economic environment it has wrought.

The Bayoumi and Eichengreen (1994) study is widely cited for its empirical underpinnings to the predictions of many euro-pessimists that the European Monetary Agreement will fail. The latter author recently has changed the emphasis of his writings on the subject. In an article found on his Web site (Eichengreen, 2000) he links labour market flexibility and exchange rate regimes by suggesting that dollarization is a good capstone on the series of the market reforms in Argentina. At the same time he doubts that dollarization in Ecuador will force market reforms to occur before it causes severe economic and social dislocations.

I think it is very important that increasing attention be given to the possibility that a fixed exchange rate through dollarization or monetary union will make labour markets and other institutions more flexible and able to deal with economic shocks. If this insight is correct, a North American Monetary Union would bring no macroeconomic costs and would improve the longer run performance of the economy — on top of the microeconomic benefits of lower interest rates and exchange costs.

The Politics of Currency Integration

However, even if there is the postulated link between exchange rate regimes and economic flexibility, there remains a question about speed and political will. Changes to the behaviour of labour and other institutions require time. If a North American Monetary Union were created tomorrow, would the economy become flexible quickly enough to prevent severe economic distress after the next economic shock? Will politicians let this flexibility develop or will they give in to organized labour and adopt policies that serve that interest group and shelter it from the need to be flexible?

I do not know the answers to these questions. But I can offer the following public choice perspective on the role of politicians in the determination of labour market flexibility and exchange rate regimes. Under the flexible exchange rate system, politicians in democratic countries are caught in a trap. The system and especially the competition among parties force them to make promises to special interest groups which will bring electoral support from the beneficiaries and little electoral punishment by the majority paying the costs. Politicians are forced to play these games even if they know that these policies are bad for their country. While politicians have begun to understand the nature of this trap, the point I am making is that international agreements and self-imposed restraints on their freedoms are a way out of it.

Thus, international free trade agreements like NAFTA, constitutional balanced-budget requirements, the privatization of publicly owned enterprises, central banks' commitments to price stability, membership in the IMF, World Bank and United Nations agencies constrain the freedom of parliaments. These constraints allow politicians to say "no" to their special interest group clients. Monetary union in North America would analogously remove monetary policy from the influence of politicians and serve the same purpose as the other restraints. Opposition to monetary union tends to come from politicians and bureaucrats in the old mould. They believe that their role is to substitute their own judgement on short-term issues to produce outcomes superior to those resulting under the institutional restraints just discussed. The road to economic crisis is littered with good intentions.

Conclusion

Let me close with a reference to an historical and almost ideological context for the call for fixed exchange rates and institutions capable of assuring their operation. The Keynesian model was designed to deal with the problem of unemployment. Its key assumption was that real wages are rigid in the downward direction. Inflation and budget deficits were therefore considered necessary to deal with this problem. The experience of the last 30 years has shown that inflation and deficits did not lower unemployment, but raised it. For this reason, Keynesian economics is discredited. Price stability and balanced budgets are again major policy goals.

The need for flexible exchange rates is the last important institution considered to be necessary to deal with unemployment and imperfect labour market flexibility. It is time that exchange rate flexibility joins inflation and deficits on the scrap heap of policies inspired by Keynesian economics.

Toward North American Monetary Union   *251*

References

Bayoumi, T. and B. Eichengreen (1994), "Monetary and Exchange Rate Arrangements for NAFTA", *Journal of Development Economics* 43, 125-165.

Commission of the European Communities (1990), *European Economy: One Market, One Money* (known as the Delors Commission Report).

Delors Commission Report, see Commission of the European Communities (1990).

Eichengreen, B. (2000), "Dollarization and Sense: More than the Big Mac, Coca Cola, or Levi", *Strategy and Business* (May).

Friedman, M. (1953), "The Case for Flexible Exchange Rates", in *Essays in Positive Economics* (Chicago: University of Chicago Press), 157-203.

Grubel, H. (1999), *The Case for the Amero: The Economics and Politics of a North American Monetary Union* (Vancouver: The Fraser Institute).

_____ (forthcoming), "The Merit of a Canada-US Monetary Union", conference volume to be edited by James Dean and Steve Globerman.

Mundell, R. (1961), "A Theory of Optimum Currency Areas", *American Economic Review* 51(4), 657-665.

_____ (1998), "The Case for the Euro - I", "The Case for the Euro - II", "Making the Euro Work", *Wall Street Journal*, March 24, March 25 and April 30.

Murray, J. (1999), "Why Canada Needs a Flexible Exchange Rate", Working Paper No. 99-12 (Ottawa: Bank of Canada).

Unilateral and Multilateral Currency Integration: Reflections on Western Hemispheric Monetary Union

George M. von Furstenberg

Free international movements of capital and free trade and e-trade in financial services have combined to make more regional currency consolidation inevitable. Looked at from an international portfolio perspective, the forces of financial integration now may have become so strong as to drive out low-credibility currencies. Having scores of financially small countries retain separate currencies keeps these countries excessively vulnerable to financial sector shocks that may lead to crises disrupting their entire economies. As currency proliferation has not served the causes of efficient adjustment and investment in the world economy, financial markets appear to be pushing to reduce it. Some governments, particularly in the Western Hemisphere, are ready to concede and to jettison their own money and exchange rates in favour of formal dollarization. By adopting the dominant currency in the region, a financially "small" country can avoid some of the recurring crises that are both triggered, and accompanied by, sharp changes in currency risk.

Editor's Note: This is an excerpt from the author's longer paper "U.S. Dollarization in Latin America: A Second-Best Monetary Union for Overcoming Regional Currency Risk" (available from the John Deutsch Institute).

While complete dollarization may be a useful step for the period immediately ahead, it is second-best in the short run and unsustainable in the long run even in its hemisphere. Specifically, uncooperative unilateral monetary unions, such as those brought about by formal dollarization, are inferior to the multilateral sharing model of monetary union pioneered in Europe. Dollarization involves a very high financial tribute to the United States. Countries will be reluctant to forgo, say, a billion dollars' worth in flow seigniorage year after year once they have become accustomed to monetary stability and have internalized the virtues of low inflation. Rather than paying for this lesson indefinitely, they will reclaim co-ownership and co-management of their monetary asset in a multilateral monetary union with like-minded countries. Frankel (1999); Ortiz (1999); Sachs and Larrain (1999); Stein (1999); U.S. Senate Banking Committee (1999); von Furstenberg and Alexander (1999); and Berg and Borensztein (2000) debate the issues.

At the formal level, countries that are major exporters of financial services such as the United Kingdom, Switzerland and Canada may be successful in resisting the pressures to join monetary unions, at least over the medium term. As such, they are explicitly excluded from the ensuing analysis. Nonetheless, while unilateral monetary union (or dollarization) may not appeal to Canada or Canadians, such a union could be a stepping stone towards some version of multilateral monetary union more congenial to Canada.

In what follows, the first section focuses on pressures leading to unilateral monetary union (or dollarization). This will be followed by a comparison of unilateral and multilateral models of regional currency integration, including an analysis of why unilateral dollarization is unlikely to be stable over the longer term and why it will tend to evolve in the direction of monetary union.

The Short-Lived Appeal of Unilateral Monetary Union

If currency consolidation can indeed make a major contribution to the development and stability of a number of developing countries, how might it be achieved safely and equitably? In open, international economic and investment markets, a financially small currency is increasingly hard to shelter against competition from the best-managed currency denomination in the region: use of the latter yields the greatest service potential and the deepest liquidity and lowest funding costs around. In principle, every country, regardless of size, has a right to its own, homemade, monetary base by virtue of the national product of its citizens that gives transactions value to this base. Yet if the country is small and wide open to international financial flows, it may encounter growing difficulties with continuing to exercise that right for its national currency if it acts alone. Regulations and restrictions affording local currency protection are up against more and more rules of international finance and investment and trade-in-services liberalization. The local money may still be needed to pay wages, taxes and retailers, and local banks may have to keep it on their balance sheet if the government says so. Yet all the big financial transactions and contracts will eschew denomination in an internationally obscure and volatile denomination that has little liquidity or accounting use.

Buffeted and made expensive by country and currency risks even when kept on a strict regimen of internationally prescribed best practices, the small currency loses out to a currency that is in wide international use. Thus there is creeping eurozation at the eastern and southeastern periphery beyond the 12 current members of Euroland and creeping U.S. dollarization in many other countries, particularly in the Western Hemisphere. This imposes first the risks of bi-monetarism on a country in which two moneys with variable exchange rates co-exist in a manner that cannot fully be hedged in many facets of ordinary economic and financial life. It then poses the question of formal dollarization by which the U.S. dollar would become sole legal tender in the country to rid it of the vulnerability associated with the uneasy co-existence of two moneys. The attraction of taking this extra step would also lie in further cost savings for top-quality borrowers, who need not be sovereigns. For example, in the second half of 1999, Argentine banks charged about 12% interest on U.S.-dollar-denominated loans to prime domestic loan clients when the comparable loan rate in the United States was a little over 6%. Would the rate charged by Argentine banks have been closer to the former or to the latter rate if the country had been completely U.S.-dollarized? Surely much closer to 6% than 12%, provided Argentina's banking system had strengthened to the point of being able to attract low-cost funds from home and abroad, and to identify credit risks. Even if the locally-owned part of that system does not strengthen but shrivels away under foreign competition, qualified borrowers increasingly will be able to choose from loan suppliers and securities' underwriters from throughout the region

Unilateral and Multilateral Currency Integration   *255*

in a way that is now assisted by standardization and the Internet. They need not bear the cost of using low-credibility local intermediaries who must try to pass on their high funding costs or go out of business.

If currency consolidation is indeed indicated within several regions, the question becomes what alternative to their own currency small countries should pursue without surrendering something of value — their domestic transactions base — for nothing. Though multilateral monetary union may not be on offer, it is clearly superior to the unilateral kind in this regard. For not just their fool's gold of national monetary-policy sovereignty but genuine national income is lost when financially small countries end up importing or renting the money they use. They then pay in goods and services exports and through interest payments on foreign loans for something they could have, by prudent policy and international cooperation, for free.

Foreign holdings of U.S. currency are now separately identified and reported in the official accounts for the international investment position of the United States published in the (U.S.) Department of Commerce's *Survey of Current Business*. A member of the Board of Governors of the Federal Reserve System (Meyer, 1999) recently rejoiced that, "with about $300 billion of U.S. currency in the hands of foreigners, the United States earns roughly $15 billion per year in seigniorage". The last figure is twice the current U.S. budget for non-military foreign aid[1] and could soon be triple or quadruple.

It may be useful to elaborate further on what the United States stands to gain from dollarization. National currency, being subject to strictly enforced government "copyright", can be viewed as part of a country's marketable and exportable intellectual property. Foreign use indirectly involves the payment of "royalties" to the United States. Even though paper money costs the U.S. monetary authorities next to nothing to produce physically, foreigners have to pay full value in goods to acquire it, or to relinquish interest earnings or make interest payments as long as they hold it. (Of course, U.S. taxpayers do not get the greenbacks for free either, but whatever seigniorage profits and interest savings they provide as non-tax receipts for their own government they get back in lower taxes or increased government services.) In addition, dollarization gives a significant competitive advantage to those, mostly U.S.-owned, financial institutions that have the widest and

---

[1] Budget of the United States Government, *Fiscal Year 2000*, p. 143. The spending proposed for international development and humanitarian assistance is $7.6 billion.

lowest-cost access to federal funds and a dollar-deposit funding base in the United States. As U.S.-owned, home-country-regulated, multinationals take over more and more of the financial business of dollarized countries, that system in fact becomes subject to U.S. controls and extra-territorial application of its sanctions and directives to some degree. So while external dollarization is good business and good politics for the United States that can easily draw nationalistic cheers (e.g., Barro, 1999), the question is whether it is also the best the Latin American and Caribbean countries can do by and for themselves in the medium and long run.

One of the risks of wider adoption of foreign money as sole legal tender is that the quality of that money may decline on account of a change in the originating central bank's management incentives. Because unilateral monetary union gives the currency-issuing country taxing power over the other countries in the region, this power could be enhanced through somewhat higher average rates of inflation. For in a unilateral monetary union, the currency monopolist in the region can impose (i) an inflation tax and (ii) a real growth tax on other countries, as detailed below. By contrast, multilateral monetary union internalizes, and thereby discourages, incidence of the inflation tax and frees peripheral countries from a tax on economic growth that would otherwise be implied by their dependence on a foreign source for their currency growth. In addition, the financial convergence produced by deep economic and regulatory integration in a multilateral monetary union makes currency demands, along with what needs to be done to preserve approximate price stability, much more predictable than for the region covered by unilateral monetary union. For this reason, the latter may be expected to produce somewhat higher and more variable inflation rates than the former type of union on average for given degrees of national inflation aversion.

Under unilateral as opposed to multilateral monetary union, the peripheral countries depend on the sole currency-issuing country in the region for the maintenance of real currency balances. For this reason, the centre country will have an incentive to tax the peripheral countries through accommodating somewhat higher average levels of inflation than it would be inclined to tolerate otherwise. In other words, the objectives governing the management of the supply of high-powered money by the issuing country may be affected by opportunities to garner foreign-source income from domestic seigniorage. The extent to which the avoidance of inflation will be compromised in the issuing country on account of there being both foreign and domestic demand for its currency depends on the perceived domestic welfare costs of inflation and on the constraints imposed by international currency competition among the few regional currencies that will remain.

Under unilateral monetary union, the centre country benefits not only from the existing but also from any increased demand for real currency balances that accompanies financial development and economic growth in peripheral countries of its region. These countries will have to reduce absorption and generate higher net exports of goods and services (or costly capital imports) to be able to afford higher imports of foreign currency. If the financially small countries in a region are specialized in production or produce Armington-type goods that face finite elasticities of foreign demand, they will incur some deterioration in their equilibrium terms of trade when their money is imported rather than home-produced. Such deterioration is equivalent to a tax on imports and a subsidy of exports causing a loss of real income to domestic residents. This reduction in real consumer income, which could have been produced equivalently by a domestic tax making up for the loss of seigniorage proceeds from money creation reveals the real cost of importing money to the small country. This cost is to be incurred year after year as long as the unilateral monetary union is maintained.

It is doubtful that this continuing sacrifice of national income and output will remain economically worthwhile and politically defensible indefinitely once living under unilateral monetary union has taught the peripheral countries in a region to adopt prudent fiscal and financial policies and the benefits of living with low inflation. However, it is not yet clear how soon feasible alternatives to dollarization that are credible to financial markets and individual money holders could emerge. Since multilateral monetary union is the capstone of economic integration and of all the joint arrangements in a region, it cannot be pushed beyond that region. This would prevent the European monetary union (EMU), for instance, small European possessions aside, from reaching into Latin America or the Caribbean even though (unilateral) eurozation of a few of the smaller or southern countries in the Western Hemisphere, while not particularly likely or practical, would not be categorically excluded.

Realistically it appears therefore that the United States must either eventually evolve a model of a U.S. dollar-based monetary union whose features are increasingly multilateral, or South American countries, led by Brazil and Argentina, ultimately will be tempted to sponsor a separate multilateral monetary union for their mutual benefit. At least one scattered harbinger of the former strategy already has come into view.

First Steps to Making Dollarization more Attractive

Recently, there has been a legislative proposal to permit the United States to provide some financial support for formal dollarization of reformed countries in the Western Hemisphere. The *International Monetary Stability Act* of 1999, S. 1879, introduced November 8, 1999 and referred to the Senate Committee on Banking, Housing, and Urban Affairs, for the first time indicates that the U.S. Congress could be willing actively to encourage dollarization. The Act recognizes that official dollarization of the Western Hemisphere is not easily attained or subsequently sustained without some financial consideration being given to the dollarizing countries. It is emphatic about the Federal Reserve System having no obligation to act as lender of last resort or to consider the economic conditions of dollarized countries when formulating or implementing U.S. monetary policy.[2] But it offers partial conditional compensation for the loss of seigniorage by the dollarizing country.

Compensation is to be given for 85% of the interest forgone by a country that exchanges its own holdings of U.S. Treasury securities for Federal Reserve notes (currency) for the purpose of official dollarization. Such a country would receive a free allocation of consols for taking the final step. In other words, no compensation would be granted for seigniorage lost by pre-existing informal dollarization of a country, and the compensation to be offered for going all the way with dollarization would be fractional. Compensation also would be insufficiently adjusted over time for the especially rapid growth of currency holdings expected in dollarized *developing* countries. Furthermore, the spirit of unilateralism prevails in some other respects on the U.S. side, as the consols to be issued to the dollarizing country may be declared null and void under certain conditions other than de-dollarization. These conditions are unlikely to remain fixed at the hands of the U.S. Congress and the administration when penalizing or pressuring an officially dollarized country becomes politically attractive for any reason. For instance, when Panama became a target of U.S. official wrath in 1988–89, it was clamped into financial stranglehold by the United

---

[2]Of course, if the economic conditions of dollarized countries affect U.S. financial markets and the global demand for U.S.-produced high-powered money appreciably, the Federal Reserve could not help but factor the economic conditions of dollarized countries into its deliberations even when adopting a purely selfish perspective.

Unilateral and Multilateral Currency Integration   *259*

States using its control of dollar flows and of assets with U.S. banks. Interest on the consols may also be attached under what could be a broadening list of conditions. Congressional staffers (Schuler and Stein, 2000, p. 9) have touted "[t]he latitude that the Secretary [of the Treasury] has [as] one factor that should induce countries interested in official dollarization to cooperate fully with the United States". Although representing progress towards a concept of making formal dollarization less costly to the adopting countries in certain respects, the Act thus still would leave dollarization a clearly second-best form of currency consolidation. This leads naturally into a discussion-cum-analysis of, arguably, the first-best form: monetary union.

Unilateral versus Multilateral Models of Regional Currency Consolidation

Countries that wish to use a strong international currency as their own can do so only through a costly unilateral act unless they are both prepared and allowed to become partners in a multilateral monetary union. However, the requirements for gaining membership in a multilateral monetary union are fairly strict. Even when such a union is developed outside Europe, qualifications may include achieving Maastricht-type norms of fiscal rectitude and low inflation. Candidate countries would have to resolve their internal conflicts over tax effort and incidence and over government spending policy so that they could show that they have learned to live without the option of monetizing fiscal deficits to paper over such conflicts. A country must also maintain fixed exchange rates with the union it seeks to join for long enough to demonstrate the appropriateness of the terms of conversion to a common currency. If its commitment to stability is credible, it will be rewarded with interest rates that are indicative of deep financial integration with the union even before joining, indeed, as a condition for joining. At the same time, moral hazard and cross-subsidization arising from excessive risk pooling would be contained by the cost of providing emergency liquidity to troubled institutions continuing to be borne nationally and not multilaterally.

Given the rigours of preparing for any multilateral monetary union that involves deep integration and confident interlinking of financial systems, some countries might be tempted to opt for a quick fix by choosing unilateral monetary union rather than attempting to qualify for the multilateral kind.

For instance, in its former state of disarray, Ecuador could not possibly be admitted to any integrated monetary grouping. When it dollarized formally, as a disorderly succession of its Presidents had proposed in January 2000, such an act was the default solution remaining after hyperinflation, and not a reward for having achieved economic stability or fiscal problem resolution and financial development. During the same month, Estonia made noises, judged to be disagreeable by the European Union's president, about adopting the euro unilaterally rather than working to qualify for joining the EMU some years down the road. Hence some countries may choose unilateral monetary union over the rigors and reforms of preparing for a superior alternative although an eventual conversion to the multilateral form may be intended. Genberg (1999, pp. 26-27) has made the interesting observation that once accession to an existing monetary union is expected, as in Greece, Denmark and Sweden, there will be widespread substitution of the expected future, for the current national, unit of account, so that there is a relation between currency substitution and prospects for monetary union in any event. Exchange rate fluctuations are not helpful when the prices of more and more domestic goods and services come to be fixed in euro in the expansion zone of Euroland, or in U.S. dollars in the Western Hemisphere.

Many applaud complete dollarization, the least adaptable and least giving form of monetary union, as more stable and efficient than carrying on with heavily protected, poorly maintained, and ultimately doomed mini-carriers of monetary services, particularly in South and Central America and in the Caribbean. Others would say that taking a dangerous toy away from a small country is all to the good without acknowledging that its customer base should be worth something. Dornbusch (2000), for instance, has urged "unconditional surrender, close the central bank, [and] give up funny money" in this regard.

Multilateral union, while more demanding, is also much kinder to small countries and promises systematically lower rates of inflation than joining a monetary union unilaterally, as per unassisted formal dollarization. It does not expropriate their national monetary asset through annihilation and replacement with a foreign money. Rather it transforms this asset from a national to a multinational form and makes it whole in the process. For even if a country had lost part of the domestic component of its monetary base, and hence part of its national seigniorage, through currency substitution to the dominant international currency in the region, its seigniorage share would be based on estimates of *all* of the common currency circulating within it after monetary union. The Deutschmark notes which account for 10 to 20%

Unilateral and Multilateral Currency Integration   *261*

of Poland's currency supply together with U.S. dollars and zloty, now still yield a flow of seigniorage benefits to Germany — via interest saved on the debt which the German government otherwise would have issued. However, this foreign fraction will become part of Poland's own euros and seigniorage share once Poland has joined the EMU[3] as well may happen in the course of the next decade. In addition, the head of Poland's national bank (NBP) then will have a seat on the Governing Council of the European Central Bank (ECB), like every other member, thus acceding through a merger of equals to a body whose principles and rules are already set. Financial and banking systems, once cleaned up and properly provisioned and mutually supervised, will start to mesh throughout a wider European monetary region, so that even country risk will drop sharply. Poland, incidentally, has had a per capita GDP that was about the same in 1997 as that of Mexico at the prevailing average exchange rates. Hence multilateral monetary union need not be a rich-country exclusive: If one of these countries can qualify for such a type of union, then so perhaps can the other. Ultimately qualified borrowers will be able to choose from loan suppliers throughout the region in a way that is now assisted by the Internet. The most highly rated among them need not bear the cost of depending on low-credibility local financial intermediaries or share their government's (low) credit rating.

The process of implementing monetary union in Europe has revealed that the country with the most internationally respected currency in the group, Germany, may help confer credibility by implanting its proven culture of monetary stability in the entire group, as Corsetti and Pesenti (1999, pp. 300, 312-313) elaborate. Yet it "pays" for inculcating its core principles by yielding on many peripheral matters, such as banking and fiscal structure, and personnel appointments, to its partners in Euroland. Hence, within a multilateral monetary union, there is a partnership of give and take.

---

[3]This statement applies to the extent that Poland's future capital share in the ECB, which is the seigniorage distribution key based 50% on its share of population and 50% on its share of GDP, mirrors its share of high-powered euro-money demanded.

Why Dollarization May not Be Sustainable Indefinitely

A unilateral monetary union is not anchored in international treaties or binding undertakings but predicated on the convenience of the adopting country. Once the 33 OAS member countries of the Western Hemisphere roughly to the south of the United States have been completely U.S. dollarized long enough to be used to world-standard stable prices, there may be nothing, not even the market, to stop them from eventually seeking to leave the unsettled state of unilateral monetary union with the United States. For seigniorage recapture and self-respect, they may try to form a multilateral sub-union of their own by creating popular demand for changing legal tender, tax and unit-of-account rules. With some nudging, they thus may be able to induce their public to swap U.S. dollars for a new common currency minted and printed by a future Latin American and Caribbean system of central banks. It is worth quoting what Mundell (1978, p. 32) had to say on this point a generation ago:

> The LDCs have been shut out of the seigniorage from global monetary expansion ... Since most of the individual countries are too small to form their own "Eurobanks" on a global basis, their best chance is to combine their resources in the creation of a counterpart to the dollar and the proposed ECU.

Forced de-dollarization, of the kind practised in Mexico during the crisis of 1982 when there was forced conversion of dollar-denominated bank accounts at below-market exchange rates (Lustig, 1992, p. 25; Gruben and Welch, 1996, p. 399), is unthinkable in open financial markets. In free financial markets governments can not guarantee the successful launch of a new common currency that is deconsolidating an existing unilateral monetary union whose lead currency will continue to be in wide international use. Yet those markets may accept Latin American countries' sharing a hard currency other than the U.S. dollar eventually. It appears unrealistic to think that increasingly confident countries like Brazil, Argentina and Chile will accept and then stay with U.S. dollarization for much of the present century no matter how "American" it will be. Even Mexico, whose determination to keep down the dollar portion of its money supply appears to be flagging, could eventually come to resent dollarization. Such a formal step would tax

Unilateral and Multilateral Currency Integration   *263*

it more than 1 billion dollars per year[4] right now, and then more each year as the demand for currency keeps growing with the economy, compared with enjoying the flow of seigniorage from all the currency used inside the country. The model of shared control and ownership of the type pioneered in Europe is more sustainable as it contributes to the wealth of a plurality of nations and does not just make the monetary wealth flow from the periphery to the centre, or *e pluribus ad unum*.

Summary and Conclusions

Free international movement of capital and free trade and e-trade in financial services have combined to make regional currency consolidation inevitable.

Compelled by the high and volatile currency risk premiums incurred in doing business in, or hedging, low-credibility denominations in open financial markets, advocacy of rapid dollarization, in some cases of this entire hemisphere, has spread beyond the United States. Business and government groups in countries from Argentina to Ecuador, El Salvador and Mexico openly have expressed interest in formal dollarization. This advocacy is spurred by the desire to shed exposure to interest- and exchange-rate pressures and crises in which a rise in the currency risk premium imparts the equivalent of a strong adverse supply shock to the entire economy.

While complete dollarization may indeed be a useful step for the period immediately ahead under these conditions, it may be viewed as distinctly

---

[4]Mexico's monetary base, consisting almost entirely of peso currency, has been equal to about 3.5% of Mexico's GDP in recent years (Banco de Mexico, 1999, p. 237). Adding U.S. dollar bills in Mexico would raise this percentage to around five. At an interest rate of 5.5% otherwise earned on U.S. government securities, the annual cost of complete dollarization would be equal to 0.275% of Mexico's GDP. With that GDP estimated at around $460 billion for 2000, the annual loss of seigniorage would start at $1-1/4 billion. This figure is expected to rise every year at about the same rate as GDP so that the discounted present value of all the seigniorage lost under just three decades of dollarization could easily be 20 times as large. Hence, in terms of seigniorage forgone, the present cost of a unilateral decision to dollarize and to remain dollarized for 30 years would be $25 billion for Mexico.

second-best in the short run and unsustainable in the long run even in this hemisphere. Specifically, uncooperative unilateral monetary unions, such as those brought about by formal dollarization, are inferior to the multilateral sharing and co-determination model of monetary union pioneered in Europe. Hence regional currency consolidation may have to evolve towards some form of multilateral monetary union, even if it should remain U.S. dollar-based in the Western Hemisphere. Staying with uncooperative dollarization ultimately involves too high a tribute to the United States. Countries will be reluctant to continue paying billions of dollars' worth in forgone seigniorage once they have become accustomed to monetary stability and have inter-nalized the virtues of low inflation. Rather than paying indefinitely for this lesson, they will reclaim co-ownership and co-management of their monetary asset in multilateral monetary union with like-minded countries.

Eventually, therefore, unilateral monetary unions will be doomed and destabilizing unless they evolve towards a multilateral form from within. It is time for the United States to take a careful look at Europe's multilateral model of monetary union and to develop a variant that could remain beneficial for the Western Hemisphere as a whole in the long run. Until then, there is no transplanting the European model to American monetary union, or matching EMU with an American monetary union. Prolonged lack of a multilateral option then leaves financially small countries in the Western Hemisphere worse off than those in the vicinity of Euroland.

References

Banco de México (1999), *The Mexican Economy 1999*, Banco de México, Mexico d.f., annual.

Barro, R.J. (1999), "Let the Dollar Reign from Seattle to Santiago", *Wall Street Journal*, Midwest edition, (March 8), A18.

Berg, A. and E. Borensztein (2000), "The Dollarization Debate", *Finance and Development* 37(1), 1-6.

Corsetti, G. and P. Pesenti (1999), "Stability, Asymmetry, and Discontinuity: The Launch of European Monetary Union", *Brookings Papers on Economic Activity* (2), 295-358.

Dornbusch, R. (2000), "When Funny Money is No Joke", *Financial Times*, January 3, 13.

Frankel, J.A. (1999), IMF Economic Forum, "Dollarization: Fad or Future for Latin America?" <http://www.imf.org/external/np/tr/1999/TR990624.HTM>, 2-6.

Genberg, H. (1999), "EMU and the Changing Structure of Macro Risks", *Swedish Economic Policy Review* 6(1), 7-33.

Gruben, W.C. and J.H. Welch (1996), "Default Risk and Dollarization in Mexico", *Journal of Money, Credit and Banking* 28(3, pt. 1), 393-401.

Lustig, N. (1992), *Mexico: The Remaking of an Economy* (Washington, DC: The Brookings Institution).

Meyer, L.H. (1999), "The Euro in the International Financial System", *Federal Reserve Bank of Minneapolis: The Region* 13(2), 25-27, cont. 58.

Mundell, R.A. (1978), "The Santa Colomba Conclusions 1978: 'The Great Adjustment Controversy' ", *Economic Notes by Monte dei Paschi di Siena* 7(2-3), 3-33.

Ortiz, G. (1999), IMF Economic Forum, "Dollarization: Fad or Future for Latin America?" <http://www.imf.org/external/np/tr/1999/TR990624.HTM>, 6-10.

Sachs, J. and F. Larrain (1999), "Why Dollarization is more Straitjacket than Salvation", *Foreign Policy* (116), 80-92.

Schuler, K. and Stein, R. (2000), "The Mack Dollarization Plan: An Analysis", paper presented at the Federal Reserve Bank of Dallas conference on "Dollarization: A Common Currency for the Americas?", March 6.

Stein, E. (1999), "Financial Systems and Exchange Rates: Losing Interest in Flexibility", Inter-American Development Bank, *Latin American Economic Policies* 7 (Second Quarter), 8.

U.S. Senate Banking Committee (1999), *Citizen's Guide to Dollarization*, Committee Documents Online – 106th Congress. This online publication contains two additional pages of references. See <http://www.senate.gov/~banking/docs/reports/dollar.htm>.

von Furstenberg, G.M. and V. Alexander (1999), "The U.S.-Dollarization Approach to Regional Currency Consolidation: Second-Best in the Short Run, Doomed in the Long Run", *Problemas del Desarrollo* 30 (119), 105-117.

Money, Markets and Mobility

Part VIII:

The Future of National Currencies

Exchange Rate Systems and Currency Integration: Prospects for the Twenty-First Century

Robert A. Mundell

Editor's Introduction

Robert Mundell concluded his Nobel Lecture with the following observations:

> Today, the dollar, the euro and yen have established three islands of monetary stability, which is a great improvement over the 1970s and 1980s. There are, however, two pieces of unfinished business. The most important is the dysfunctional volatility of exchange rates that could sour international relations in time of crisis. The other is the absence of an international currency.

With Robert Mundell's permission, what follows is an edited version of a much longer paper entitled *Currency Areas, Exchange Rate Systems, and International Monetary Reform*. This paper was delivered at Universidad del CEMA, Buenos Aires, Argentina, April 17, 2000. The full version is available on Mundell's Website at: <www.columbia.edu/~ram15/cema2000.html>.

The present paper addresses these two issues.

In the remainder of this introduction, I replicate the relevant aspects of the spirit, if not the precise wording, of Bob's introduction to his Universidad del CEMA paper.

Strong currencies are the children of empires and great powers. The dollar became the greatest currency of the twentieth century because it was comparatively stable and America became the superpower. As the U.S. came to dominate the international monetary system, the dollar elbowed out gold as the principal asset of the system. When General de Gaulle in the 1960s wanted to attack the United States and its "dollar imperialism", he served up a demand for a return to the gold standard, the only conceivable rival to a dollar-based system. The U.S., of course, wouldn't hear of it and after the Americans went off gold in 1971 the dollar, instead of sinking into oblivion, had no rivals. What killed the gold standard was the financial supremacy of the United States and its delivery system, the dollar.

Currency power configurations, however, are never static. They evolve along predictable lines with the growth and decline of nations. Looking at the international monetary system as a constantly-evolving oligopoly, it seems inevitable that a countervailing power would develop to challenge the dollar. Now, at the close of the "American century", the euro has appeared as a potential rival, the countervailing power, to the dollar.

The advent of the euro may therefore turn out to be the most important development in international monetary arrangements since the emergence of the dollar as the dominant currency shortly after the creation of the U.S. central bank, the Federal Reserve System, in 1913. But there are several hurdles to negotiate. For example, globalization is much less efficient than it might be because of some telling defects in our international monetary system. The inefficiency of our current "system" is reflected in the hundreds of trillions of dollars of wasted capital movements that cross international borders every year solely as a consequence of uncertainty over exchange rates. In this respect we should look with more respect at the international monetary system at the beginning of the century when the gold standard provided a highly efficient international monetary system. If we cannot recreate that system, we should at least be able to duplicate it with a more modern alternative.

Toward this end, the analysis begins with a focus on currency areas and currency unions. This is followed by a discussion of alternative monetary rules. The analysis then shifts to Canada and addresses the pros and cons of dollarization and its alternatives. In the penultimate section Mundell draws on Keynes' *A Tract on Monetary Reform* to highlight the need to pursue both internal and external stability. In the concluding section, "Towards a World Economy", Mundell elaborates on his preference for a *common* world currency, if a single world currency proves unattainable.

This concludes my editor's introduction, and we now join the Mundell analysis "in progress", as it were.

Currency Areas and Currency Unions

The growing importance of the dollar was a little-noticed event at the start of the twentieth century. The advent of the euro is the big news at the close. It has led to a redrawing of the map of currency areas. When the euro was created it instantly became the second most important currency in the world.

Monetary mass is important. Judging by its monetary mass the euro is more important than the yen, but less important than the dollar. The eleven countries of the EU that went into monetary union have a GDP of something like seven trillion dollars, which compares to a U.S. GDP of nine trillion and Japan's GDP of five trillion dollars.

These currency areas are of course evolving. The euro area — and possibly the dollar area — are getting bigger. The euro area has eleven countries now, and Greece is already on board. In a few years we can expect the EU-12 to be joined by Britain, Sweden and Denmark. By the end of the decade, the EU will contain several more of the thirteen countries that have been invited to apply for membership. Though meeting the requirements pose a significant challenge, entry into EU and EMU represents the best chance they have to lift their standards of living toward EU levels and most of the countries are working very hard towards meeting them.

In ten years, therefore, there could be as many as 28 member countries in the European Union. In addition, thirteen CFA franc countries in West and Central Africa, since 1946 tied to the French franc, are also tied to this euro area. If, as seems plausible, a few countries in North Africa and the Middle East also choose to fix their currencies to the euro, the euro area could easily contain as many as 50 countries with a population exceeding 500 million and a GDP substantially larger than the United States within a decade.

Turning to Asia, what about the chances of a currency area forming in that burgeoning continent? There has been some discussion of a kind of

Exchange Rate Systems and Currency Integration   *271*

APEC Monetary Fund, and even a currency area based on the yen. But the European model of single currency would not fit at the present time in Asia. The stumbling block is not economics but politics. The single-currency project of the European Union became possible because Europe became a security area, i.e., an area within which war could be, in all probability, ruled out; the long-standing Franco-German enmity was laid to rest. An Asian currency area would be possible in the future only if a formula could be found for correcting the political disequilibrium. An Asian Monetary Fund could, however, be a catalyst for constructive political developments and might pave the way eventually to a viable Asian currency area.

We mustn't forget the dollar! The dollar area will also expand over the next ten years. Some countries in Latin America and elsewhere will be inclined to follow the path pioneered by Argentina in 1991. They will be using the dollar as an anchor for their currency, just as countries in Africa and elsewhere will be using the euro as an anchor for their currencies. The dollar area is likely to expand. New currency areas may form. A currency area has been talked about for Brazil, Argentina, Uruguay and Paraguay, the countries that form the Mercosur Free Trade Area. It might even be possible to establish some kind of currency union for all the Americas, a kind of Latin dollar.

There are many models for currency areas. The tightest form is a single currency monetary union. Dollarization represents a hegemonic approach to a single-currency monetary union. The alternative of a new currency created by political agreement (such as the euro, or Herbert Grubel's plan for an "amero" in North America), involves a high degree of political cooperation and sharing of sovereignty. Multiple-currency monetary unions could include currency board arrangements, and a parallel currency system, both of which could be looked at as stages toward a more complete single-currency monetary union. The less tight monetary unions depend for their success on credibility.

When one fixes exchange rates to a currency area, there are many ways to buy credibility for the exchange rate commitments. One way is to build up reserves. After nine years with a currency board — an enormously important step toward monetary stability — Argentina still has credibility problems especially in times of crisis. These problems are reflected in high interest rates in dollars. But I doubt Argentina would have any problems with the credibility of its exchange rate if it had the foreign exchange reserves of Taiwan. Taiwan has more than US$100 billion in foreign exchange reserves. That's very high for a country of 22 million people, and it has to be high partly because of the political isolation and vulnerability of Taiwan. Nevertheless, larger rather than smaller currency reserves are a big plus, and that's one alternative. By and large, I believe most countries have too few currency reserves.

Convertibility is a unilateral fix. Another way to achieve credibility is through a bilateral approach. Would a monetary agreement with the U.S. help? The answer is yes, certainly. If the Federal Reserve or Treasury guaranteed the peso rate whenever there was a run on the peso it would be unnecessary for interest rates to rise. There is a problem (or worry), though, about moral hazard. Instead of building up reserves or keeping to the strict requirements of a currency board, the country might rely on the guarantee to do the job! The U.S. might be more willing to give Mexico a guarantee, because Mexico is part of NAFTA and Mexico's problem is thus the U.S.'s problem too. There might be more willingness still if Mexico had a currency board with the United States. I could well imagine the Federal Reserve being willing to guarantee this in a time of crisis, and to avoid the need for a complete dollarization of the economy with which that was associated.

The Importance of Monetary Rules

At the Davos meeting of the World Economic Forum this year [2000], the governor of the central bank of a Latin American economy said that one thing we have learnt from the recent currency crises is that fixed exchange rates are no good! I think nothing could be more opposite from the truth. I'm sure that he was thinking of pegged rates.

It is essential to make a distinction between "pegged" and "fixed" rates. The difference lies in the adjustment system. A fixed rate is one where intervention in the exchange market is allowed to affect the money supply. If a country has a surplus the central bank has to intervene to prevent its currency from appreciating; it buys foreign exchange in return for domestic currency. The increased supply of domestic currency increases the reserves of the banking system and increases domestic expenditure, automatically correcting the surplus. Similarly, a deficit requires intervention in the opposite direction. The central bank sells foreign exchange to support the domestic currency and gets back domestic currency, which reduces the reserves of the banking system, the money supply and domestic expenditure,

Exchange Rate Systems and Currency Integration

and thereby corrects the deficit. A fixed exchange rate system is a monetary rule that contains a self-adjusting equilibrating mechanism of the balance of payments.

By contrast, a pegged rate is an arrangement whereby the central bank intervenes in the exchange market to peg the exchange rate but still keeps an independent monetary policy. To maintain an independent monetary policy it may offset the monetary effects of intervention in the exchange market by sterilization operations. For example, when a country has a surplus, the central bank must intervene to prevent the pegged rate from appreciating; it buys foreign exchange and supplies in return domestic currency, increasing reserves as before. But now, to neutralize the monetary effects of intervention, the central bank sells an equal quantity of domestic assets (say government bonds) canceling the effects on the money supply. It then makes a separate decision to expand or contract the money supply, increase or lower interest rates. The result is that there is no mechanism of adjustment for ensuring balance of payments equilibrium. This is in fact the automatic practice of the U.S. and British central banks (in the event of intervention in the exchange market), which adhere to flexible rates. A pegged exchange rate may be defended as a temporary expedient in certain situations, but as a general rule, because it matches an international system with a domestic monetary policy, it involves conflicts that lead to crises and breakdowns. Pegged exchange rates sooner or later always collapse.

The gold standard was a good example of fixed rates. Countries defined their currencies in terms of weights of gold and exchange rates represented the ratios of the weights. When gold left the country (a balance of payments deficit) the money supply shrunk, domestic expenditure (total spending) was cut and the deficit was corrected; when it arrived, the money supply increased, expenditure rose and the surplus was eliminated. The system got into trouble only rarely when, as during war, countries turned to deficit finance. Success of the gold standard depended of course on fiscal prudence.

Panama is a contemporary example of a country that has a fixed exchange rate. Its currency is the balboa, which is a metallic currency equivalent to and freely convertible into the U.S. dollar. Upon its creation as a country, in a treaty with the United States, the government committed itself not to create a paper currency. As consequence, Panama is "dollarized" and the paper dollar circulates freely in Panama and is equivalent as legal tender and unit of account. Panama could of course at any time abrogate this "self-denying ordinance" but has chosen not to because the dollar anchor has given it a degree of monetary stability that is quite unique in Latin America.

The balance of payments is kept automatically in equilibrium by the unhindered exports and imports of dollars, shrinking and expanding the money supply in the process, and Panama gets the same core inflation rate as the United States.

A currency board represents a rigorous form of a fixed exchange rate system. A country fixes the exchange rate between its currency and an important foreign currency. Intervention to keep the rate fixed automatically affects the money base of the system. When a central bank buys (say) dollars, it pays for them with national currency and that expands the reserves in the monetary system; similarly, a sale of dollars contracts reserves. A currency board lets this intervention determine monetary policy, and it works automatically to preserve equilibrium in the balance of payments: a deficit, for example, leads to a contraction of the money supply, which lowers expenditure and corrects the deficit. Currency boards were commonly used in small countries or colonies of the great European empires of the twentieth century but they have made a come back in independent and much more important countries today. Several of the transition countries of Central and Eastern Europe have used currency boards as an anchor for their monetary policy, and Hong Kong's currency board has been in place since 1983. But the outstanding example in the modern world is, of course, Argentina.

It is worth taking time out to reflect on why "currency boards", as a special case of fixed exchange rates, have come back into fashion. It is mostly because of the common confusion between pegged and fixed exchange rates. Largely because of the way international economics has been mis-taught in many of our schools and our international financial institutions, fixed exchange rates have been identified with pegged rates; i.e., a system with a built-in mechanism of re-equilibration has been confused with a system with no adjustment mechanism at all. The practice is reinforced by the absurd classification of exchange rate arrangements in the *IMF International Financial Statistics*, which lumps together (amidst several other confusions) under the same system — "currency pegged to the US dollar" — Panama and Iraq! This misinformation has cast discredit on the phrase "fixed exchange rates" which has become mixed up with "pegged" exchange rates so that, to avoid confusion, some writers now speak of a "currency board" in order to describe a fixed exchange rate system that lets the balance of payments influence the money supply in an equilibrating way.

Argentina, for example, does not have a currency board in the sense that this term was used before World War I. But it has a fixed exchange rate system with an automatic adjustment mechanism, governed by the Convertibility

Exchange Rate Systems and Currency Integration   275

Law that every new peso created is backed by one U.S. dollar. Under convertibility, Argentina by and large gets the U.S. inflation rate, modified according to the differences in the Argentine basket of goods in the price index. Currency boards represent one extreme end of the spectrum of fixed exchange rate systems. Other viable fixed exchange rate systems that differ substantially from currency boards are those of Austria and the Netherlands, two countries that kept their currencies fixed to the DM.

Let us come back to the question which has been posed in much of the literature: Should countries have fixed or flexible exchange rates? But to me it is not a good question. First of all it is not clear what "fixed" exchange rates mean in the question, so that economists who debate the issue are often talking about quite different animals. How many times have I heard young (and sometimes old) economists rant on about the superiority of flexible rates over "fixed" exchange rates, proving their case by pronouncing as a theorem that fixed exchange rate systems always break down! The alert student will see this theorem as an oxymoron.

But even if "fixed rates" refers to truly fixed rates, the question is a terrible one. As I defined it, a fixed exchange rate is a monetary rule. It's a rule that gives the country the monetary policy of the partner country. How can you compare a fixed rate, which is a monetary rule, to a flexible rate, which is a non-committal absence of a monetary rule? Fixed exchange rates imply a precise monetary policy that will give the country the inflation rate of its partner countries. By contrast, a flexible exchange rate is consistent with any monetary policy at all — hyperinflation, hyperdeflation or price stability! You can only legitimately compare a fixed rate, which is a monetary rule, with other monetary rules.

The proper question is, I think, what is the best monetary rule? What variable should be fixed? Should it be a currency fix? A currency fix would fix the domestic currency to a currency, or a basket of currencies. Should it be a commodity fix? A commodity fix would anchor the domestic currency to a commodity (e.g., gold) or a basket of commodities (inflation targeting). Should it be a monetary fix? That would stabilize the level or growth rate of some definition of the money supply. Which of these three systems is the best? Just asking the question in this way should caution against glib and dogmatic answers. The choice of monetary rule depends on the size configuration of countries. Some countries don't have the option of fixing the exchange rate.

Some countries are too small not to fix, but at least one country is too large to fix! The United States cannot have a fixed exchange rate. What currency would it fix to? You can fix the Canadian dollar or the Mexican peso to the U.S. dollar (not a bad idea!), but you can't fix the U.S. dollar to the Canadian or Mexican currencies. If there were a single world currency, you could never have a currency fix! With a single world currency, the only choice is between inflation targeting or monetary targeting.

The choice between inflation- and monetary-targeting depends on the inflation rate. Monetary targeting comes into its own in cases of hyper-inflation and at very high inflation rates, say over 3 per cent a month. Very high inflation rates are typically caused by budget deficits financed by the central bank. Stabilization policy depends on getting the rate of monetary expansion down.

After inflation has been brought down below 3 per cent a month, inflation targeting becomes a superior rule. Monetary targeting is too heavy-handed a weapon for fine-tuning at low rates of inflation and it is completely dominated by inflation targeting. Every country that has tried it has found out sooner or later that the ratio between monetary growth and inflation rate fluctuates too much to be relied on. Some leading countries continue to publish monetary "targets" they have tended to become predictions rather than policy determinants. Quite apart from their use as targets, however, it must always be remembered that monetary aggregates contain important information about the economy.

At low inflation rates the serious choice is between inflation targeting, using a goods-and-services basket, and exchange rate targeting, using a currency basket. With a commodity basket, a country is free to choose its own inflation rate. Its inflation target rate is a matter of national preferences. By and large, however, the major currency areas — the dollar, euro and yen areas — have adopted 0–2 per cent as the inflation target and there are strong arguments for inflation rates to remain within this range. Alternatives outside this range tend to be arbitrary and readily subject to change.

Stability of the inflation rate is an important policy goal and low inflation rate targets produce in general more stable inflation rates. But if a country wanted to maintain a higher inflation rate than that which prevailed in one or more of the major currency areas, it would have to rule out the possible alternative of a fixed exchange rate.

Argentina's system can be contrasted with Chile's. Argentina gets the inflation rate of the United States by fixing its peso to the dollar, and it has been successful in that respect for nearly a decade. Chile, by contrast, has managed to use inflation targeting with a considerable degree of success, and achieved a good record on growth, but it has nevertheless had to rely on

Exchange Rate Systems and Currency Integration

controls over capital movements. It remains to be seen which method will be more successful in the long run.

Capital controls are not necessary if uncertainty over the exchange rate is eliminated. Remember the eleven European members of EMU that will soon be twelve when Greece comes in. The eleven countries now have an absolute fix of the exchange rate and they have no need for controls over capital movements. It is the fix that gives you market freedom, if you can find an appropriate currency to which to fix!

. . .

Central Banks, Dollarization and the Maastricht Conditions

While the Europeans are completing their transition to a currency union, recent discussion in the Americas has been about the benefits of dollarizing. Dollarization and its alternatives are options open not only to Latin America but to other countries with substantial trade and connections to the United States, such as Canada. The same arguments have been applied to Canada and thus our examination of the merits and costs of dollarization in Canada will generally apply to most nations in Latin America.

The interest in dollarization stems at root from the belief that the central bank movement has been a failure. People need to be reminded that central banks are in most countries a comparatively recent phenomenon, a product of the 1920s or 1930s. It is true that the Riksbank in Sweden and the Bank of England were created as early as the late seventeenth century. But most central banks in the world were creatures of the twentieth century and, specifically, the period after World War I when the international gold standard had broken down. Even the largest economy (by far) in the world did not have a central bank until the Federal Reserve System was created in 1913. Most colonial countries had currency boards or allowed their commercial banks to manage the gold standard.

Central banks were introduced to fulfill a deeply-felt need. Even under the gold standard, periodic crises had created a demand for a more "elastic" monetary system, and the central bank became an instrument of that elasticity. In time of crisis, when gold was flowing out, the central bank

278   Robert A. Mundell

could mitigate the harsh effects of contraction by the provision of domestic credit, sterilizing the effects of gold outflows. There was of course a danger: if carried too far, sterilization would undermine the adjustment process and confidence in the gold parity. The Federal Reserve System was created to eliminate defects in the U.S. banking system but during the process, the "solution" created new problems with which the System was ill-prepared to cope.

With the instability of gold during World War I and its aftermath, new arguments appeared for central banks. Rather than submit to imported price fluctuations under the gold standard, a country could set up its own central bank and use it to create a managed currency. In an age where colonialism was beginning to be unpopular, a central bank as well as a national currency could be looked upon as a badge and confirmation of sovereignty. It was not realized until much later that these central banks would become instruments of inflationary finance under the thumb of the ministry of finance or treasury.

The Bank of Canada was a comparatively young central bank, created only in 1935. A quick glance at its subsequent history will set the stage for a discussion of dollarization. During World War II, the Bank of Canada served as a handmaiden of the Ministry of Finance, assisting in the war effort by providing credit to the government that doubled the price level. (In this respect the Bank was no better and no worse than its peer group, the Federal Reserve and the Bank of England.) The traditional parity of the Canadian dollar with the American dollar was maintained by exchange controls and "austerity" in the post-war period. After September 1949, following the great 30 per cent devaluation of sterling, Canada devalued by 10 per cent. However, after the opening of hostilities in Korea, capital inflows swamped the monetary authorities and they reacted, not by returning to parity (it would have focused attention on what could be called the mistake of 1949), but by moving on to floating exchange rates. This was in violation of the IMF charter, but Canada was given permission to float pending its determination of a new parity. By accident, therefore, Canada pioneered in the development — for what would become a G-7 country — of floating exchange rates.

The Canadian dollar was kept strong, at a premium over the U.S. dollar, by the Bank of Canada's tight monetary policy, but it proved to be at the expense of growth and caused excess unemployment. In the early 1960s, the Canadian authorities came to believe that the Canadian dollar was overvalued and the Minister of Finance announced its determination to use the resources of the Bank of Canada to depreciate the rate. This action proved to be a mistake as the bottom fell out of the market. In a panic, the

Exchange Rate Systems and Currency Integration

authorities reacted by supporting the rate at US$0.925, fixing the rate at that level and drawing on the International Monetary Fund. The Canadian dollar was then kept fixed throughout the rest of the decade, and during this period Canada experienced the U.S. inflation rate and the great growth boom of the United States. In 1970, however, in the midst of the U.S. recession of 1970–71, the Canadian dollar was again set loose, and it promptly appreciated. Since that time Canada has had a floating exchange rate. The experience from 1970 until the present therefore constitutes a useful test case of the efficiency and effectiveness of flexible rates. In fourteen of the twenty years between 1972 and 1991, Canada had a higher inflation rate than the United States, but in the 1990s, the Canadian inflation rate has been in general lower than the American. The Canadian dollar, however, which had once in the 1970s been as high as US$1.07, fell to a (so far!) all-time low of US$0.62 in 1998. A fixed exchange rate would obviously have given Canada a lower rate of inflation over the period. At the same time Canada's employment rate and growth rate were in general significantly lower than those in the United States and Canada, contrary to the long-term pattern, did not participate in the magnificent boom that got its start in the early 1980s. The prima facie evidence is that Canada has paid a price for its flexible exchange rate in the form of a poorer economy.

Now let us consider dollarization. One quick and brutal way to accomplish it would be to abolish the Bank of Canada. If you abolished the Bank of Canada, and destroyed all the Canadian dollars in existence, what would Canadians do? First of all, they would have suffered a capital loss and would feel poorer. They would need a new money and it would be natural for them to turn to import the currency south of the border, the most important currency in the world. Of course Canadians would have to earn U.S. dollars by generating an export surplus or by going into debt. This would involve a real cost, which is a factor that on balance must be taken into account. Putting that issue aside for the moment, Canada would have the same money as the United States, the same price level and inflation rate, and the same interest rates. Trade between Canada and the United States would soar and Canada's standard of living would converge toward that of the United States. The two countries would become much more closely integrated economically. Instead of having a purely local currency, Canadians would now participate in the benefits of a world currency.

The case for dollarization rests not just on the gains from monetary integration but also on the fact that American monetary policy is better than Canada's. In 1974, the Canadian dollar was as high as US$1.07, but it fell

280   *Robert A. Mundell*

in 1998 to a low of US$0.62 cents. In this respect the Canadian currency was more like the Australian dollar, which depreciated from US$1.5 in 1974, to around US$0.50. Both central banks arrogantly thought they could improve upon U.S. performance when the United States inflation rate increased, but both subsequently did much worse.

The gains from dollarization are substantial if, as can generally be assumed, it implies a better monetary policy in addition to the gains from a world-class currency. But what about the costs, which have to be balanced against the benefits. There are three costs: One is the loss of seigniorage. The second is the loss of a national symbol. The third is the loss of sovereignty arising partly from the fact that the United States would not adjust its inflation rate to take into account the policy interests of Canada. The importance of these costs are likely to differ between countries, but would have to be weighed against the advantages of a monetary policy that, I am assuming, would be superior as well as the benefits from using in a world-class currency.

What would happen if suddenly the whole hemisphere became dollarized? It would surely result in a great increase in the gains from trade and investment and probably economic growth. The gains would be greater the more countries participated. Whatever gains Argentina might capture due to dollarization would be much enhanced if Chile and Brazil and other countries joined. Similarly, Brazil would gain additionally if Argentina and Chile were dollarized. Dollarization of the hemisphere would represent a considerable gain to all the countries in the hemisphere, including the United States.

Of course it is necessary to anticipate objections. A clever economist might say: "We don't need complete dollarization. Why not create a central bank and create some of our own money and have 50% dollarization. Every country could have its national dollar, convertible into U.S. dollars, saving both seigniorage and national face!" A Latin American dollar freely convertible into U.S. dollars would give Latin America the best of both worlds.

Theoretically, this alternative is an attractive one. The problem arises from the vicissitudes of human nature, always hoping to get something for nothing. Back in the 1920s, when Edwin W. Kemmerer, Professor of International Finance at Princeton University, was helping to create central banks all over Latin America, no one anticipated that they would be transmogrified into instruments of inflation, handmaidens of the fiscal authorities. If central banks were created to produce national dollars, what would prevent them from exceeding the limits of prudence and rendering the national currency inconvertible? How can we prevent history from repeating itself? It would be

Exchange Rate Systems and Currency Integration   *281*

necessary to impose some statutory limit on the fiduciary component of the backing for domestic money.

If there existed a single world currency (say gold, for example, as in the past), countries would always have an incentive to economize on the expense of gold payments by bank money or national currencies, the pattern historically since the seventeenth century. Even if countries agreed to prohibit national currencies they would take steps to economize on the use of foreign currency and find money substitutes at home, creating an inflationary bias in the world economy. You would get a gradual decline — or more exactly a slower rate of growth — in the demand for money that would, if not taken into account, create more inflation than otherwise.

If dollarization were good for Latin America, would it not be even better for the entire world? Let us suppose that the whole world were dollarized! Essentially, then, the world would have a common currency and a world central bank called the Federal Reserve System. As long as the Federal Reserve kept to its policy of stabilizing the American basket of goods — representing between a fifth to a quarter of world output — it would have the merit of being a very stable currency, more stable even than the gold standard or its bimetallic predecessors.

There is, of course, always a danger that Federal Reserve policy might lapse into the inflationary pattern of the 1970s or (much less likely) the deflationary pattern of the 1930s. But these historical episodes have produced their lessons and are not likely to be repeated. In the discussion below, I shall assume that U.S. monetary policy continues to be as exemplary as it has in the recent past.

The benefits from a world currency would be enormous. Prices all over the world would be denominated in the same unit and would be kept equal in different parts of the world to the extent that the law of one price was allowed to work itself out. Apart from tariffs and controls, trade between countries would be as easy as it is between states of the United States. It would lead to an enormous increase in the gains from trade and real incomes of all countries including the United States.

Another dimension of the benefits from a world currency would be a great improvement in the monetary policies of perhaps two-thirds of the countries of the world. The benefits to each country from a stable currency that is also a universal currency would be enormous. If the whole world were dollarized, there would be a common inflation rate and similar interest rates, a considerable increase in trade, productivity and financial integration, all of which would produce a considerable increase in economic growth and well-being.

Two arguments against dollarization relate to the transfer of seigniorage and the political barrier or "cost". Global dollarization would involve a transfer of seigniorage to the United States, greater than the already substantial seigniorage gained from the use of the dollar as an international reserve asset and money. The seigniorage transfer could be substantial, perhaps amounting to more than $100 billion per year. But the seigniorage issue is not insuperable. The bill proposed in the U.S. Senate by Senator Connie Mack represents one way the seigniorage issue could be handled. An alternative approach would be to set aside the seigniorage profits for international public uses.

The political issue or cost is more difficult to quantify. Countries would have transferred monetary sovereignty to the United States in return for a better money and (probably) monetary policy without receiving any share of a global sovereignty. Unlike members of the euro area, which have a share in the ownership and control of the central bank, members of the dollarized world simply transfer sovereignty to another country.

An analogy may help to make this issue clear. Many countries in the world are poorly managed. By contrast, the United States is well-managed. Why not turn over the tasks of government to the United States? By internalizing the problem of foreign relations, military conflict would be eliminated and the gains from disarmament put toward an improvement in welfare. The U.S. government as the world government would be a force for stability and peace! But whatever the potential gains, how much of the rest of the world would be willing to scrap their sovereignty for membership in an American Empire?

The costs and benefits of dollarization are not independent of the number of countries that participate. With economies of size the gains are larger when more countries participate, and thus economic gains would be greatest if the entire world were dollarized. But in the other direction consider costs that arise when only a part of the world is dollarized. If major countries stay outside the dollarized zone, exchange rate volatility appears as a new problem. When there are two or more blocs, as in the present, dollar, euro and yen currency areas, getting locked into a dollar area that is appreciating (or depreciating) strongly against the other currencies would impose substantial adjustment problems.

Taken from the starting point of a barter economy, dollarizing is easy. In the absence of an existing currency, people would be quite willing to

Exchange Rate Systems and Currency Integration   283

import a foreign currency to fill its monetary requirements. History is replete with examples of countries that have used a foreign currency. Most of the colonies in the Americas used Spanish, Portuguese, English, or French currencies — in some cases all of them — over that period. There is no need for Maastricht-type conditions in a barter economy, because if you have a barter economy the government has no means of creating an unbalanced budget or an erring monetary policy. Once the economy is dollarized, and people start to use dollars, the new monetary economy makes it possible for the government to make mistakes. But because the government can't print any money, it can't have an unbalanced budget. It can borrow and run a deficit, but it can't run an inflationary deficit. It can run deficits up to the limit of its borrowing capacity, but discipline is assured without any Maastricht type conditions.

But in our actual economies, the problem is different. The experience of Europe is instructive. Monetary union would have been easy immediately after the Hague summit in December 1969 because the European currencies were fixed to the dollar and had converged to dollar variables and therefore one another's; under the Bretton Woods arrangements countries knew that it was dangerous to run budget deficits that would threaten convertibility. But monetary union was not politically possible in the first years and by the time the international monetary system had broken down, in two steps in 1971 and 1973, countries lost their convergence around the dollar. As a consequence of flexible exchange rates, the European countries went their own way and coordinated policy became much more difficult. The Maastricht conditions were imposed as a result of the undisciplined policies of the 1970s and 1980s and the commendably-stern insistence of the Bundesbank on fiscal and monetary rectitude. Gradually, they worked their way back to monetary stability. Take the case of Italy. Italy had a fixed exchange rate from the post war period until 1971, and throughout this period recognized that it had to maintain fiscal balance as well as pursue a monetary policy that would keep the balance of payments in equilibrium. The exchange rate was 620 lire to the dollar and Italy had one of the fastest growing economies in the world, with a stable price level and a low level of unemployment. Flexible exchange rates, however, led to the breakdown of discipline. Monetary inflation was the result. By the end of the decade, Italy decided it had enough inflation, so it joined the Exchange Rate Mechanism (ERM). Its monetary stability was improved, but Italy then succumbed to fiscal instability, running up its Debt/GDP ratio to over 100 per cent of GDP.

The Maastricht conditions were needed to strap down ministers of finance. Like naughty children, they kept running deficits and forcing the central banks to buy government bonds when the market no longer wanted them.

In my Nobel Lecture (Mundell, 1999 [reproduced in this volume]), delivered in Stockholm on December 6, 1999, I called the first and last decades of the twentieth century "bookends" of the century, in the sense that they were decades of monetary stability separated by a long period of instability. In both decades there was monetary and fiscal discipline. The gold standard imposed it automatically in the first decade of the twentieth century. In the last decade, when almost all the OECD countries had inflation rates below 3–4% a year, many of the countries achieved stability not automatically but by self discipline or, in the case of Europe, the Maastricht conditions. The creation of the euro zone in fact prepared countries for the kind of gold standard mechanism that would be automatically imposed on them when their currencies were locked to the euro. It was a kind of replay — an automatic programming of the conditions that existed under the gold standard. The eleven countries of Europe are now following a gold standard type mechanism that gives these countries automaticity.

Exchange Rate Volatility and Internal vs. External Stability

The dollar, euro and yen areas make up nearly 60 per cent of the world economy. Because there is a high degree of price stability in each area they can be seen as three islands of stability. Despite the stability, however, exchange rates are very volatile. The dollar-yen rate has in the past been very unstable. The dollar-euro rate may be in the future, equally unstable — we do not know yet.

If we judge the future of the dollar-euro rate by the history of the mark (the backbone of the ecu, which became the euro), we'd have to be pessimistic about volatility. As for the DM-dollar rate, in 1975 the dollar was about 3.5 DM. Five years later, in 1980, the dollar was worth half that, 1.7 DM. Five years later, by February 1985, the dollar had doubled to 3.4 DM. By 1992, the dollar had plummeted below 1.4 DM — a fall to 40% of its value —, and now the dollar is up around DM2. It is hard to believe this

Exchange Rate Systems and Currency Integration

extreme volatility isn't a very serious problem. Think of the problems at the time of the 1992 ERM crisis in Europe. A doubling or halving of the rate would be devastating for Europe. If the euro went down to 50 cents that would be awful for inflation, and if it doubled to US$2 that would be terrible for unemployment.

How much flexibility is good? How much can a country stand? Well, flexibility of the kind that existed between the dollar and the mark rate over the past 25 years would crack euro-land apart. And when the dollar-euro rate changes, it creates hard problems for the countries on the periphery of Europe that are doing business with both currency areas. It's disturbing to third countries and to the rest of the world.

The same difficulty exists for Asia. Look at the volatility of the dollar-yen rate: in 1985 the dollar was 250 yen. Ten years later, in April 1995, it was 79 yen (one third the value). In June 1998, the dollar had soared from 79 yen to 148 yen, and speculators were saying it was going to go up to 200 yen. Instead it came down to about 105 yen. This volatility is terrible for countries that are closely involved with the Japanese and American markets. This volatility played a big role in the so-called Asian crisis.

Why "so-called"? Because the crisis hit only a few countries in Asia. It was a crisis for four countries: Thailand, Malaysia, Indonesia and Korea. Their currencies were pegged, not very efficiently, to the dollar, which was strongly appreciating against the yen. They lost markets in Japan. Many had debts fixed in dollars, which exacerbated their debt burdens. To understand the crisis better, however, one must also look at the countries that did not have a crisis, to see why Singapore, China, Hong Kong, Taiwan, and Japan were able to avoid it. What were these economies doing differently from the others? The differences were remarkable. Each of these countries had a very explicit target for their monetary policy. Their targets were transparent and automatic, and everybody knew they were. Singapore, Taiwan and Japan had commodity basket targets (inflation targeting), China had a fixed exchange rate with the dollar with capital controls, and Hong Kong had a currency board fix against the dollar. They had a successful track record in following that policy, and everybody knew what they were going to do when important things were happening such as changes in the exchange rate elsewhere. They also had huge amounts of international reserves, so they didn't have to draw on the IMF or listen to advice, whether bad or good. They could follow their own policies, which in the past had been successful.

Keynes, in his book "A Tract on Monetary Reform" (Keynes, 1923), made the crucial distinction between "internal stability" and "external stability". Internal stability refers to a stable price level. External stability refers to a stable exchange rate and equilibrium in the balance of payments. He said it was good to have both. But if you had to make a choice, choose internal stability first and make external stability only a secondary choice.

When Keynes wrote that book, he was looking at the world economy in the economic crisis after World War I, and one important event especially: the fluctuation in the U.S. price level and gold (because the dollar was tied to gold). The price level in the U.S. had soared from 100 in 1914 to 200 in 1920. At this point, belatedly, the Federal Reserve System shifted to tight money and the U.S. economy went into a nosedive. The price level came from an index of 200 down to an index of 140. This fall in the dollar price level (and consequent appreciation of gold) posed a great problem for the pound and other currencies.

Keynes clearly recognized the consequences for Britain. If Britain kept the exchange rate stable, it would suffer deflation too. On the other hand, if she kept the price level stable, Britain would have to allow the pound to appreciate against the dollar and gold. Because the dollar, now the dominant currency, was unstable against commodities, Britain could not have both internal and external stability; she would have to choose between them.

Keynes' distinction between internal and external stability, and his preference for internal stability is well known. What is often ignored is the importance he attached to external stability, even though it was secondary to internal stability. He was quite explicit in saying it was better to have both, if it were possible. If the United States and gold are stable against commodities, Britain could have both internal and external stability. There is a contemporary lesson for our three islands of stability eight decades later.

If there is price stability within each of the dollar, euro and yen areas, why should there be exchange rate fluctuations between them? Volatility of the exchange rates aggravates instability of the financial markets, disrupts trade and the efficiency of capital flows. Exchange rate uncertainty is an immediate cause of gross, excessive volatility in financial markets and the massive shifts in cross-border funds today. Capital market transactions in foreign exchange currently amount to something like two trillion dollars a day! It's largely capital that is going in and out, in and out, every five or ten minutes. People with their computers are pushing the funds back and forth, and it's nearly all pure waste. Only a tiny part of these shifts represent legitimate and beneficial capital movements.

Exchange Rate Systems and Currency Integration   *287*

Towards a World Currency

Earlier, we discussed the possibility — and the costs and benefits — of dollarizing the world economy. That would be the quickest and most effective way to produce a world currency. The political limitations of that solution, however, would make it difficult if not impossible to negotiate. It would greatly increase the power of the United States and leave the world at the mercy of potentially aggressive unilateralism. The temptation to exploit its monopolistic position and raise the inflation rate to maximize off-shore seigniorage would be too tempting. The power of nationalism continues to rule emotions and sovereignty is the last asset to be pawned. The idea was in the air at the 1944 Bretton Woods meeting but it was dropped at the insistence of the United States. A world currency could only have legitimacy within the framework of a new Bretton Woods-type international agreement.

The advent of the euro, however, invites a reconsideration of the need for and possibility of a world currency. Historically, the superpower has been an obstacle to monetary reform because it has the most sovereignty to lose. England, the producer of the dominant currency in the nineteenth century, rejected the efforts of France and the United States to establish a world currency in that century. In the twentieth century, the United States has been the obstacle. The creation of the euro, however, diminishes the monopolistic position of the dollar and in this respect U.S. power in the international arena will increasingly have to be shared. The United States may therefore find it in its interest to become less of an obstacle to international monetary reform in the future than it has in the past. At the very least, the need for some guidelines in conflict situations over management of the dollar-euro-yen exchange rates will become increasingly apparent.

It is entirely possible that in the future the United States may adopt a sympathetic approach to international currency management and even a genuine international currency. Let us experiment with some possibilities. Imagine an agreement for the world economy modeled after the monetary union forged by the eleven countries of the euro area. Instead of doing it for 11, do it for 200 countries. If everyone used the same currency, wouldn't that make a great improvement in the way in which prices are compared, transactions are effected, and payments are made? There would be no currency crises and the two trillion dollars worth of cross-border transactions that exist only because of uncertainty over exchange rates would disappear. Good riddance!

Robert A. Mundell

Of course there would be problems of management. A Governing Council modeled on that of the ESCB, with more than two hundred members, would be much too unwieldy. It would be necessary for the Board of Governors to designate a few leading countries to manage the new system and the new currency.

Is it realistic to think of international monetary reform along the lines, pioneered by EMU, of a single currency for the world? I myself doubt it. The single-currency option adopted by the European Union was a gamble that happened to pay dividends at a time when members of the European Union were and still are considering closer political integration. But in the absence of closer political integration, a single-currency monetary union, requiring that national currencies be given up, would probably not be successful on the world stage. Quite apart from the preferences of smaller countries, the United States is not likely to be willing to give up the most successful currency of the twentieth century, and the rest of the world is not going to be content with the dollar as its world currency. Nor would the countries of the euro area be willing to scrap their new currency after decades of negotiations to bring it into being, which in any case they want partly for political reasons. And if Americans and Europeans keep their currencies, the Japanese will not be willing to give up the yen. A single currency monetary union is not feasible in the present world and could not be negotiated in the absence of greater political integration.

Let's be more modest and consider a multiple-currency monetary union for two or three of our three islands of stability, the dollar, euro and yen areas, and then consider how this union might be generalized to accommodate the interests of the rest of the world. There are no technical obstacles to a three-currency monetary union among the G-3. It could be patterned on the EMU construction, stopping short of replacing the three currencies by a single currency. Europe has locked its currencies. There is no speculation whatsoever for or against the franc, lira, mark, peseta and all the other currencies in the euro area. Even before the new currency has been introduced in tangible form, there is a fixed exchange rate multiple-currency monetary union.

The same approach could work with two or three of the three main currency areas. Given convergence of inflation rates, it would be possible to lock exchange rates and bring interest rates into line with one another. The mechanism for locking exchange rates could be simplified by assigning different tasks to the three central banks. One of the three currencies could be chosen as the pivot currency. It is best to choose the currency with the

Exchange Rate Systems and Currency Integration

largest monetary mass, at the moment, the dollar. The other countries could be assigned the task of fixing exchange rates. Japan could fix the yen to the dollar at a rate of 100 (to make use of round numbers), 100Y=$1, so that 1 yen equals 1 cent. The Bank of Japan would stand ready to buy and sell dollars at that rate for all spot and forward offers and cease open market operations in domestic assets. Similarly, the ECB would stand ready to buy and sell dollars at (say) a one for one exchange rate between dollars and euros.

The assignment for the Bank of Japan and ECB would be to keep exchange rates fixed while that for the expanded Federal Reserve would be to stabilize the price level. The Policy Committee of the Federal Reserve (now the Open Market Committee) would incorporate Japanese and European as well as American experts. A nine-member Committee might include four Americans, three Europeans and two Japanese. Members of the Committee should be independent of their governments (as are, theoretically, members of the Governing Council of the ESCB).

The expanded Fed would make the decisions about tightening or loosening credit. There would be a common target for monetary policy. The price index would incorporate goods representative of all areas, much like the harmonized index of consumer prices in Europe (Eurostat's HICP). The next step would be to agree on a common target for inflation. Members would then cast votes for tightening or loosening credit just as the three central banks do today. There would also be a formula for redistributing seigniorage, just as in the ECB. The system would be very similar to a single currency monetary union, but it would preserve the individual currencies. The system would work in much the same way as in a single-currency monetary union.

The arrangement would work best if all three areas participated. But it would also be possible with any two of the three areas. Any two of the three areas would become the dominant currency force, the mainstream of the world economy. The costs of being left out might be substantial, however, and an exchange rate fix of the three currencies would be superior to a currency fix of only two.

In the example given, the numbers accidentally work out neatly, with the yen being a cent and the euro and dollar at parity, the currencies are like different denominations and the need for a parallel currency is not so apparent. In general, however, it would be useful to introduce a common numeraire for denominating prices. All members would quote prices in this numeraire currency in addition to local currencies.

Robert A. Mundell

Let us now see how the exchange rate stability of the three major currency areas could be used to create a multiple-currency monetary union for the world as a whole. The International Monetary Fund could be turned into a world central bank (WCB) and granted the authority to produce a world currency. The three largest currency areas could be designated as agents of the Board of Governors of the IMF. The numeraire currency might be equated to a dollar or a euro or 100 yen. We might call this new currency "intor" or "unor". Each participating member in the union would fix its local currency to the world currency, following the adjustment principles of a currency board, and denominate prices in the world currency as well as the local currency. The world currency itself would be backed by the currencies of the three largest central banks. The WCB would stand ready to buy and sell the world currency on demand so that it would not add to or subtract from the world money supply. Some provision could be made for redistributing seigniorage on a global rather than tripartite basis, perhaps with the three designated leaders setting up a special fund that could be used to finance agreed international projects.

Think of the great benefit to the rest of the world, including Latin America, if it never had to worry about changes in the dollar-euro, the dollar-yen, or the euro-yen exchange rates and could link its currencies to a true international currency in the production of which they participate. There would be no currency crises in participating countries as long as they adhered to the rules for fixed exchange rates. A world currency would provide a universal unit of account for transmitting values and be a source of a substantial increase in the gains from trade.

The link between language and currency has often been noted. Language is a medium of communication and currency is a medium of exchange. National, ethnic and liturgical languages are here to stay, but a common world language, understood as a second language everywhere, would obviously facilitate international understanding. By the same token, national or regional currencies will be with us for a long time in the next centuries, but a common world currency, understood as the second most important currency in every country, in which values could be communicated and payments made everywhere, would be a magnificent step toward increased prosperity and improved international organization.

References

Keynes, John Maynard. 1923. *Tract on Monetary Reform*. London: Macmillan.

Mundell, R. A. 1968. "A Plan for a World Currency", *Joint Economic Committee Hearings*. Washington, D.C. September.

_____ 1971. "The Optimum Balance of Payments Deficit and the Theory of Empires" in *Stabilization Policies in Interdependent Economies*, (eds. P. Salin and E. Claassen). Amsterdam: North Holland Press: 69–86.

_____ 1995. "The International Monetary System: The Missing Factor". *Journal of Policy Modeling*, October 1995, 17(5): 479–92.

_____ 1998a. "The Case for the Euro: Part I", *Wall Street Journal*. March 24.

_____ 1998b. "The Case for the Euro: Part II", *Wall Street Journal*. March 25.

_____ 1998c. "Making the Euro Work", *Wall Street Journal*, April 30.

_____ 1999. "Reconsideration of the Twentieth Century", Nobel Memorial Prize Lecture, December 8. Stockholm (Nobel Web Site and this volume, 17–37).

_____ 2000a. "Threat to Prosperity", *Wall Street Journal*, March 30th.

_____ 2000b. "A Reconsideration of the 20th Century". *American Economic Review*. June.

_____ 2000c. "Money and the Sovereignty of the State". *Zagreb Journal of Economics*.

Money, Markets and Mobility

Appendix

A Plan for a European Currency

Robert A. Mundell

The Problem

Europe today stands at a cross-roads, in politics, in technology, in economics, in culture. I shall have to mention why this is so at the end of my discussion. But my thesis today is that Europe stands at a monetary cross-roads.

The cross-roads represent a choice. What is the best choice among the alternatives?

First, we have to see the problem. Does Europe have a monetary problem? What solutions are available? What solution is best?

Editor's Note: As I noted in the Introduction to the present volume, this paper is appended in order to apprize readers of Mundell's early role in the analysis and evolution of the euro and (as Ronald McKinnon notes in his contribution to this volume) on the comparison piece to Mundell's AEA article on optimum currency areas.

This is a reprint of Chapter 9 of *The Economics of Common Currencies*, edited by Harry G. Johnson and Alexander K. Swoboda (London: George Allen & Unwin, 1973). The paper was originally presented at the *Optimum Currency Areas* Conference in Madrid in March of 1970.

The place to start is with the present arrangements. What are they? Can they be improved? What solutions are compatible with other economic, social, political and cultural objectives?

I shall begin with a discussion of the present arrangements. Then I shall show that these arrangements cannot last. Then I shall argue that the best technical solution is a European currency managed by a European monetary committee. And, finally, I shall argue that this solution is not only compatible with, but actually would promote, other European objectives.

The ABCs of the Present System

All the European countries define the par value of their currencies in terms of gold, although they usually quote them in terms of the 1949 gold dollar (see Table 1).[1]

Things that are equal to the same thing are equal to one another. The dollar is the unit of account and all exchange rates can be conveniently quoted in terms of dollars. The dollar exchange rates are calculated by

Table 1

	Gold "Content" (grams)	U.S. Cents Equivalent	Units per U.S. Dollar
Pound	2.13281	240.00	0.416667
Deutschmark	0.242806	27.3224	3.66
French franc	0.16000	18.004	5.55419
Lire	0.001421	0.160	625.000
Guilder	0.245489	27.624	3.620
Belgian franc	0.017773	2.28167	43.726
U.S. dollar	0.888671	100.00	1.000

[1]Switzerland is an exception because she is not a member of the IMF. The value of the Swiss franc is undefined. Although in what follows I shall discuss explicitly only the six EEC countries and Britain, the impact of my remarks is not meant to exclude other European countries that would most certainly be included in a wider European currency area.

dividing the gold content of the national currencies by the gold content of the dollar; the national currency prices of the dollar are the reciprocals of the dollar prices of the national currencies. Market exchange rates, however, are determined by demand and supply. To keep the exchange rates fixed the European central banks buy and sell dollars at upper and lower support points. Thus the Bank of England intervenes in the exchange market to sell dollars (and buy pounds) when the market price of the pound goes down towards $2.38; and to buy dollars (and sell pounds) when the market price goes up towards $2.42. Each of the European countries intervenes at support points three-quarters of 1 per cent above and below the dollar parity.

By keeping their exchange rates fixed to the dollar the European currencies are fixed to one another within exchange rate margins. The monetary integration of the European economies is achieved through the intermediation of the dollar.

In order to intervene in the dollar exchange markets the central banks have to keep working balances in New York banks, the active component of their reserves. In addition, of course, the European countries keep reserves of dollars in time deposits, treasury bills, certificates of deposit and some long-term bonds yielding higher interest rates.

Balance-of-Payments Policies

When the demand and supply of dollars against national currencies in the exchange market is not in balance the exchange rate adjusts, within limits permitted by the margins, until the European central banks intervene, leading to a change in reserves. The size of reserves determines how long imbalances can continue. Generally, however, if a central bank allows too much fluctuation in reserves, confidence in the exchange parity may be undermined and induce speculation and mass movements of funds. This can go to the point of forcing a closing of the markets and devaluation or upvaluation. This happened in the third week of November 1967 against the pound and in September 1969 for the Deutschmark; in the first case the British devalued; in the second case the mark was set free and later was upvalued. Such aberrant events are a symptom of a faulty *adjustment mechanism*, that is, a system of policies to bring demand and supply in the private market into balance.

The balance of payments is a monetary phenomenon and its correction implies monetary policies. There are, broadly speaking, only two monetary means of bringing about equilibrium. One is to change the price of money — the flexible exchange rate solution; the other is to change the quantity of money — the flexible money solution. The debate is on whether it is better to fix the stock of money (or its rate of change) and let the price of one money vary in terms of others; or to fix the price of money and let the quantity vary. All the major countries today adhere to the second method. Let us consider how adjustment is brought about.

Under fixed exchange rates, demand and supply of currencies are brought into balance by national monetary policies. This is automatically brought about by the act of intervention itself. Thus when the Netherlands Bank is in surplus it has to buy dollars with guilders to prevent appreciation of the guilders. This increases the supply of guilders outstanding, eases liquidity in the Dutch money market and increases spending, leading to increased capital exports (or reduced capital imports) and increased imports. Both factors help to correct the balance of payments, bringing about equilibrium between demand and supply of guilders and rendering further intervention unnecessary while opposite responses take place in the rest of the world. Thus the balance of payments equilibrates itself, unless the central bank takes active steps to prevent the mechanism from operating.[2]

---

[2]The United States and Britain are exceptions. The U.S. balance is a very special case because many countries want to accumulate dollars. The Bank of England has been another exception for a different reason; it used to try to follow an independent monetary policy until reserve losses forced it to put on the brakes. The history of this policy in Britain is a curious one. In 1932 when Britain had a floating exchange rate, the government set up an exchange equalization account to integrate Treasury and Bank of England policy with respect to intervention in foreign currency markets and to simplify monetary policy. When the Account bought foreign currency or gold it automatically sold Treasury securities to prevent any change in the money supply. This was a sensible system as long as the pound exchange rate was flexible. The problem was that they kept the system after 1945 when Britain went back to the fixed rate! It is an institution that now performs a disequilibrating function and has been responsible for the series of very harmful balance-of-payments crises that Britain has suffered by contrast with her Continental neighbours for more than two decades now. The failures of British monetary policy have largely been a failure of British intellectuals and the quite unfortunate influence of the Radcliffe Report.

It is too much to expect a bureaucracy to cut off one of its limbs. The rule of a bureaucracy is to add, not subtract, so instead of suggesting that the EEA be abolished, the Bank of England should set up a new bureaucracy to offset EEA.

Generally speaking, however, the process of adjustment works automatically in most of the countries except when there is a loss of confidence in currency values. The adjustment mechanism, if it is run correctly, works just like the inter-regional mechanism of adjustment between the twelve districts of the United States, which runs so smoothly that most people are not even aware that there are twelve district currencies, one issued for each of the twelve Federal Reserve Districts.

The Weaknesses of the European Currencies

It is important not just to see the similarities between interregional adjustment, such as takes place between different monetary districts of the United States, but also to be aware of the differences. The fact that exchange rates are fixed between districts (subject to only minor qualifications) means that interest rates are the same on equivalent assets. But the fact that exchange rates within Europe can change, and are often expected to change, means that interest rates may differ substantially from one country to another. For example, at the end of 1968 the U.K. money market rate was almost 7 per cent and the French rate 8 per cent, but the German rate was barely more than 2 per cent. These differences reflected the expectations of appreciation of the mark, and the weaknesses of the pound sterling and the French franc. But after the exchange rates were altered, with the devaluation of the franc and the appreciation of the mark, the money market rates adjusted, reducing the disparities between yields in the different centres. Currently, however, we see low interest rates in the Netherlands and Switzerland that reflect the market opinion that there is some probability of an upward adjustment of the guilder and Swiss franc. These differences in rates are reflected in forward exchange rates since, after taking into account default risk (exchange control), covered interest rates on equivalent assets have to be the same.

Thus when the Bank of England loses dollars the supply of pounds is reduced by the equivalent. The EEA then replenishes the stock of pounds by buying government securities. The new institution, the anti-EEA can then sell an equal amount of government securities and recapture the pounds. This would restore the *status quo ante* EEA without disrupting the bureaucratic apparatus. In fact, to avoid disrupting the money markets the clerks operating could work in adjoining rooms and conduct the transaction between themselves.

A Plan for a European Currency   *299*

The expectations of exchange rate changes greatly unsettle the money markets, make planning difficult, and, in the long run, weaken the control a government has over economic policy. There is a pure welfare effect associated with the interest difference that involves transfer of seigniorage from one country to another and a deadweight loss for Europe as a whole. The money markets of Europe have not been as disturbed as they have over the past three years since the chaotic periods of the 1930s. We can see these costs on the international crisis index (Figure 1).[3] Note the jump upwards after the 1960 gold bubble, the period of calm and the renewal of tension until just recently. This period of crises involved real economic costs in loss of efficiency. Since I have developed this point elsewhere[4] I shall not go into

Figure 1: World Crisis Index

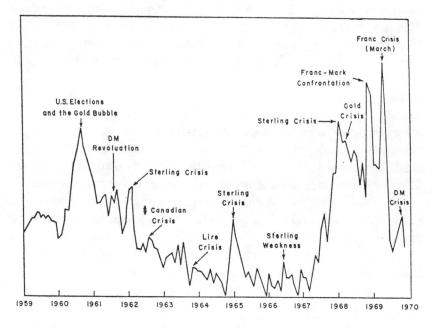

---

[3]Calculated by Houston Stokes.

[4]See Robert A. Mundell, "The Cost of Exchange Crises and the Problem of Sterling", in *International Economics*, Ch. 19 (The Macmillan Co., New York, 1968) pp. 272-81.

details here. Suffice it to say that Europe could reap appreciable gains from establishing a centralized financial market, not in the sense of a single location, but in the sense of unified rates on assets of different currencies.

This is not fully appreciated. The only way to establish a unified money market is to kill the sporadic and unsettling speculation over currency prices that ravaged the European markets between 1967 and 1969, and permit discounts and premia to develop on currency futures. The exchange rate should be taken out of both national and international politics within Europe.

I recognize that this suggestion seems to be blowing against the wind at a time when a number of influential economists have suggested the adoption of a crawling parity system, with a widened margin. I believe their emphasis is wrong and would be a disastrous system for the European countries to adopt. And for the United States the system is totally irrelevant.

It is wrong economically because it treats the exchange rate "as a price like any other price". The exchange rate is a price but it is not a price like the price of cabbage. It is a special price which establishes the goal of monetary policy, provides a basis for expectation of future policy and this links the national money as a unit of account to the international price level. An exchange parity is an expression of the long-run commitment of the monetary authorities to a monetary policy. Leaving the parity of the smaller national currencies to arbitrary and frequent changes is to make the exchange rate the hostage of any monopolistic attack, whether internal or external, on currency. The arguments for changing the exchange rate are short-run arguments based on a money illusion that is increasingly disappearing.

I am speaking here of the currency fluctuations between areas as closely connected through trade and lending as the different currencies within Europe. Brazil and many other countries with unstable or rapidly expanding money supplies have adopted such a system, but I do not believe the system has any applicability within Europe. The size of the European currency domains have become too small relative to other assets to make continual fluctuation among the exchange rates a desirable system. Nor do I believe it would be desirable to break up the currency system of the United States in order to allow fluctuations in exchange rates between different districts. Both the United States and Europe possess enough of the characteristics of an optimum currency area to move towards narrower, rather than wider fluctuations in exchange rates. In matters of finance it is better for Europe to move towards the U.S. pattern of high capital and labour mobility than to break up, by the crawling peg system, the degree of integration already achieved.

A Plan for a European Currency   *301*

My argument can best be illustrated by asking how the crawling peg system would have benefited France after the May-June 1968 events, or Britain in the November 1967 attack on sterling, or Germany in September 1969. The answer is not at all.

Rather than moving to more flexibility of exchange rates within Europe the economic arguments suggest less flexibility and a closer integration of capital markets. These economic arguments are supported by social arguments as well. On every occasion when a social disturbance leads to the threat of a strike, and the strike to an increase in wages unjustified by increases in productivity and thence to devaluation, the national currency becomes threatened. Long-run costs for the nation as a whole are bartered away by governments for what they presume to be short-run political benefits. If, instead, the European currencies were bound together disturbances in the country would be cushioned, with the shock weakened by capital movements.[5]

The fact must be faced that if the United States had separate currencies for each one of the fifty states rather than for the twelve districts, the local exchange rate would be at the mercy of the few big companies or labour monopolies in that state; and there would be little if any chance of keeping a stable monetary system in operation. To some extent the same problem would result even if there were twelve separate district currencies (which there are) subject to exchange rate changes (which they are not). The larger the currency area the greater is the resistance of the exchange rate to any given economic disturbance. But the European currencies now cover too small a domain of contract and information to resist the social disturbances to which they may be subject. The same argument holds with respect to the movements of funds controlled by the giant international corporations. A wider currency area, with the exchange rate taken out of politics, would ensure protection against disturbances arising in a world in which big companies, big labour unions and large international banks can threaten the viability of the national currency. If Europe created a common money it might well find flexible exchange rates or the crawling peg scheme a desirable basis for external currency relations.

---

[5]This argument has been very forcefully made by A. Laffer (see Chapter 1 of *The Economics of Common Currencies*, edited by Harry G. Johnson and Alexander K. Swoboda, London: George Allen & Unwin, 1973).

The Dependence on the Dollar

The appropriateness of an exchange system cannot be judged independently of the size configuration of national states in the world economy. One exchange system may work well in a world of equal-sized states. Another exchange system may be effective in a world dominated by a single nation. And yet a different system is appropriated in a world composed of a super-state, a few large powers, and many smaller states.

Our world of 1970 fits the last-mentioned configuration. The United States super-economy, Japan, the European powers, and many smaller states dominate the economic environment. This leaves aside the role of Russia, China and India, giants in different dimensions, but they are not dominating forces in the economic trading sphere with which we are now concerned.

If the world were composed of a super-economy like the United States and a large number of very small states there would be no alternative to a dollar standard, except insofar as the small nations could combine to form a single political unit and, by joint action, match in strength the power of the super-state. That is not in the realm of possibility today. The fact is that collective economic strength of the European powers matches in certain dimensions the U.S. super-economy. Its weaknesses in technology, military strength and organizational efficiency derive from its diversity and the dispersion of its energy. The diversity, however, is not an unmixed evil for that promotes protection of cultural depth and philosophical dispersion.

There is an inherent tendency for a common international money to develop based on economies of scale in the production of information. Historically this is seen in the use of gold. No one invented the gold standard. It developed through its adoption by a few countries as money as a result of its efficiency in trade, based on its low transport costs per unit of value. But when gold substitutes became cheaper, like the pound sterling in the nineteenth century, gold was replaced for many of its functions. The same holds today with the dollar which in almost every conceivable international function of money has replaced other assets.

In a world of a super-economy and very small states, this process would be inevitable and irresistible. The world would be dollar-dominated and the world central bank would be the U.S. Federal Reserve System. There would be no alternative. This appears to be the model of Kindleberger, Salant and Despres.

But our world is not really like this. In the world we live in there are, besides Japan, in Western Europe alone four powers of substantial size —

A Plan for a European Currency   *303*

Britain, France, Germany and Italy — besides other financial powers like Switzerland, Holland, Belgium and Sweden that are by no means insignificant.

In this world it is not at all inevitable that the dollar is irresistible for there are alternatives to it. They do not exist at the present time, but they can be created. The important question is whether they are worth creating.

In order to understand the thrust of my argument it is necessary to look closely at the path the financial world is now taking and at the dominating position of the dollar in that world. From 1945 to 1960 the dollar became the international currency for central banks, as intervention currency unit of account, unit of quotation, reserve asset, store of value of asset or settlement. Especially from 1960 it began to assume its important functions as a vehicle currency. The 1960s saw the rise to prominence of the international corporations which use the dollar and the international banks which produce them. The Eurodollar market is the international short-term capital market, dominated by the dollar and the vehicle through which excess reserves are lent and borrowed.

The Eurodollar market is also the international money market, analogous at the international level, to the Federal Funds market. It is not a passing phenomenon. It is a systematic force, an extension to the world sphere of American banking. Estimates of its importance in Europe range from $15 to $30 billion. Actually all these figures grossly understate its practical importance even now and far more so its potential for growth over the next few years. A rough index of its growth can be obtained from the liquidity definition of the U.S. balance of payments which has shot up from $1 billion yearly in the 1950s to $3 billion in the early 1960s to almost $9 billion in 1969. Dollars and other quasi moneys have become the major U.S. export.

The Spectre of the Eurodollar

International banking means the private creation of international or multinational money. Low-powered money in the United States becomes high-powered money in Europe. The European central banks have increasingly lost control over domestic money supplies. This is seen not just in the sense that the maintenance of the parity demands a commitment of monetary policy, or in the aggregate sense that Europe has lost control over the sum of the pounds, francs, marks, lire, etc., that provide the basis for European spending power. In a more important sense if European countries try to tighten monetary policies new dollar-creating banks will sprout up and create Eurodollars to replace pound-franc-mark-lire creation. In this sense the supply of European money, defined in terms of the work it can do, has become highly elastic. Every business with international connections is concerned about the exchange value of its assets, and this now means, increasingly, their dollar value. The dollar is undercutting the national currencies, cannibalizing, through private international banks, the national money supplies of Europe. As business becomes more outer-directed and internationalized, Eurodollar accounts replace national currency accounts, where laws permit, and the seigniorage gain from national money creation at the government level is shifted to rents accruing to the international banks, most of which have connections and credit lines in the United States and can rely on the credit worthiness of a famous name.

Consider the following question: Which bank is more likely to "fail", the Bank of France or the First National City Bank? Hardly anyone believes in failures of the great American banks or of their branches in Europe. But there is still widespread speculation against the currencies of Europe issued by the central banks. The reason is not just size. To be sure, the big American commercial banks are larger than the central banks of Europe. Any economist or banker who ignores this development is an ostrich. But there are other reasons.

Eurodollars have already begun to replace national currencies in national uses. *Public* banks in Europe compete with *private* banks in America. Why should an international business in Italy maintain lire deposits when (or if) it can use Eurodollar deposits on virtually equal terms? Gresham's Law operates in the competition between private American banks and European public banks.

Anything a lire can do a Eurodollar can do better. The big American commercial banks are safer, judged by records since the war, than European central banks. An overseas branch of a big American bank is less likely to fail than a national bank is to devalue. The overseas branch is backed up by the home office which is in several cases bigger than the European central banks. But it is also reinforced by confidence in the American banking system arising in the belief, from insurance (FDIC) and a belief probably justified, that the American government would not permit a bank failure of one of the big commercial banks; in this sense they are semi-public institutions.

European countries can, of course, impose controls and restrictions against U.S. banks or the European banks who "counterfeit" dollars. But the

A Plan for a European Currency   *305*

big banks are big enough to play one country off against the other much like the international corporations. Even though collective action is desirable, it is not in a country's interest to take an individual stand. And there is no convenient avenue in Europe for advancing the collective interest.

One could, of course, argue that private European banks are protected by their own central banks. The Bank of France bought assets in 1968 rather than let the French commercial banks fail. But as the sequel makes clear the internal liquidity crisis is converted to an external liquidity crisis. The European central banks have to keep their currencies convertible into the dollar. They are not banks of last resort in the world setting. The dollar has become the apex of the international monetary pyramid. The U.S. central bank has no problem maintaining convertibility.

It is often said that gold is the apex of the monetary pyramid though less so now than a few years ago. Could not the Europeans exchange dollars for gold and threaten the convertibility of the dollar?

The formal answer is, yes. But that record has been played for a decade. Threatening the dominant power is a thankless task and it is not costless. The French attempt to raise up gold in opposition to the dollar failed because it was a unilateral move, badly prepared, and not part of an acceptable plan. The gold standard of the nineteenth-century variety lacked economic truth in 1965. But the failure served as a warning to Europe that relative power positions had fundamentally changed.

The gold convertibility threat is now too heavy-handed a weapon — at least in a poker game among friends. It is like a doomsday machine. No European country wants to bring down the collapsible house of cards pinned on the strength of the European dollar even if it could do so. Far better to drift along with the present system, the changes of which seems distant and remote, than for any single country attempt to weaken confidence in the dollar.

Consider then the problem. For a decade or more U.S. officials and U.S. detractors (strange bedfellows) have been bemoaning the weakness of the dollar and the problem arising from the balance of payments. The balance-of-payments "programme" involved a series of measures including controls of one kind or another that a few economists (including myself) repeatedly warned would not work; the deficit in the control period almost tripled to its current level of almost $9 billion. Many of the same economists who advocated controls in the 1960s are now advocating flexible exchange rates in one or another of its variations, joining forces with many libertarians who have always opposed controls — again strange bedfellows. But the point is

306   Robert A. Mundell

not whether one's heart is in the right place, but whether one's theory of the process is right. It is my opinion that the theory of the process, used by flexible rate advocates and control mongers alike, is too short-run in its scope.

What would be the effect of introducing floating rates (or crawling pegs with widened margins)? Clearly the balance of payments on an official settlement basis would disappear except insofar as additions to reserves were freely bought. But what would be the effect on a liquidity basis? It would worsen. For the reserves that the central banks were previously accumulating would now be acquired by the commercial banks and used as the basis of Eurodollar expansion. Private money creation would replace central bank money creation and the domain of the national currency would shrink and shrink in the unequal battle for survival in a dollar-dominated world. A movement in the direction of flexible exchange rates is no solution for the European countries. It would enhance rather than weaken the in-roads of the dollar.

What, then, is the solution? The United States is powerless to correct its deficit short of forbidding other countries to buy or use dollars, which would be absurd. Hope for correcting or reducing the U.S. deficit lies with Europe. Only by creating a substitute for the dollar can Europe free itself from dependence on it, and only through this means can the United States correct its balance of payments. There is thus only one solution.

That solution, I believe, lies in the creation of a European money. One of the advantages to Europe of the common money is to restore to European governments the sovereignty that is being whittled away by the Eurodollar explosion and to enable Europe to resume command over its own monetary policy. Its immediate advantage to the United States is to eliminate the U.S. balance-of-payments deficit which U.S. officials (for reasons not entirely clear) have long proclaimed to be undesirable. But in the long run it would enable Europe, eventually in equal partnership with the United States, to develop instruments for the rational monetary management of the world economy.

The major objection does not of course come from the United States but from those in Europe who regard a monetary unit as the symbol of national sovereignty, and are distrustful of any ideas likely to threaten that sovereignty. The point is, however, that monetary sovereignty is already threatened. The relevant question is simply whether sovereignty should be allowed to pass to America or whether it would not better serve the interests

A Plan for a European Currency   *307*

of European countries if the sovereignty were restored to Europeans in a common European enterprise.

The case for a European money must be made primarily on political grounds, just because politics in the widest sense of the word has to override economics. I shall make a case for a European money in the third section. Before doing so, however, it is necessary to clear away the economic underbrush in order to make clear that there are no economic difficulties in the way or any technicalities that cannot be resolved. As it turns out, the economic case for a European money is a very strong one.

The Plan

A New Anchor

I have argued that the gains from European financial integration are considerable, that integration at both the official and private level is being achieved through the intermediation of the dollar, but that the costs of intermediation through the dollar are exceedingly high, striking at the nerve centres of monetary control and sovereignty itself. In this section we have to consider some of the alternatives to the present arrangements.

Let us take it as given that we want to avoid the complete dependence on the dollar in which Europe today finds itself. What steps must be taken to achieve this end?

The first thing is to establish the destination and then consider the best means of getting there, taking into account technical and practical problems. The first requirement, the *sine qua non*, is to lay the anchor to which the European currencies are to be moored. Currently, as we have seen, currencies are pegged to the dollar. What is needed is an alternative to the dollar.

There are three possibilities. One is to choose gold. Second is to create a synthetic unit of account. Third is to choose one of the existing national currencies. Some combination of the three possibilities may be desirable.

Let us first consider gold. The European currencies could all peg to gold. But this option is, at least for the present, impractical. No one in the United States wants to leave the fortunes of monetary policy to the vicissitudes of the available stock of gold and such an arrangement for Europeans would

308   *Robert A. Mundell*

either imply huge fluctuations in reserve levels if the dollar price of gold were fixed or fluctuating exchange rates if the dollar price of gold were allowed to remain free. To be sure, a managed gold standard — managed by Europe and America collectively — is possible and may ultimately become desirable. But it does not meet the present European problem of finding a satisfactory anchor to which the European currencies can be pegged — together. The relations with gold are concerned with extra-European relations to which we shall presently turn.

The second possibility is to establish, by fiat, a unit of account in Europe. The European countries could agree on a common piece of paper, and hitch their currencies to that. They could then set up a European monetary authority and central bank to govern the connections between that unit and the dollar or gold. This is a possible solution, perhaps it is even an ideal solution. But it is politically very complicated, almost utopian. The reason is that it starts in the wrong direction, at the end of a process rather than at the beginning. It is very hard to make political leaps of the magnitude which such a path would take.

The third possibility is to take a European currency and use it as a temporary anchor. This process has the disadvantage of having to select a particular country and that involves problems of national jealousies. No one wants to repeat inside Europe the problems Europe as a whole has had with the dollar. For this reason any solution in this direction would have to be looked upon only as a first step in a process.

I believe, however, that this is the best way to start. It is practical and informal. The choice of currency as a key currency lies within the realm of technicalities and can be decided by the central banks and governments. No country in Europe has legislative approval for a dollar standard, yet that is the system they now use. I think it would be a mistake to attempt to deceive parliaments in this respect, and it would be best to show that the method works before putting a drastic change up for parliamentary approval. So the best first step is to shift from the dollar as intervention currency to one of the currencies within Europe.

Which? Each of the central banks would have some claim. Italy and Belgium have had the best record of exchange stability over the past two decades. France has the oldest central bank. Germany has had a strong currency for over fifteen years, a good inflation record and is the largest industrial power. The Netherlands have some of the oldest central banking traditions and probably, with the possible exception of Italy, the best

A Plan for a European Currency 309

management. Britain is the largest financial power and the pound is still a world currency.

The issue is not really that important. Actually any of the countries would do although there are technical reasons why there are advantages to using the currency with the largest financial base, the best connections and thickest money market. The question could be decided informally. For purposes of the present discussion I shall suppose that the pound is chosen, since Britain's transfer to the decimal system removes one of the difficulties that would formerly have barred or weakened the pound's advantages.

Here, then, is how the transition would be made. Britain continues, at least initially, to peg to the dollar, while all the other countries shift over from pegging to the dollar to pegging to the pound. Everything else goes on as before. No change in exchange rates would have occurred.

But what about reserves? Britain will now need larger dollar reserves because she will have to take upon herself the combined deficits of Europe when Europe as a whole is in deficit. (She will also have to accumulate reserves when she is in surplus while other countries will have to have more pounds.) The solution is simple enough. The other countries can deposit a pile of their dollars in a special account set up by the Bank of England, and get in return credits in pounds. There is no reason why all accounts cannot, in the initial period, be dollar-guaranteed.

This first step would solve the anchor problem. Now Europe as a whole could easily adopt any stance necessary in relating to the dollar. If the United States inflated or went into a depression Europe could always change the pound parity of the dollar and thus the parity of Europe as a whole. Or they could widen the margins, let the dollar float or even peg to gold. A new degree of freedom would have been achieved.

Of course the other European countries would not be able to allow the Bank of England to make exchange rate decisions in isolation. The second problem is the determination of *policy*. The weakest stage of co-operation is consultation. But it should not be a difficult matter to go beyond this to the setting up of a European monetary advisory committee analogous to the U.S. open market committee. This committee would have to concern itself with two kinds of decisions: (i) British open market policy and (ii) external exchange rate policy.

The third step is to ensure that the benefits of the system are divided. It would not be fair for the United Kingdom to have complete freedom to run up sterling debts to European central banks, at least not without a *quid pro*

Robert A. Mundell

quo. There are informal ways of handling this through the appropriate setting of interest rates, and there are more formal methods.

One of the most straightforward formal methods is to pool reserves. All, or a certain fraction of, reserves could be put in a pool and a new asset — a claim on the pool — could be issued to the European countries in the form of either a deposit at the Bank of England or a special asset. In the long run the creation of a special asset would be desirable because the money that ultimately may circulate in Europe should not be the pound sterling, but a fresh asset that is a symbol of the step that has in fact been taken.

The Making of Europa

In the making of such a symbol acts of parliament may be required in some countries. This is a politically sensitive issue but it has to be brought home to the public how much sovereignty on money matters has already been lost to the dollar, and the bleak future in the event that no changes are made. The parliaments and the public have a right to be informed of the threat to their national financial independence that already exists.

At the stage of creating the symbol, one might ask: What is to be its nature? One could take up an old European name for a currency, such as thalers, ducats, florins, livres, ecus; one could adopt a new name for it such as Eurodollar or use the name suggested by Giscard d'Estaing, the Euror, in his plan for a European currency. I shall refer to it as the EUROPA.

What would the Europa be? It has to have a definition. The simplest is to define it in terms of gold, e.g. a Europa could be equal to 1 gramme of gold, which would make it worth about $1.13. But it seems rather petty to fix an even figure with respect to gold when most people are used to the dollar as a unit of account, so defining it in terms of the IMF unit of account, which is the 1944 gold dollar, would give it a gold "content" of 0.888671 grammes, the same value as the dollar.

The existing exchange rates would then be

$$
\begin{aligned}
1\ \text{EUROPA} \ &= 0.888671\ \text{grammes of gold} \\
&= 41.6\ \text{new pence U.K.} = 1/2.4\ \text{pounds sterling} \\
&= 3.66\ \text{Deutschmark} \\
&= 625\ \text{lire} \\
&= 5.55\ \text{French francs} \\
&= 50\ \text{Belgian francs} \\
&= 3.62\ \text{guilders}
\end{aligned}
$$

A Plan for a European Currency

In this way the Europeans would have found their way to a European money.

The European Monetary Pool

We cannot, however, stop at this point. Formalities have to be observed with respect to the use of reserves and monetary policies. I do not propose to go into details because they are best cleared up by negotiation. A few suggestions, however, may facilitate discussion. We have to ask: What would the central banks do with their reserves and what is the appropriate quantity of Europas to issue?

It is very convenient to establish quotas. Current European reserves are about $25 billion, counting the Six and Britain, of which about $15 billion are in gold (the rest in dollars). If this sum were put in a pool it is clear that it would be a larger reserve than is really necessary. The reason is partly the insurance principle: all countries will not get into deficit at the same time so that pooling reserves automatically permits an economizing of them. But there is a second reason. The European countries hold reserves now, not just to cover deficits related to trade with the rest of the world, but also to trade with one another. A reserve saving is possible with respect to intra-European trade. Pure intra-European credit can be created to cover reserves needed because of intra-European trade, with hard reserves kept for transactions with the rest of the world. This represents a gain in the real purchasing power of existing reserves.

There are various ways of establishing a scientific basis for determining a sound fraction of intra-European to extra-European reserves. It is sufficient for our purposes, however, to note that the intra-European reserve saving would be related to the ratio of intra-European to extra-European trade, which would thus involve a saving of the order of 50 per cent. If we add to this the insurance saving it is possible that Europe as a whole would not need more than $10 billion in total external reserves, or about 40 per cent of the total they now possess.

This assumes, however, that reserves are presently adequate. Actually U.K. reserves are too low, and too large a proportion is borrowed. Moreover it might be better at the outset to establish a level of reserves that will enhance the securities of the currencies. For this reason a pool of, say, $30 billion would be appropriate, of which half should be backed by hard currency.

The appropriate size of quotas can be established by negotiation, although a degree of arbitrariness cannot be avoided. Taking into account population, GNP, IMF quotas, variance of imbalances, etc., one can arrive at the following quotas for purposes of discussion:

United Kingdom	7
France	7
Germany	7
Italy	5
Netherlands	2
Belux	2
Total	30 billion Europas

If this figure appears very high (it is higher than the IMF total) one should recognize that it is not much larger than the big American banks and less than half the size of the U.S. Federal Reserve Bank.

Each of the countries would earmark to the pool, administered by the Bank of England, reserves of gold or dollars equal to *half* its quota, while the rest of its quota would be paid in national currency (much like the IMF system); and it would get in return a deposit of Europas equal to its quota. Thus France would pay 3.5 billion of gold or dollars and get in return 7.0 billion Europas which it could use to fix the franc exchange value of the Europa.

The balance sheet of the Pool would then look something like Table 2.

Table 2: The Pool's Assets and Liabilities

Assets		*Liabilities*	
Gold and federal exchange	15.0	To United Kingdom	7
Pounds	3.5	Germany	7
Deutschmark	3.5	France	7
French francs	3.5	Italy	5
Lire	2.5	Netherlands	2
Guilders	1.0	Belux	2
Belgian francs	1.0		
	30 Europas		30 Europas

A Plan for a European Currency

Policies

Countries could in principle follow the same policies with respect to balance-of-payments adjustment they now follow, although it would serve the interests of financial integration better to squeeze the intra-European exchange rate margins together. In view of the increased connections between financial markets, however, it would be desirable to make adjustment policies more automatic, moving in the direction of the traditional equilibrating rules of the game, setting adjustment policies in motion promptly, and thus taking both the exchange rate and adjustment process out of political manoeuvring. Two policies must now be considered.

The first is the appropriate policy of adjustment of the money supply of Europe as a whole. How rapidly should the money supply in Europe be allowed to move and to what extent should this be related to movements in the United States and the rest of the world?

On the supposition that U.S. monetary policy is stable there is no reason why European and American monetary policies cannot be harmonized. Given similar price level goals in Europe and the United States, fixed exchange rates can be maintained between the two blocs. If, however, the U.S. or European monetary goals should become very different some exchange flexibility between the blocs would be required.

Mutual co-ordination of policies with respect to the use of reserves will become more important. The European monetary pool will have a bloc of dollar and gold reserves of about $15 billion, about the same stock of reserves as the United States. Correct monetary management of the two areas will require continuous consultation of monetary policies. Thus Europe and the United States would have to decide not to dump or demonetize gold. There is no reason why an arrangement cannot be worked out by which the existing par value of the Europa and the dollar in terms of gold is maintained. Only in the event of an avalanche of gold arising out of vast new discoveries would it be necessary to give up the use of gold or lower its price. On the other hand an increase in the price of gold would serve no valid monetary purpose.

There remains the question of gold pegging arrangements. The United States could peg to the Europa. Europe could peg to the dollar. Or both blocs could peg to gold within suitable margins, established by the degree of exchange flexibility considered desirable, with joint action to control the world monetary stock of gold.

314   *Robert A. Mundell*

These two areas, Europe and the United States, would constitute the twin pillars around which the free world monetary system revolved. Third countries could peg their currencies to either bloc and hold their reserves in the currencies of either bloc. But because the United States and Europe would represent such a large part of the world they would each have to share responsibility for sound, non-inflationary policies. The creation of the European bloc would economize on reserve and in this sense would contribute to the inflation potential in the world economy unless discretionary management were carefully observed. To guard against premature spending of additional reserves the Europeans could decide to self-discipline their spending of additional reserves, treating extra reserves as conditional, rather than unconditional liquidity.

Control would be necessary over the extent to which banking systems were allowed to overlap between the two areas. We have already seen the enormous inflation potential that is created by the extension of the Eurodollar market, to which bank money in one country, the United States, becomes high-powered money in another continent. It would be necessary to keep a close rein also on the reserve process by which European banks nearly secured the existence of their own money, were not permitted to explode into the United States. Zones of currency and banking domains could be defined.

Let us summarize the steps needed in moving towards a European money.

The first requirement is to have an *anchor* which will provide Europe with an extra degree of freedom, namely, the right to let its currencies move collectively with respect to the dollar, reducing European subservience in this dimension and affording an alternative — a degree of protection — in the event that the U.S. economy becomes unstable. This is provided by the Continental countries' fixing their currencies to one another through the medium of one of the European currencies.

The second requirement is to have a *policy*. Taking for illustrative purposes the Bank of England as agent for Europe, she could convene a board of advisers from the Continental banks, a committee set to the task of formulating a European monetary policy. Alternatively, this same leadership could be at the initiative of the President of the BIS.

The third requirement is to *divide the benefits*. This can be accomplished formally or informally. An attractive solution here is to form a reserve pool, with quotas, and a European bank, with suitable adjustments of interest rates and quittance rights.

A Plan for a European Currency   *315*

The fourth requirement is to have a *symbol*, a unit of account, that properly forces attention on the fact that a significant step has been taken. The name suggested for purposes of discussion is the Europa, but that is obviously a detail that can be worked out when the need for it arises. In the longer run it might be worth issuing Europa notes to the public for purposes of tourists and other international travellers, replacing the current reliance on the dollar and recouping the seigniorage.

The final step is to arrange *external connections*. Relations could be established on a gold basis or through a continuation of existing pegging arrangements through the United Kingdom. Thus the Bank of England could peg the pound to the dollar and the Europa to the pound (flat), while the other countries could peg to the Europa flat or with very narrow margins. In the event that the pound or the Bank of England ceased to be a satisfactory unit for pegging, an equivalent arrangement could be transferred to one of the other European currencies.

It is not perhaps fully realized how exceptionally propitious is the present time to the creation of a European money. There are various reasons for this. First, there is now a fairly generally accepted view of how the international financial system works and of the key role played by U.S. monetary policy in determining the world price level and the rate of world inflation. Second, European currencies are pegged to the dollar at rates *vis-à-vis* one another that can be thought of as equilibrium rates if they are properly backed up by appropriate monetary policy. Third, central bank management has become far more sophisticated and includes a number of men of the highest calibre in several countries. Fourth, the governments in power are in general more sympathetic to an extension of the European concept than ever before. Fifth, Britain is in the process of going on to a decimal system.

Not all these factors are of equal importance. But they combine to make 1970 a very favourable year in which to get the feet wet. There is, indeed, far less time available than is commonly realized as the gush of information, new technology, conglomerates, international corporations and banks are rapidly turning the Atlantic into an American lake. The friendly financial imperialism of the United States is powerful not because it is ugly, but because it is so attractive.

Transition Problem

Before turning to historical-political considerations it seems advisable to face squarely some political-economic problems raised by the transition. The creation of a new monetary unit on the scale envisaged would mark a dramatic new bid for monetary power on the part of Europe. It would be disingenuous to imply that such a development does not have important implications for the United States and that the United States does not, therefore, have a right to be kept informed and consulted and given assurances that its vital interests will not be threatened. First let us consider the legal basis of the European action.

There is no provision in the IMF Articles of Agreement inhibiting the creation of a common monetary bloc in Europe. There are provisions, however, that specify the rules with respect to exchange rate and intervention policy. The United States is currently freed from exchange market intervention by its formal adherence to Article IV-4-b stating that it buys and sells gold freely; European countries are permitted to keep dollar margins within 1 per cent of par in accordance with a 1959 Regulation, even if it allows cross rates with currencies of other member countries to go up to 2 per cent. From a formal point of view there is no problem to the transition.

Big changes in the system, however, would be accomplished by the creation of a European monetary pool and a European money, and legal rights do not afford sufficient grounds for disrupting expectations. When a country "cries down" an international money it affects the world economy. Thus changes in U.S. silver policy had huge effects on silver-standard countries, especially Austria and Russia in the 1870s, and on China in the 1930s. Similarly, the U.S. "threat" echoed repeatedly by American nationalists (but not by the government) to demonetize gold by refusing to buy it, had, and still could have, big effects on Europe.

A similar problem would arise if a misplaced European nationalism decided abruptly to "demonetize" the dollar. The European pool would have a huge bloc of dollars on hand as well as gold, and any threat to demonetize the dollar by dumping dollar holdings abruptly would be an act of irresponsibility. What might eventually be required is an arrangement between the United States and Europe not to demonetize each other's reserves and to negotiate the correct holdings of each other's money. The principle on which negotiations are set should pay some attention to the rule of thumb that bygones are bygones, that past deficits involve claims that are

A Plan for a European Currency   *317*

a *fait accompli* and cannot be unravelled at the free option of the holder. This holds with respect to sterling, dollars and gold balances alike.

I believe, with Bernstein, Triffin, Machlup, Johnson and others, that a world-wide pooling of external reserves is needed in order to lodge control of the international monetary base with the IMF, which is supposed to be the world monetary authority; but that we are unlikely to be able to negotiate a satisfactory control arrangement until the Europeans have solved their problems. In this respect most U.S. and European long-run interests, broadly conceived, are in harmony, not in conflict; and on this basis the creation of a European money, far from threatening U.S. vital interests, will promote them. It seems too obvious to mention the ease with which the U.S. balance-of-payments problem, which up to now has proved intractable to the U.S. acting alone, could be solved once Europe has created its own regional money. Europe, with a common money, could solve the bulk of the U.S. balance-of-payments problem, as it is conceived of by the U.S. officials, which currently approaches $9 billion a year on a liquidity basis, almost overnight.

The Case for a European Money

It is not necessary to rest the case for a European currency on economic arguments alone. It is true that the economic arguments favour a European money: (i) the pecuniary gains to Europe from the reserve saving; (ii) the protection from further expansion of the dollar; (iii) the increase in control over the European money supply; (iv) the recovery of seigniorage to Europe; and (v) a new instrument to correct the U.S. balance of payments.

Political Considerations

These arguments alone would make the organizational effort required to create a European money worthwhile. But there are more compelling gains. Even if there were no economic case for a European money there is a political case for one, for the creation of a European money would represent a strong step in the direction of European integration. The case for a European money is therefore tied up with the case for integration. Since the case for integration rests on social, political, military, cultural and intellectual grounds our arguments for a European money based on economic grounds alone is as if we had just examined the tip of the iceberg and left untouched the seven-eighths of the true case lying underneath. Of course most political judgements involve questions of values but I believe the values are widely shared on both sides of the Atlantic.

What are the political arguments? It would be a hopeless task to summarize them here and millions of words have already been written about them. Yet some perspective can be obtained if we are willing to take a longer look at the evolution of the European economy, and its monetary fortunes. I think when that is done we shall find that the present is unique, characterized by a transition of unprecedented significance. The transition represents the reversal of a trend begun several centuries ago.

Europe achieved a kind of monetary unity under the Roman-Byzantine Empire, a unity implied by the recognition by the princes of the newly emerging European nations of the exclusive monopoly of the pontiff-emperor of gold coinage. The symbolic turning point came at the beginning of the thirteenth century with the sacking of Constantinople, the seat of Byzantium, by the third Crusade in 1204. Prior to that date a myth had always been maintained of the sacred character of gold and the authority — to be sure mainly spiritual — of the Eastern Pontiff to create and stamp gold coins. After 1204 Europe turned its back on the universal money of Byzantium, the last tangible manifestation of the unity of Christendom, the effective end of the Crusades, and the yoke of the Romans. European monetary integration of a sort had been achieved through the intermediation of Roman-Byzantine money.

After that date the kings and princes of the emerging European nations went their own way in matters of money and a great period of monetary experimentation set in. Monetary independence and political decentralization found their expression in the wave of independent gold coinages; even the formality of the rule of the Holy Roman Emperor was dropped when Edward III in 1347, as Vicar-General of the German Emperor, was given the legal authority to make his own gold coins.[6] A coin achieved the status of international money on competitive grounds and the reputation of its quality; exceptionally trustworthy coins, like the Venetian ducat, were extensively

---

[6]Actually Henry II had made gold coins, but without authorization; the emperor was giving away a privilege that most kings had already usurped fifty years before.

A Plan for a European Currency

used as European money for centuries. Other important units of account, like the florin, various Spanish coins, and the guilder, were used until the rise of dominance of the pound sterling through the eighteenth and nineteenth centuries. Sterling became the ducats of the nineteenth century and dollars the ducats of the twentieth century.

There is an important difference, however, between the earlier Venetian, Florentine, Spanish and Dutch monies and the pound sterling and the dollar, however. The former were full-bodied gold coins and did not involve such substantial seigniorage gains to the producer as the credit monies of the pound and the dollar. This has an important political significance because it meant that to be trustworthy, credit arrangements either had to be immune to political disturbances, especially war, or else the domain of the currency had to be inside a security area. It is for this reason that the success of the pound sterling was closely tied up with the security domain of the British Empire and that the success of the dollar was and is contingent on the security umbrella of the United States.

Who would doubt the usefulness of the dollar in the post-war monetary system? It was through the intermediation of the dollar that a great step forward was taken in restoring the monetary unity of Europe that had existed, in certain dimensions, up to the thirteenth century. Who would not prefer the quarter-century since 1945 based on the dollar to the monetary chaos of the thirty-year inter-regnum of common sense from 1914 to 1945? What I am questioning is rather whether a creative and independent European development is consistent with a continuation of the dollar system as it penetrates deeper and deeper into every dimension of European business.

The power of the dollar is based on its efficiency in performing financial services, an efficiency based on economies of scale in the production of a multiple-attribute commodity money, or more generally, liquidity. The U.S. monetary system can be thought of as a vast cartel where bank deposits, time deposits and quasi monies produced by different institutions are convertible into cash at a fixed price. European national monies cannot compete.

Along with the dollar comes American civilization. America is no longer Europe overseas; it is a civilization on a new key with a new technological and organizational structure, and a process of change built into the system itself, a strange, worried civilization as different from Europe as Rome was from Greece. Its production is highly efficient and beneficial to Europe. There can be no question of its benefits in enhancing European productivity. But its costs have been underrated. These costs involve a loss of control and sovereignty. Under the current system the gains, which are short-run, are acquired at a high price in the long run. The overall gain, the net benefit, may be negative.

We thus come to the heart of the argument. No one can dispute the short-run benefits; everyone will concede the long-run costs. Which are greater? It is like asking whether the sale of birthright for a mess of potage is worthwhile. The answer depends on the interest rate, on how urgent immediate requirements are, relative to long-run requirements, and also on the opportunities.

If Europe were faced with a choice of American technology, gained at the price of European sovereignty, it would probably be worth paying something in sovereignty for the technology if those were the only terms available. However, if there were another way out, if the bulk of the gains in technology could be achieved without loss of sovereignty and independence, it would be irresponsible of European leaders not to explore that possibility to the fullest extent. Why cannot Europe create its own technology, engaging in free trade with America in the field of ideas?

The answer is that she can. But the trade can be achieved on the most beneficial terms only if European leaders in the field of knowledge are given comparable facilities that allow the exploitation of economies of scale implicit in the knowledge industry. Exploitation of these gains implies a higher degree of centralization in the production, distribution and utilization of ideas, and the development of suitable vehicles of transmission of ideas.

The English language has become the primary language of science and this confers an incredible advantage on the U.S. techno-structure in competition with the tongues of European nations, because language is the medium of exchange of ideas. It is probably not possible to resist this development as English becomes the second language of most people in Europe. It is not possible to go back to Latin or take up Esperanto except in the time scale of centuries, far beyond any considerations relevant here.

The dollar becomes the medium of exchange of commodities. As long as the dollar is the world currency, which it is increasingly becoming, America will maintain the commercial and financial advantages, intrinsic in its vastness. But currency rights are man-made and reversible, the prerogative of the sovereign state. We have seen that hope for the national currencies of Europe is slim in the very long run. But there is possible in the field of money a development ruled out in the field of language, namely, a European money — if there is a political will and if it is felt that European

A Plan for a European Currency

independence is worth preserving. For a European money can be created in a year, and the balance of advantages, now weighed overwhelmingly on the side of the United States, redressed.

Money is the key that can unlock the doors that are currently barriers to the flow of information and finance. Instead of gratuitously ceding to the United States the enormous advantages in the fields of both language and money, it can take the first fundamental steps through the creation of a money.

American technology, capital and power are transported through the media of the American language and the American money. Europe needed something like the dollar in the initial post-war period, but now the need is over. Now she needs a monetary union. A monetary union has become possible because Europe has become a security area, a war-free domain.

One must be careful to distinguish between two different approaches to the question of European integration. One is to ask: What is the appropriate degree and kind of integration taking Europe alone into account? The other involves the extra-European context.

If we take Europe alone into account we can accept the need for some degree of integration to capture the spillover effects in the fields of transport, communication, entertainment, education, technology and defence. Informal methods of co-operation, combined with a few rules and treaties, might suffice and a tight degree of integration rendered unnecessary. All the gains and pleasures associated with the universe of natural cultures could be preserved.

But such a land of Cockaigne, of delight and commodiousness, cannot exist without protection in a world of mass states and super-powers. Cheap culture drives out dear and Europe, far from becoming a land of fun and diversity, would become a museum run by American curators.

I don't know of any intelligent human who has the bad taste to be proud of the twentieth century, with its record in the span of thirty years, of world war, hyperinflation, hyperdepression, fascism, Stalinism, genocide and atomic war. But it is in the aftermath of that period of tragedy that Europe's problem now lies. The extra-European environment cannot be avoided even if one wanted to draw a *cordon information* around the boundaries of Europe. It just is not possible. Europe has to cope not only with the advanced civilization in America, but also with the backward, if powerful, Russian super-state, and with the other half of the world living in varying states of poverty, degradation and misery. And in this world it has to recognize not only its right to protect those nerve centres that define its existence and

322   *Robert A. Mundell*

uniqueness; but also its responsibility to take an active role in keeping order and raising the standard of life in other parts of the world.

It is worth emphasizing responsibility because Europe has not contributed its share in the positive developments of this century. Twice it has dragged the world into war and from 1945 to 1970 it has concerned itself almost exclusively with the selfish but understandable pursuits of reconstruction and the drive towards affluence. The age, starting in 1500, when Europe became — to adopt Weber's metaphor — mistress of the world is past. But the mistress is not in her dotage; the matron still has life and responsibilities.

Yet that life needs a power centre, and money, the creation of the state, is the seat of the power base. The provinces of Europe are getting a money, but it is the U.S. dollar.

Thus the famous myth of the rape of Europa — the beautiful daughter of a Phoenicean prince, transported over the sea to Crete on Zeus in the form of a beautiful bull, to consummate with her bullish lover her dream of two continents — would have its sequel in the Oedipus, a new rape of Europe by her son, America.

Europe has for three decades now huddled with relief under the umbrella of a friendly America. The dollar has served as the anchor for a degree of European integration. As long as this system continues the U.S. balance-of-payments deficit will grow; and as long as it grows European independence will be increasingly undermined; her economic power diminished; the franc, pound and mark humbled; and America, however mistakenly, pushed into control. Mutuality of interests in the Atlantic area is served by a European revival, beginning in finance, and the *sine qua non* of that revival is a European money serving all the provinces of Europe.

Can there be a transformation of attitudes in Europe? A shift away from the concept of competitive national interest and rivalry so destructive in the past of the whole? A shift away from the idea that there is time to spare, that independence and integration will still be possible two decades from now? That the world will stop and wait and the technological explosion and the communications revolution will be arrested while Europe catches her breath? That European youth will be content with third-rate intellectual fare while Americans plant themselves on the moon?

A final historical analogy. Just two years after Columbus found America, a united France invaded a divided Italy, an act symbolic of the new age of the great European nation states. France and Spain, the technologically superior barbarian giants of the West, cajoled and coerced the

A Plan for a European Currency

over-civilized Italian duchies into despair at their inability to cope with the new more-powerful civilizations around them. It was then that "Italy" became a concept for patriots. In the closing words of *The Prince*

> . . . For, sure, the ancient worth,
> That in Italians stirs the heart, is not yet dead.

Machiavelli quoted Petrarch. But it took Italy over 300 years to become united.

It is time for Europeans to wake up.

Contributors

Russell S. Boyer — Department of Economics, University of Western Ontario

Thomas J. Courchene — School of Policy Studies, Queen's University

Michael B. Devereux — Department of Economics, University of British Columbia

Pierre Fortin — Département d'économique, Université du Québec à Montréal and Canadian Institute for Advanced Research

Herbert Grubel — The Fraser Institute and Department of Economics, Simon Fraser University

Richard G. Harris — Department of Economics, Simon Fraser University and Canadian Institute for Advanced Research

Philip R. Lane — Trinity College, Dublin

John McCallum — Secretary of State (International Financial Institutions) (formerly Royal Bank of Canada)

Ronald McKinnon — Department of Economics, Stanford University

James R. Melvin — Department of Economics, University of Western Ontario

Robert A. Mundell — Department of Economics, Columbia University

Sylvia Ostry — Centre for International Studies, University of Toronto

George M. von Furstenberg — Graduate School of Business Administration, Fordham University

Robert Waschik — Department of Economics and Finance, La Trobe University

Queen's Policy Studies
Recent Publications

The Queen's Policy Studies Series is dedicated to the exploration of major policy issues that confront governments in Canada and other western nations. McGill-Queen's University Press is the exclusive world representative and distributor of books in the series.

John Deutsch Institute for the Study of Economic Policy

The State of Economics in Canada: Festschrift in Honour of David Slater, Patrick Grady and Andrew Sharpe (eds.), 2001
Paper ISBN 0-88911-942-2 Cloth ISBN 0-88911-940-6

The 2000 Federal Budget: Retrospect and Prospect, Paul A.R. Hobson and Thomas A. Wilson (eds.), Policy Forum Series no. 37, 2001
Paper ISBN 0-88911-816-7 Cloth ISBN 0-88911-814-0

Room to Manoeuvre? Globalization and Policy Convergence, Thomas J. Courchene (ed.), Bell Canada Papers no. 6, 1999
Paper ISBN 0-88911-812-4 Cloth ISBN 0-88911-810-8

Women and Work, Richard P. Chaykowski and Lisa M. Powell (eds.), 1999
Paper ISBN 0-88911-808-6 Cloth ISBN 0-88911-806-X

School of Policy Studies

Knowledge, Clusters and Regional Innovation: Economic Development in Canada, J. Adam Holbrook and David A. Wolfe (eds.), 2002
Paper ISBN 0-88911-919-8 Cloth ISBN 0-88911-917-1

Lessons of Everyday Law/Le droit du quotidien, Roderick Alexander Macdonald, 2002
Paper ISBN 0-88911-915-5 Cloth ISBN 0-88911-913-9

Improving Connections Between Governments and Nonprofit and Voluntary Organizations: Public Policy and the Third Sector, Kathy L. Brock (ed.), 2002
Paper ISBN 0-88911-899-X Cloth ISBN 0-88911-907-4

Institute of Intergovernmental Relations

Comparaison des régimes fédéraux, 2ᵉ éd., Ronald L. Watts, 2002
ISBN 1-55339-005-9

Health Policy and Federalism: A Comparative Perspective on Multi-Level Governance, Keith G. Banting and Stan Corbett (ed.), 2001
Paper ISBN 0-88911-859-0 Cloth ISBN 1-55339-000-8, ISBN 0-88911-845-0 (set)

Disability and Federalism: Comparing Different Approaches to Full Participation, David Cameron and Fraser Valentine (ed.), 2001
Paper ISBN 0-88911-857-4 Cloth ISBN 0-88911-867-1, ISBN 0-88911-845-0 (set)

Available from: McGill-Queen's University Press
Tel: 1-800-387-0141 (ON and QC excluding Northwestern ON)
1-800-387-0172 (all other provinces and Northwestern ON)
E-mail: customer.service@ccmailgw.genpub.com

IRPP
Recent Publications

A State of Minds: Toward a Human Capital Future for Canadians,
Thomas J. Courchene, 2001, ISBN 0-88645-188-4

Adapting Public Policy to a Labour Market in Transition
W. Craig Riddell and France St-Hilaire (eds.), 2001, ISBN 0-88645-186-8

The Review of Economic Performance and Social Progress
The Longest Decade: Canada in the 1990s
Keith Banting, Andrew Sharpe and France St-Hilaire (eds.), 2001
ISBN 0-88645-190-6

Pulling Against Gravity: Economic Development in New Brunswick During the
McKenna Years, Donald J. Savoie, 2001, ISBN 0-88645-192-2

These and other publications can be purchased on-line at www.irpp.org or
through McGill-Queen's University Press.